Integrated Treatment for Mood and Substance Use Disorders

PUBLISHING FOR THE WORLD
125 Years

THE JOHNS HOPKINS UNIVERSITY PRESS

Integrated Treatment for Mood and Substance Use Disorders

Edited by

Joseph J. Westermcycr, M.D., M.P.H., Ph.D.
Professor, Department of Psychiatry, University of Minnesota
Chief of Psychiatry and Mental-Behavioral Health Service Director,
VA Medical Center, Minneapolis, Minnesota

Roger D. Weiss, M.D.
Associate Professor of Psychiatry, Harvard Medical School,
Boston, Massachusetts
Clinical Director, Alcohol and Drug Abuse Treatment Program,
McLean Hospital, Belmont, Massachusetts

Douglas M. Ziedonis, M.D., M.P.H.
Associate Professor and Director, Division of Addiction Psychiatry,
Robert Wood Johnson Medical School, Piscataway, New Jersey

THE JOHNS HOPKINS UNIVERSITY PRESS
Baltimore & London

The Johns Hopkins University Press
2715 North Charles Street
Baltimore, Maryland 21218-4363
www.press.jhu.edu

Library of Congress Cataloging-in-Publication Data

Integrated treatment for mood and substance use disorders / edited by Joseph J.
Westermeyer, Roger D. Weiss, and Douglas M. Ziedonis.
      p. ; cm.
Includes bibliographical references and index.
   ISBN 0-8018-7199-9 (hardcover : alk. paper)
   1. Substance abuse — Treatment.   2. Affective disorders — Treatment.   3. Dual
diagnosis.
   [DNLM: 1. Mood Disorders — therapy.   2. Diagnosis, Dual (Psychiatry).
3. Mood Disorders — complications.   4. Substance-Related Disorders —
complications.   5. Substance-Related Disorders — therapy. WM 171 1585 2003]
I. Westermeyer, Joseph, 1937–   II. Weiss, Roger D., 1951–   III. Ziedonis, Douglas.
   RC564 .1546   2003
   616.85'2706 — dc21   2002007591

A catalog record for this book is available from the British Library.

Contents

Acknowledgments

The editors acknowledge funding from numerous sources during the preparation of this volume.

For Joseph Westermeyer, sources include: principal investigator, "Development and Pilot Study of a Daily Symptom Chart for PTSD," Bristol-Squibb (developmental grant) (1996–2000); principal investigator (Jose Canive, M.D., co–principal investigator), "Delivery of Mental Health Services for PTSD and Alcoholism to American Indian and Hispanic American Veterans in New Mexico and Minnesota," VA Merit Review grant (1997–2000); co–principal investigator (James Jaranson, M.D., principal investigator), "Population-Based Survey of Torture and Violence [in African Refugees]," NIH grant (1998–2003); site principal investigator, multisite study, "Double Blind Controlled Study of Venlafaxin (Effexor) in the Treatment of PTSD," Wyeth-Ayerst (2001–2003). Dr. Westermeyer's employment during these grants involved funds from the Minneapolis VA Medical Center and the University of Minnesota Department of Psychiatry.

For Roger Weiss, sources include National Institute on Drug Abuse Grants DA00326 and DA09400 and the Dr. Ralph and Marian C. Falk Medical Research Trust.

For Douglas Ziedonis, sources include National Institute of Drug Abuse, Center for Substance Abuse Treatment, and Robert Wood Johnson Foundation.

Contributors

Dennis C. Daley, Ph.D., Associate Professor and Chief, Addiction Medicine Services, Department of Psychiatry, Western Psychiatric Institute and Clinic, University of Pittsburgh School of Medicine, Pittsburgh, Pennsylvania

Melissa P. DelBello, M.D., Assistant Professor, Department of Psychiatry, University of Cincinnati College of Medicine, Cincinnati, Ohio

Caroline Eick, M.A., Director of Education, Pavillon International, Mill Spring, North Carolina

Shelly F. Greenfield, M.D., M.P.H., Assistant Professor of Psychiatry, Harvard Medical School, Boston, Massachusetts, and Medical Director, Alcohol and Drug Abuse Ambulatory Treatment Program, McLean Hospital, Belmont, Massachusetts

Jonathan A. Krejci, Ph.D., Instructor, Department of Psychiatry, and Project Director, Co-occurring Disorders Program, Robert Wood Johnson Medical School, Trenton, New Jersey

Ihsan M. Salloum, M.D., M.P.H., Associate Professor and Medical Director, Addiction Medicine Services, Department of Psychiatry, Western Psychiatric Institute and Clinic, University of Pittsburgh School of Medicine, Pittsburgh, Pennsylvania

John Slade, M.D. (deceased), Professor and Director, Program in Addictions, School of Public Health, University of Medicine and Dentistry of New Jersey, New Brunswick, New Jersey

Stephen M. Strakowski, M.D., Professor and Director, Bipolar and Psychotic Disorder Research Program, Department of Psychiatry, University of Cincinnati College of Medicine, Cincinnati, Ohio

Michael E. Thase, M.D., Professor, Department of Psychiatry, Western Psychiatric Institute and Clinic, University of Pittsburgh School of Medicine, Pittsburgh, Pennsylvania

Betty Vreeland, M.S.N., R.N., N.P.-C., C.S., Clinical Instructor, Departments of Psychiatry and Family Medicine, Robert Wood Johnson Medical School, Piscataway, New Jersey; Clinical Assistant Professor, School of Nursing, and Consultant and Advanced Practice Nurse, University Behavioral HealthCare, University of Medicine and Dentistry of New Jersey, New Brunswick, New Jersey

Jill M. Williams, M.D., Assistant Professor, Department of Psychiatry, Robert Wood Johnson Medical School, Piscataway, New Jersey

Integrated Treatment for Mood and Substance Use Disorders

Addressing Co-occurring Mood and Substance Use Disorders

Joseph J. Westermeyer, M.D., M.P.H., Ph.D.

Why Focus on Comorbid Mood and Substance Use Disorders?

The goal of this book is to enhance the care of patients with comorbid mood and substance use disorders, including those patients who present to clinicians or programs specializing in substance use disorders and those who present to facilities devoted to the care of mood disorders. We inform the clinician-reader about integrated, concurrent treatment for mood and substance use disorders, as opposed to merely describing the separate or sequential treatments of these disorders. For example, we describe the special aspects of care for these patients and how their care differs from treatment-as-usual for substance dependence or mood disorder alone. To achieve our objective we provide some background information on the integrated course of these disorders in patients with such comorbidities. Topics of much research interest but less immediate clinical relevance (e.g., genetics, epidemiology, neurobiology) are addressed only insofar as background knowledge is useful for providing care. In pursuing these ends, we endorse the following principles.

1. *Reputable clinicians and investigators do not always agree on important*

issues in the assessment and care of patients with comorbid addiction and mood disorder. For example, some clinicians experienced in the treatment of these comorbid conditions prefer not to administer pharmacotherapy or psychotherapy if patients are still abusing psychoactive substances. They prefer to undertake care only if the patient is in a secure setting where substance use is unlikely to occur (e.g., a hospital, halfway house, or residential facility) or when the patient has achieved a period of stable sobriety. Other physicians will administer pharmacotherapy or psychotherapy to patients who are abusing psychoactive substances, usually under special circumstances (as in bipolar disorder). Still others will prescribe for the patient who is not yet stable but recommend that the patient discontinue medication immediately on resuming substance use at any level. The latter approaches might be used for the patient who has been mostly abstinent but still has occasional slips, who has reduced the frequency of usage to specified times (such as over weekends only), or who has reduced the dosage of use (say, attempting to resume moderate social usage after a period of heavy or excessive use). Certain circumstances or patterns of substance use preclude active, successful treatment of either the mood or the substance disorder. For example, an insight-oriented session with an intoxicated patient is not feasible. For a substance-dependent person using heavy doses daily, having frequent blackouts, or using medications to increase sedation, pharmacotherapy involves excessive risk with minimal or no gain likely. Psychoeducation during the first week or two of sobriety wastes time and resources, since the acquisition of new knowledge during this period is impaired. We also agree that physicians must not prescribe medications for mood disorder in the blind hope that addiction will remit without addiction treatment; therein lies folly.

2. *Clinicians caring for patients with comorbid mood-substance disorder must cope with ambiguity, that is, not having all of the desirable information at hand before making a decision.* In this book, we suggest means of proceeding with treatment before a final or clear diagnosis is known. For example, it may not be clear for some weeks or months whether a patient has a substance-induced mood disorder (which may or may not need specific treatment beyond abstinence alone) or an abstinence-onset mood disorder (which is likely to require specific treatment for mood disorder). The clinician may not be able to establish whether the substance disorder preceded the mood disorder or vice versa. Despite incomplete information, clinicians must make decisions regarding care.

3. *Distinguishing between the primary and secondary disorders (i.e., whether*

the addiction or the mood disorder began first) may be feasible in research stud-
ies but may not be readily accomplished during the early phases of clinical man-
agement. Such distinctions are not critical to early care in most cases. Some
research suggests that the sequence of the disorders may be important in terms
of ongoing treatment or prognosis, or both. However, this differentiation into
primary versus secondary disorders is generally not critical in early phases of
care, when withdrawal, establishment of abstinence, and treatment of medical
and psychiatric emergencies (e.g., hemorrhage, psychosis) are priorities. We
do, however, recognize the need of medical records offices and third-party payers to have a "primary diagnosis" for record-keeping or fiscal purposes. Although we do not promise to solve these practical problems for the reader,
some information in the book should prove useful in approaching this com-
monplace problem for clinicians.

Health services research is beginning to define gaps in the detection and
treatment of comorbid mood disorders in patients with substance abuse. Craig
and DiBuono (1996) examined psychiatric conditions as compared to psychiatric referrals in a detoxification unit. They found that only 20 percent of the
patients receiving detoxification were referred for psychiatric assessment.
Among those referred, 84 percent were found to have an axis I or II DSM-III-
R condition—a finding that points up the skill of the detoxification staff in
identifying "true positive" cases with comorbidity. However, in the remaining
80 percent of patients who were not referred, the rate of major axis I or II psychiatric disorder was 21 percent. Thus, the detoxification staff failed to identify about half of the patients who should have been referred for psychiatric
care. Among those in the "unreferred group" who had a psychiatric disorder,
about half had a mood disorder. Were this some other disabling, life-threaten-
ing condition, such as tuberculosis or cancer, a missed identification rate of 50
percent false-negative cases would be unacceptable. Information in subsequent chapters will help the reader achieve the most efficient, cost-effective,
and best-timed screening for comorbid disorders. Treatment efficacy, cost, and
benefits are also addressed.

Audience

The audience for this book is clinicians of several disciplines: alcoholism and
drug abuse counselors, physicians (including psychiatrists), psychologists, social workers, nurses, occupational and recreational therapists, and clergy.

Some readers will have extensive knowledge and experience with mood disorders but not with substance abuse; others will have expertise in substance abuse but not mood disorders. This book is targeted to both audiences.

Because this is not a book exclusively for addiction psychiatrists or for researchers into these comorbid conditions, we have eschewed an extensive reference list and critique of research methods in favor of practical clinical strategies. We have not avoided useful references that might be of interest to the reader, concise comments on method as a limiting factor on our knowledge, or relevant reviews of the scientific literature, all in an attempt to enrich our understanding of clinical situations and their management.

The chapters in the first half of this volume review the research literature for the following reasons:

• Clinicians need to have state-of-the-science knowledge to practice their art. This is especially the case for clinicians designing treatment programs for clinical facilities and for clinicians devising treatment plans for individual patients.

• The science is always incomplete. Extrapolation of research findings to particular cases and programs requires having some information on the limitations of the studies. These limitations are typically related to the patients in the study (their demographic and clinical characteristics), the methods of data collection, and — in some cases — the interventions used. Clinicians need a modicum of knowledge of these issues because scientific knowledge can never cover all eventualities. Extrapolation from known but limited facts to the complexities of the clinical "real world" poses daily challenges for all clinicians.

• Most clinicians with master's or doctoral degrees will have no difficulty reading the literature reviews because they have been exposed to such presentations during their training and in their professional journals. Clinicians with bachelor's degrees should be familiar with all of the terms as a result of their training and clinical experience.

• Some level of "overeducation" (i.e., of material above and beyond that needed to make everyday decisions) is part and parcel of pedagogy. The critical issue lies in not overloading the clinician-learner with unnecessary detail.

• The people who wrote the chapters are clinicians, albeit clinicians who also conduct studies of patients with mood and addictive disorders.

We did not write this volume for clinician-investigators. Had we done so, we would have emphasized several topics that we did not include here (e.g., influence of sampling on the data, evaluation of various research instruments, other research data, such as animal studies).

Terminology

The generic terms *mood disorder* and *substance use disorder* cover the entire panoply of specific diagnoses in each of these categories; they are written in lower case. Particular diagnoses, such Major Depressive Disorder and Alcohol Abuse, are capitalized. The generic term *depressive disorders* includes several diagnostic categories, including Major Depressive Disorder, Dysthymia, Substance-Induced Mood Disorder, and Mood Disorder due to a General Medical Condition. *Mood disorder* includes not only the depressive disorders but also Mania and Bipolar I and Bipolar II Disorders. *Substance use disorder*, or *substance-related disorder*, includes all DSM-IV categories associated with substance use (i.e., dependence, abuse, intoxication, withdrawal, intoxication delirium, withdrawal delirium, dementia, amnestic disorder, psychotic disorders, mood disorders, anxiety disorders, sexual dysfunctions, and sleep disorders), as well as the various psychoactive substances that can cause these disorders (i.e., alcohol, amphetamine, caffeine, cannabis, cocaine, hallucinogens, inhalants, nicotine, opioids, phencyclidine, sedative-hypnotic-anxiolytics, and other substances). *Depressive symptoms* refers to the numerous symptoms that accompany depressive disorders (e.g., appetite and weight changes, fatigue, sleep disturbance, lowered pain threshold, decreased attention and memory, anhedonia, nihilistic outlook, suicidal ideas or acts). Such symptoms can vary in duration and intensity, can occur as normal human experiences (e.g., during bereavement), and can accompany many disorders besides depressive disorders. For our purposes here, the adjectives *affective* and *mood* have the same meaning.

The reader will note that authors use the term *patient* in some places and the term *client* in other places. The editors have chosen to let the chapter authors use either term. Clinicians working in hospitals and medical centers tend to use *patient*, whereas those working in community outpatient settings are more apt to use *client*. There are also some differences by discipline, with many physicians and nurses preferring *patient* and many psychologists and social workers preferring *client*.

Epidemiological Studies

One of the earliest epidemiological studies indicating a high rate of comorbid mood and substance use disorders was conducted in the 1970s using DSM-II diagnostic criteria. Among those with a lifetime diagnosis of alcoholism, 44 percent had experienced a lifetime history of major depression and 15 percent had experienced minor depression (Weissman and Miers, 1980). Of course, these lifetime rates do not necessarily imply that the disorders occurred at the same time.

The Epidemiological Catchment Area (ECA) study was conducted in five urban areas during the early 1980s using a structured psychiatric interview administered by trained interviewers (Regier et al., 1990). This study confirmed the higher-than-expected coexistence of mood and substance use disorders. Among those with a lifetime history of Alcohol Abuse/Dependence, 13.4 percent had a history of mood disorder, nearly twice the rate of mood disorder in those without Alcohol Abuse/Dependence. Conversely, among those with a lifetime history of mood disorder, 21.8 percent met DSM-III-R criteria for Alcohol Abuse/Dependence at some point in their lives, also twice the risk for this disorder among individuals without a mood disorder. Thus, with either mood or substance use disorder, the risk for comorbidity of both disorders was about twice what would be expected on the basis of chance alone.

A more recent epidemiological study from the early 1990s, the National Comorbidity Study, suggested that comorbidity in general (including all psychiatric diagnoses) may be increasing in the United States (Kessler et al., 1994). Co-occurrence of two or more disorders was found in 14 percent of the general adult population. With lifetime Major Depressive Disorder, the risk of lifetime Alcohol Abuse/Dependence was increased by about twofold — very similar to the ECA study conducted earlier. The risk for lifetime Alcohol Abuse/Dependence associated with lifetime Dysthymia was even higher, approximately fourfold (Swendsen et al., 1998). The severity of impairment was greater among those with comorbid conditions than among those with only one disorder. These data also suggest that rates of mood disorder can differ depending on whether one is studying individuals with alcohol abuse versus alcohol dependence and that gender can also affect the rates of comorbidity (Kessler et al., 1997).

During the last decades, several epidemiologists have addressed Nicotine Dependence and mood disorder, especially depressive disorders. In a study conducted in New Zealand, 63 percent of women with psychiatric disorders were tobacco dependent, as compared to 23 percent of those without psychiatric disorders (Romans et al., 1993). In a survey of 1,007 young adults in the United States, Breslau and coworkers found a high association of depression and tobacco dependence (Breslau, Kilbey, and Andreski, 1991). Another New Zealand group found that, among depressed teenagers in the general population, Nicotine Dependence was 4.6 times more frequent than in teenagers without depressive disorder (Fergusson, Lynskey, and Horwood, 1996). In their longitudinal cohort study of 947 children, the latter group also observed that comorbid depressive disorder and Nicotine Dependence were both "well established" by age 16.

Clinical Studies of Substance-Abusing Patients

The rates of mood disorder in various groups of substance-abusing patients have differed, usually within fairly narrow limits but sometimes greatly. This is true even among more recent studies conducted since the introduction of the DSM-III diagnostic classifications, which brought enhanced reliability into psychiatric diagnosis. To convey some notion of the variability, we reviewed studies that met the following criteria:

• published from 1984 until now by refereed journals in psychiatry and the addictions
• included 50 or more subjects, with subjects drawn from clinical settings providing treatment for alcohol and/or drug abuse
• focused on depression (rather than mania, which is covered in a subsequent chapter)
• provided sufficient data to characterize the patients and describe the timing of data collection (whether in the early phase of abstinence or after prolonged abstinence)

See table 1.1 for rates of depression observed in 15 clinical studies that met these criteria. Despite the great variability in rates of depression among all 15 studies (i.e., 10–59%, a difference of 49%), 11 studies showed considerably less variability (22–43%, a difference of 21%). Some of the difference in rates is due to differences in definition of "depression," timing of the study in relation to abstinence, duration of time over which the patients were studied, and clin-

Table 1.1 Rates of Depression in Patients Presenting with Substance Use Disorder

Depression Rate (%)	Sample Size	Demographic and Clinical Characteristics	Study
59	64	women with alcohol problems	Rowe et al., 1995
43	106	men with alcohol problems	Rowe et al., 1995
42	2,945	alcoholics, 6-center genetics study	Schuckit et al., 1997
39	71	predominantly male alcoholics	Mason et al., 1996
36	928	middle-aged VA alcoholics	Penick et al., 1994
34	92	young adult intravenous drug users	Dinwiddie, Reich, and Cloninger, 1992
33	339	current/previous depressive symptoms, inpatient alcoholics	Roy et al., 1990
33	78	inpatient alcoholics	Dawes, Frank, and Rost, 1993
30	273	current severe mood disorder, inpatient alcoholics	Schuckit, 1983
27	72	MDD after 3–6 weeks of sobriety	Abou-Saleh, Merry, and Coppen, 1984
24	52	adolescents with alcohol, cannabis, polydrug abuse	Neighbors, Kempton, Forehand, 1992
22	642	current prevalence, 16% MDD and 6% Dysthymia	Westermeyer and Eames, 1997; Westermeyer, Kopka, and Nugent, 1997
15	72	"severe depression," 64 months abstinence	Behar, Winokur, and Berg, 1984
14	101	mostly employed, male alcoholics	Kranzler et al., 1995
10	494	drug abusers, current prevalence, 10% MDD, 5% Cyclothymia, 4% Bipolar Disorder	Weiss, Griffin, and Mirin, 1992

ical instruments used. For example, the study with the highest rate (59%) in-cluded only women, whereas the three studies with the lowest rates (10%, 14%, and 15%) used predominantly male samples or data collected after several years of abstinence. Patients in the middle 11 studies (with depression rates of 22–43%) included a diversity of addicted patients (i.e., men and women, in-patients and outpatients, patients in youth to middle age). Data in these 11 studies were typically collected in the treatment setting several weeks to several months after abstinence began.

Some of the variability in comorbid rates inevitably reflects the multitude of patterns and pathways exhibited by substance and mood disorders. The following case exemplifies one such pattern.

A 66-year-old married man retired from his job as a successful salesperson one year ago. Twenty-two years ago he received inpatient treatment for alcoholism. During the interim, he had been active in local Alcoholics Anonymous (AA) groups and had helped to establish a halfway house. He had remained abstinent until about 6 months ago, when he suddenly resumed drinking heavily. When he began drinking again, he also began to experience insomnia, loss of interest and pleasure in his usual activities, anorexia, poor concentration and memory, crying spells, and feelings of hopelessness, helplessness, and worthlessness. Over the entire year he had lost 30 pounds. At the time of admission to alcoholism treatment, he had a blood alcohol level of 373 mg%, bruises over his arms and shins, evidence of dehydration, and epigastric pain and tenderness. After detoxification and hydration, subsequent evaluation failed to reveal medical disease. His Mini-Mental State exam was normal at 29/30. He was cooperative, was logical in his speech, denied hallucinations, showed no evidence of delusions, and was goal-directed in his speech and behavior. His depressive symptoms persisted despite abstinence, and treatment for Major Depressive Disorder was initiated along with abstinence-oriented treatment for alcoholism. One year later he remained abstinent and euthymic.

The Influence of Demographic Characteristics on Rates of Comorbidity

Younger patients with substance use disorder may have lower rates of comorbidity (see table 1.1). Studies of younger patients have tended to show that the course and severity of substance abuse were comparable with and without mood disorder. This may be because younger patients have not had as long a life period in which to demonstrate comorbidity. On the other hand, many patients with comorbid disorders tend to have early onset of their substance abuse during adolescence (Westermeyer et al., 1994). Thus, the age at which comorbidity is studied may affect the conclusions drawn. These data suggest that clinicians treating adolescent substance abusers may not find high rates of mood disorder. However, clinicians treating adults whose substance use disorder began early in adolescence can expect to see high rates of mood disorder.

In studies of alcohol abusers, women have higher rates of Major Depressive Disorder than do men (Westermeyer, Kopka, and Nugent, 1997). However, in a study of drug abusers, men and women had equivalent rates (Rowe et al., 1995). Men and women may not differ so greatly in their rates of comorbid Dysthymia (Westermeyer and Eames, 1997) and Bipolar Disorder.

Historical Changes

Two or three decades ago, many clinicians recommended against treating depression in alcoholic persons who manifested depressive symptoms. In particular, treatment with antidepressant medications was especially anathema (O'Sullilvan, 1984; Viamontes, 1972). Many self-help groups in that era vigorously prompted members "not to treat one drug with another." This attitude against treating comorbid mood disorder probably affected some of the older studies that showed a poor prognosis for comorbid mood and substance use disorders.

Interest in psychiatric comorbidity has increased over the last decade. This can be attributed in part to a new diagnostic schema, the *Diagnostic and Statistical Manual of Mental Disorders*, third edition (DSM-III), which appeared in the early 1980s. Before that time, diagnostic practice favored the use of only one diagnosis, based on psychodynamic theory and a preference toward one etiology to explain each patient's psychiatric condition. DSM-III revolutionized psychiatric thought in the United States, replacing a diagnostic system based on theory with one based on clinical phenomena. Under the phenomenological approach, any one patient might have as many diagnoses as warranted by the patient's signs, symptoms, and course. The Epidemiological Catchment Area study, based on DSM-III diagnostic criteria (Regier et al., 1990), further promulgated this method, which was emulated in subsequent clinical studies. Since that time, many recovering people with substance disorder have been treated for mood disorder.

Treatment has also undergone many changes, with the addition of self-treatment with a variety of herbal pharmacotherapies, other somatotherapies (such as acupressure), and various self-help techniques (such as meditation). Accustomed to managing their own mood, some patients with this particular comorbidity use approaches of complementary and alternative medicine (CAM) at some point in the course of their disorders. Several factors probably account for the recent popularity of CAM for these and other chronic or recurrent disorders, including

• previous failure of treatment in either the substance abuse setting or the psychiatric setting

• high cost of professional care, with unwillingness of third-party payers to reimburse for care of comorbid conditions

• patient control over CAM as opposed to a perception of professional control over other approaches

• a focus on mechanistic, rapid, less-intrusive, self-directed, more easily understood treatment approaches (i.e., "take drug, feel better") as opposed to more complex biopsychosocial theories and methods used by professionals in treating these disorders

Clinicians should maintain an open dialogue with patients (as well as an open but not naive mind) regarding their use of CAM. Clinicians need to know about all therapies and therapists being used so they can identify treatment combinations that might undermine or adversely interact with each other. It is also important to appreciate patients' expectations of CAM because loss of morale, hopelessness, and even suicide attempt may result if the patient has unrealistic and subsequently unrealized expectations of CAM.

Models of Care for Comorbid Mood and Substance Use Disorders

Some models of care for this comorbid condition have grown out of theoretical perspectives. For example, drinking may be conceived as a form of "pharmaceutical self-medication" for mood disorder. Other models have arisen from clinical experience and could be viewed as after-the-fact explanatory models. For example, excessive drinking by a patient in therapy for a mood disorder could be labeled as an "acting out" of the transference relationship (rather than appropriate "acting in" of the relationship during therapy sessions). At times, some of these diverse models can be mutually reinforcing, so clinicians would want to apply the models simultaneously. At other times, the models may compete with each other, so clinicians would need to decide between diametrically opposed courses depending on which model they choose.

This dilemma is central to the treatment of comorbid disorders. For example, clinicians treating dual disorder know that they must be more flexible than those treating substance use disorder alone. Clinicians treating comorbid mood-substance problems must be willing to monitor the patient much more closely than those treating mood disorder alone. Knowing how and when to strike this balance remains largely an art, increasingly informed by an accumulating body of scientific knowledge. The first step in seeking this balance is to be aware of the varying types of models applied in these cases.

"Treatment for the mood disorder will cure the substance use disorder."

This viewpoint, carried to its extreme, would suggest that the clinician need only attend to the mood disorder, and the substance use disorder will improve on its own. In such a model the mood disorder is viewed as primary and the substance use disorder as secondary. Clinicians coming from traditional mental health training are more likely to hold this perspective.

One study was designed to assess this strategy. The National Institute of Mental Health (NIMH) initiated the Collaborative Depression Study of the five-year course in 127 patients with comorbid alcoholism and mood disorder (Hasin et al., 1996). In patients with Major Depressive Disorder (MDD), remission of depressive symptoms was associated with remission of alcoholism (as defined by 26 weeks or more without alcohol-related symptoms). The study was open-ended and descriptive, so associations can be described but causation cannot be implied. The authors concluded that "remission in MDD significantly improved the outlook for a remission from RDC (research diagnostic criteria) alcoholism." However, one might as readily conclude that remission from RDC alcoholism significantly improved the chances for remission of MDD, at least for patients receiving treatment for MDD.

Conservative conclusions regarding comorbid mood and substance use disorders, based on the uncontrolled nature of this one study, are as follows:

- Both conditions tend to remit together.
- If either condition fails to remit, the other fails to remit.
- The NIMH study does not demonstrate how best to treat such patients.
- The NIMH study does not reveal whether treatment of depression or treatment of alcoholism might be the factor predicting successful treatment.

Despite the expensive and prolonged nature of this study, we are left with the conventional wisdom that the best course is to treat both the mood disorder and the substance use disorder concurrently.

"Abstinence will cure the mood disorder."

Clinicians in the addiction field held to this belief in the 1950s and 1960s. Persisting mood symptoms might be labeled as "stinking thinking," "dry drunk," or "failure to work the recovery program." Statements to this effect could be heard as late as the 1980s, but this has become an increasingly isolated viewpoint.

Despite its current unacceptability as a general theory, this dictum does clearly apply to depressive symptoms that recur during ongoing substance abuse and remit during sobriety. Further, it applies to many patients whose mild to moderate depressive symptoms remit in the early days and weeks of sobriety. However, it clearly does not apply to patients whose mood symptoms persist despite sobriety. As discussed by Shelly Greenfield (chap. 3), patients who experience considerable depressive symptoms even while drinking heavily or abusing drugs may be different from those whose depressive symptoms are not so severe. Severe depressive symptoms even early in sobriety do portend but do not absolutely predict subsequent MDD (Westermeyer, Kopka, and Nugent, 1997). As we shall see in subsequent chapters, substance-abusing patients with MDD may have an improved prognosis with treatment for depression.

Integrated care / integrated recovery.

Before the 1980s, much care for comorbid mood and substance use disorders occurred sequentially, with one group of clinicians treating one of the two disorders initially and then another group treating the remaining condition. Patients were expected to recover from one condition first and then from the other condition. Treatment was often undertaken in inpatient or residential settings, where the patient's sobriety was reasonably assured. Still, many patients "fell between the cracks" during this transfer of treatment responsibility. Many patients with comorbid disorder never made it from substance treatment to mood disorder treatment or vice versa. Nowadays, hospitalization beyond several days is not feasible, and this means of ensuring sobriety during the early stages of treatment is removed.

Consequently, treatment professionals and programs have attempted to treat comorbid mood and substance use disorders concurrently. With this approach one relieves symptoms as soon as possible, selects venues of care other than inpatient, and applies modalities of care that fit the patient's needs. The remainder of this book focuses on means of treating the patient with comorbid disorders in an integrated fashion. The parallel changes that occur in patients are often referred to under the general term *recovery*. Despite the paucity of research data comparing sequential versus integrated care, our experience suggests that treatment for both disorders should be integrated in time, if not in place. If treatment must take place concurrently at two different locations involving two different staffs, then coordination must be close and frequent. Such an approach ultimately consumes more resources and lends itself to greater risk of misunderstanding all around.

Although fundamentally simple in theory, the actual integration of treatment can be difficult if one comes to comorbid disorder with training and experience in mood disorders or in addictive disorders, but not both. We hope that this book will serve as both a primer and an entry for those steeped in just one of these clinical traditions. These chapters will orient the reader to the challenges of recognizing and then providing care for someone with both disorders. This book also offer knowledge, experience, and case examples to meet these challenges. Of course, reading this book will not provide the experiential learning that is so crucial in developing clinical skills, judgment, and intuition. The reader will need to seek out supervised experiences to fill this gap.

Conclusion

Clinicians caring for patients with comorbid mood and substance use disorders must appreciate the integrated course of this common comorbid condition if they are to recognize and effectively treat the condition. Although much attention has been devoted to discerning which disorder is first, or "primary," this distinction probably has little import for management during acute and subacute phases of recovery. Despite abundant knowledge regarding the prevalence of this common comorbidity, much treatment for either substance disorder or mood disorder is provided without assessment for the other disorder — a major cause of treatment failure. In light of the magnitude of this problem, we prepared this book for clinicians of several disciplines who encounter either patients with substance use disorder or patients with mood disorder. For purposes of orientation, this introductory chapter includes definitions of relevant terms and an overview of the epidemiology of this comorbid condition — topics that are elaborated in subsequent chapters. We emphasize with a case report that the relationships between mood and substance use disorder are complex, so that any simple or stereotypic typology is apt to mislead the reader. Finally, a description of commonly applied models and historical changes in our models should imbue all of us with a humble and open approach to these patients.

REFERENCES

Abou-Saleh, M. T., J. Merry, and Z. Coppen. 1984. Dexamethasone suppression test in alcoholism. *Acta Psychiatrica Scandinavica* 69:112–16.

Behar, D., G. Winokur, and C. J. Berg. 1984. Depression in the abstinent alcoholic. *American Journal of Psychiatry* 141:1105–7.

Breslau, N., M. M. Kilbey, and P. Andreski. 1991. Nicotine Dependence, Major Depression, and anxiety in young adults. *Archives of General Psychiatry* 48:1069–74.

Craig, T. J., and M. DiBuono. 1996. Recognition of comorbid psychopathology by staff of a drug detoxification unit. *American Journal on Addictions* 5(1):76–80.

Dawes, M. A., S. Frank, and K. Rost. 1993. Clinician assessment of psychiatric comorbidity and alcoholism severity in adult alcoholic inpatients. *American Journal of Drug and Alcohol Abuse* 19(3):377–86.

Dinwiddie, S. H., T. Reich, and C. R. Cloninger. 1992. Psychiatric comorbidity and suicidality among intravenous drug users. *Journal of Clinical Psychiatry* 53(10):364–69.

Fergusson, D. M., M. T. Lynskey, and J. Horwood. 1996. Comorbidity between depressive disorders and Nicotine Dependence in a cohort of 16-year olds. *Archives of General Psychiatry* 53: 1043–47.

Hasin, D. S., W. Y. Tsai, J. Endicott, T. I. Mueller, W. Coryell, and M. Keller. 1996. The effects of Major Depression on alcoholism: Five year course. *American Journal on Addictions* 5:144–55.

Kessler, R. C., R. M. Crum, L. A. Warner, C. B. Nelson, J. Schulenberg, and J. C. Anthony. 1997. Lifetime co-occurrence of DSM-III-R Alcohol Abuse and Dependence with other psychiatric disorders in the National Comorbidity Study. *Archives of General Psychiatry* 54:313–21.

Kessler, R. C., K. A. McGonagle, S. Zhao, C. B. Nelson, M. Hughes, S. Eshleman, H. U. Wittchen, and K. S. Kendler. 1994. Lifetime and 12-month prevalence of DSM-III-R psychiatric disorders in the United States: Results from the National Comorbidity Survey. *Archives of General Psychiatry* 51:8–19.

Kranzler, H. R., J. A. Burleson, P. Korner, F. K. DelBoca, M. J. Bohn, J. Brown, and N. Liebowitz. 1995. Placebo-controlled trial of fluoxetine as an adjunct to relapse prevention in alcoholics. *American Journal of Psychiatry* 152:391–97.

Mason, B. J., J. H. Kocsis, E. C. Ritvo, and R. B. Cutler. 1996. A double-blind, placebo-controlled trial of desipramine for primary Alcohol Dependence stratified on the presence or absence of Major Depression. *Journal of the American Medical Association* 275:761–67.

Neighbors, B., T. Kempton, and R. Forehand. 1992. Cooccurrence of substance abuse with conduct, anxiety, and depression disorders in juvenile delinquents. *Addictive Behaviors* 17:379–86.

O'Sullilvan, K. 1984. Depression and its treatment in alcoholics: A review. *Canadian Journal of Psychiatry* 29:379–84.

Penick, E. C., B. J. Powell, E. J. Nickel, S. F. Bingham, K. R. Riesenmy, M. R. Read, and J. Campbell. 1994. Co-morbidity of lifetime psychiatric disorder among male alcoholic patients. *Alcoholism, Clinical Experimental Research* 18(6):1289–93.

Regier, D. A., M. E. Farmer, D. S. Rae, B. Z. Locke, S. J. Keith, L. L. Judd, and F. K. Goodwin. 1990. Comorbidity of mental disorders with alcohol and other drug abuse: Results from the Epidemiological Catchment Area (ECA) study. *Journal of the American Medical Association* 264:2511–18.

Romans, S. E., B. M. McNoe, G. P. Herbison, V. A. Walton, and P. E. Mullen. 1993. Cigarette smoking and psychiatric morbidity in women. *Australian and New Zealand Journal of Psychiatry* 27:399–404.

Rowe, M. G., M. F. Fleming, K. L. Barry, L. B. Manwell, and S. Kropp. 1995. Correlates of depression in primary care. *Family Practice* 41(6):551–58.

Roy, A., D. Lamparski, J. DeJong, V. Moore, and M. Linnoila. 1990. Characteristics of alcoholics who attempt suicide. *American Journal of Psychiatry* 147:761–65.

Schuckit, M. 1983. Alcoholic patients with secondary depression. *American Journal of Psychiatry* 140:711–15.

Schuckit, M. A., J. E. Tipp, M. Bergman, W. Reich, V. M. Hesselbrock, and T. L. Smith. 1997. Comparison of inducted and independent Major Depressive Disorders in 2,945 alcoholics. *American Journal of Psychiatry* 154:948–57.

Swendsen, J. D., K. R. Marikanagas, G. J. Canino, R. C. Kessler, M. Rubio-Stipec, and J. Angst. 1998. The comorbidity of alcoholism with anxiety and depressive disorders in four geographic communities. *Comprehensive Psychiatry* 39(4):176–84.

Viamontes, J. A. 1972. Review of drug effectiveness in the treatment of alcoholism. *American Journal of Psychiatry* 143:140–47.

Weiss, R. D., M. L. Griffin, and S. M. Mirin. 1992. Drug abuse as self-medication for depression: An empirical study. *American Journal of Drug and Alcohol Abuse* 18(2):121–29.

Weissman, M. M., and J. K. Miers. 1980. Clinical depression in alcoholism. *American Journal of Psychiatry* 137:372–73.

Westermeyer, J., and S. E. Eames. 1997. Clinical epidemiology of comorbid Dysthymia and Substance Disorder. *American Journal on Addictions* 6(1):48–53.

Westermeyer, J., S. Kopka, and S. Nugent. 1997. Course and severity of substance abuse among patients with comorbid Major Depression. *American Journal on Addictions* 6(4):284–92.

Westermeyer, J., S. Specker, J. Neider, and M. A. Lingenfelter. 1994. Substance abuse and associated psychiatric disorder among 100 adolescents. *Journal of Addictive Diseases* 13(1):67–83.

2

Understanding the Problem of Co-occurring Mood and Substance Use Disorders

Melissa P. DelBello, M.D., and Stephen M. Strakowski, M.D.

Substance abuse is exceptionally common during the course of affective illness. In the National Institute of Mental Health (NIMH) Epidemiological Catchment Area study, substance use disorders occurred in more than 60 percent of patients with type I bipolar disorder and 27 percent of patients with unipolar depression (Anthony and Helzer, 1991; Regier et al., 1990). This was primarily due to elevated rates of substance dependence, since nearly 70 percent of affectively ill patients with substance use disorders exhibited dependence rather than abuse. In the general population substance abuse is more common (Helzer, Burnam, and McEvoy, 1991; Regier et al., 1990). Similar high rates of substance dependence have been consistently reported from many different countries, treatment settings, and clinical and research populations (Bernadt and Murray, 1986; Gawin and Kleber, 1986; Goodwin and Jamison, 1990; Grant, 1995; Kessler et al., 1997; Miller and Fine, 1993; Miller et al., 1996a; Mueller et al., 1994; Paton, Kessler, and Kandel, 1977; Reich, Davies, and Himmelhoch, 1974; Schuckit et al., 1997a, 1997b; Strakowski et al., 1992, 1993, 1994, 1995, 1998a, 1998b; Verdoux et al., 1996; Weissman, Myers, and Harding, 1980; Weller, Aberger, and Goldberg, 1989; Winokur et al., 1995).

In both unipolar and bipolar disorders, substance dependence is typically associated with treatment noncompliance and poor clinical outcome (Goodwin and Jamison 1990; Grant 1995; Hartka et al., 1991; Hirschfeld et al., 1989; Keck et al., 1998; Miller et al., 1996a, 1996b; Mueller et al., 1994; Strakowski et al., 1998a; Tohen, Waternaux, and Tsuang, 1990; Weiss, Greenfield, and Najavits, 1995). Conversely, in substance users, the co-occurrence of an affective disorder may be associated with poorer outcome of the primary substance use disorder (Anthenelli and Schuckit, 1993; Schuckit et al., 1997a, 1997b; Tohen et al., 1990; Ziedonis and Kosten, 1991). Clearly, the co-occurrence of substance use and affective disorders represents a significant public health concern.

Despite being an important clinical problem, the reasons for high rates of substance use disorders in affective illness are unknown. However, three mechanisms might lead to the excess of substance dependence in affective disorders: (1) affective illness initiates substance dependence; (2) substance dependence initiates affective disorders in patients who would not otherwise develop affective illness; and (3) both conditions occur as a result of a common risk factor. In this chapter, we examine whether any of these hypotheses can be supported by the available literature and then discuss potential clinical implications of each of the proposed relationships between the disorders.

Hypothesis 1: Affective Illness Initiates Substance Dependence

Bipolar Disorder

One possible explanation for the high rates of substance dependence in bipolar disorder is that substance dependence is one of its sequelae. Historically, this has been proposed to occur for two reasons. The first is that substance dependence develops when patients attempt to self-medicate bipolar symptoms using drugs and alcohol (Khantzian, 1997; Sonne, Brady, and Morton, 1994; Weiss, Griffin, and Mirin, 1992). Specifically, patients are thought to use sedatives (e.g., alcohol, cannabis) to calm manic excitement and stimulants (e.g., cocaine) to relieve depression. Sonne, Brady, and Morton (1994) interviewed 25 bipolar patients with histories of substance use disorders, and 24 of them (96%) stated that they used drugs and alcohol to help their mood, consistent with this proposal. However, in many of those patients, the substance that was abused was inconsistent with the patient's state (e.g., sedative use during depression or stimulant use during mania). In contrast, Winokur, Clayton, and Reich (1969) found no evidence to suggest that patients used alcohol to relieve symptoms of mania. Moreover, Weiss and Mirin (1987) observed that some bipolar patients actually increase stimulant use during mania apparently to accentuate the manic high, rather than calm the manic excitement. In our 12-month prospective outcome study of 77 patients with first-episode mania, stimulant use was rare and did not seem to increase during depression (Strakowski et al., 1998b). Thus, there is minimal support in the literature for the self-medication hypothesis.

A second proposed mechanism is that substance abuse occurs as a result of the impulsivity, impaired judgment, and pleasure seeking of mania. Therefore, during the course of bipolar disorder, the amount of alcohol or drug use should correspond to the affective state. Supporting this, Mayfield and Coleman (1968) reported that 32 percent of 59 bipolar patients increased their alcohol use when manic, whereas only 10 percent increased their drinking when depressed. In contrast, Hensel and colleagues (Dunner, Hensel, and Fieve, 1979; Hensel, Dunner, and Fieve, 1979) found that, although 10 percent of 173 patients increased their drinking while manic, 5 percent actually decreased their alcohol use in this state. Equal numbers of bipolar patients increased and decreased their drinking when depressed (15% and 16%, respectively). Other studies provide similarly mixed results (Bernadt and Murray, 1986; Reich, Davies, and Himmelhoch, 1974; Winokur et al., 1969). When combined, these studies suggest that, during mania, approximately one-fourth of patients increase their alcohol use and only rarely do patients decrease their drinking. However, most patients do not change their alcohol consumption during a manic episode. During bipolar depression, patients are as likely to decrease as to increase their drinking (approximately 15% of each), although, again, the majority do not change their alcohol use. Notably, these studies used retrospective assessments. We recently prospectively analyzed the course of alcohol and drug abuse syndromes in 77 bipolar patients followed for one year after hospitalization for a first manic episode (Strakowski et al., 1998b). None of these patients abused alcohol in the absence of affective syndromes during follow-up, consistent with the hypothesis, although 21 percent continued to abuse cannabis after achieving remission from bipolar disorder. These results suggest that associations may be substance-specific (e.g., that alcohol and cannabis dependence develop in bipolar patients for different reasons).

If substance dependence is initiated in response to bipolar symptoms, then substance dependence should begin after the onset of bipolar illness. Several investigators studied the relative ages of onset of substance use and bipolar disorders (table 2.1) (Feinman and Dunner, 1996; Morrison 1975; Strakowski et al., 1996; Winokur et al., 1995). Taken together, they suggest that substance use disorders begin after the onset of the affective illness in only approximately 40 percent of patients. Several limitations must be considered when interpreting these studies, however. First, only one of the studies clearly stated how the age at onset for each disorder was defined, making them difficult to compare (Strakowski et al., 1996). Second, none of the studies differentiated substance abuse from dependence. Substance dependence is a more severe condition that has better diagnostic reliability and validity than substance abuse. This distinction is particularly important in bipolar patients because the excess of substance use disorders seems to be due to elevated rates of substance dependence, rather than abuse. Finally, although previous studies suggest that most patients exhibit the onset of substance abuse before the onset of bipolar illness, this still does not preclude the possibility of a relatively large minority of patients in whom substance dependence follows the onset of bipolar disorder and therefore may have been initiated by the affective illness.

Since many patients with bipolar disorder do not abuse drugs or alcohol during affective episodes, those who develop substance dependence in response to affective symptoms may have an increased familial risk for substance abuse that leads to this association. In general, as reviewed in table 2.2 (Strakowski and DelBello, 2000), studies have not reported elevated rates of substance abuse (typically alcoholism) in relatives of bipolar probands. However, few studies have specifically studied whether substance use disorders are increased in relatives of bipolar probands with co-occurring substance dependence. Indeed, Winokur et al. (1994, 1995) noted a systematic decrease in familial rates of alcoholism from bipolar probands with alcoholism to those without alcoholism to normal controls. Maier and Merikangas (1996) also found that alcoholism in bipolar probands was associated with higher familial rates of alcoholism but not bipolar disorder. In a first-episode sample, we found a higher rate of alcohol abuse in first-degree relatives of bipolar probands with alcohol use disorders as compared to probands without (Strakowski et al., 1996). These studies suggest that bipolar patients with substance dependence may have an increased risk of substance use disorders in their relatives.

Table 2.1. Relative Ages of Onset of Substance Abuse and Bipolar Disorder in Patients with Both Syndromes

Study	Total No. of Patients	No. with Substance Abuse Antecedent (%)	No. with Bipolar Disorder Antecedent[a] (%)	Comment
Morrison, 1975	18	8 (44)	10 (56)	Alcohol only
Winokur et al., 1995	64	34 (53)	30 (47)	Alcohol only
Feinman and Dunner, 1996	85	50 (59)	35 (41)	Alcohol and drug abuse
Strakowski et al., 1996	42	32 (76)	10 (24)	First-episode mania, alcohol and drug abuse
Total	209	124 (59)	85 (41)	

[a]Includes subjects in whom both occurred concurrently (<10% of patients with both in any study).

Table 2.2. Rates of Bipolar Disorder and Substance Abuse in Relatives of Bipolar Probands

Study	Total No. of Probands	Bipolar Disorder (%)	Substance Use Disorder (%)
Winokur et al., 1969[a]	56	10	7[b]
Taylor and Abrams, 1981[a]	134	6	15[b]
Morrison, 1975[d]	38	18[c]	15[b]
Dunner et al., 1979[d]	73	12	9[b]
Gershon et al., 1982[d]	96	5	5[e]
Spring and Rothgery, 1984	33	39[c]	3[b]
Dwyer and DeLong, 1987[a]	20[f]	14	13[b]
Strober et al., 1988[a]	50	15	6
Lish et al., 1993[a]	89	13	20
Winokur et al., 1995[g]	231	6	19[b]
Maier and Merikangas, 1996[a]	82	9	9[b]
DelBello et al., in press[a]	51	8[c]	9[b]

[a]Percentage is frequency of first-degree relatives.
[b]Alcohol abuse only.
[c]Includes all affective illness.
[d]Percentage is morbid risk in first-degree relatives.
[e]Includes patients with substance abuse only (i.e., does not include patients with substance abuse plus another psychiatric disorder, e.g., bipolar disorder).
[f]Includes only childhood-onset cases of bipolar disorder.
[g]Percentage is from life table estimate of total risk.

Unipolar Depression

Although clinically described, there is little research to support the hypothesis of alcohol use to self-medicate the symptoms of unipolar depression. As previously noted, alcohol is a depressant, and with chronic use, symptoms of depression rarely improve and often worsen (Brown and Schuckit, 1988; Davidson, 1995). In contrast, Mayfield (1968) found a statistically significant improvement in depressed mood after acute alcohol intoxication in both nondrinkers and drinkers. The improvement was statistically greater in nondrinkers than in drinkers, and the drinkers were not necessarily alcohol abusers. More than one-third of alcoholic persons showed symptoms of depression during drinking and the first 2–4 weeks after abstinence. However, in 80–90 percent of these individuals, conditions that resemble depressive disorders dissipate within several weeks after beginning abstinence (Brown and Schuckit, 1988; Brown et al., 1995a, 1995b; Davidson, 1995; Penick et al., 1988; Schuckit and Monteiro, 1988). In general, studies have shown that, in the short term, alcohol may lead to a decrease in symptoms of depression, although, with chronic use, it worsens depressive symptoms (Greeley, Swift, and Heather, 1992; Hartka et al., 1991).

The use of drugs other than alcohol to self-medicate the symptoms of depression is not supported by studies that have examined the effects of these drugs on depressive symptoms. Post, Kotin, and Goodwin (1974) studied the acute stimulant and euphoric effects of cocaine use on depressed patients. Orally administered cocaine did not have consistent effects on mood. Only 1 of 10 depressed patients became less depressed, 1 of 10 became more depressed, and the rest had equivocal or no change in their mood. However, intravenous cocaine, when given in large enough doses to cause large increases in vital signs, was associated in 50 percent of the cases with profound affective release and tearfulness after 1 minute of drowsiness or calmness. Other studies have also supported an increase in depression during cocaine use (Gawin and Kleber, 1986). In contrast, when given in moderate doses, stimulants, such as methylphenidate, may be useful in treating refractory depression, and case reports have described the self-medication of depression with pseudoephedrine (Diaz, Wise, and Semchyshyn, 1979; Rosenberg, Ahmed, and Hurwitz, 1991; Wallace, Kofoed, and West, 1992). However, with chronic use, pseudoephedrine and methylphenidate may produce fatigue and worsening of depression (Rosenfeld, 1979). McLellan, Woody, and O'Brien (1979) reported that chronic benzodiazepine and barbiturate abuse led to depressive symptoms in 8 of 14

(57%) subjects. Relatively few studies have examined the effects of marijuana use on depression. Ablon and Goodwin (1974) reported that 6 of 8 (75%) patients with unipolar depression had a dysphoric response after being given tetrahydrocannabinol twice daily for up to 1 week. One study suggested that decreased motivation may be the mediating factor that contributes to depression in chronic marijuana smokers (Musty and Kaback, 1995). Most studies that examine the effects of drugs on symptoms of depression fail to differentiate between depressive symptoms and disorders and substance use, abuse, and dependence. However, in general, there is little to support the use of drugs to self-medicate symptoms of depression, as most drugs, particularly with chronic use, exacerbate the symptoms of depression.

If substance use is the result of depressive symptoms, a second explanation for the relationship between depression and substance use disorders may be that substance use occurs as an alternative expression of the affective illness. However, 70–80 percent of patients with severe depression do not increase their alcohol consumption when depressed, so it is unlikely that drinking alcohol is an alternative expression of their affective illness (Anthenelli and Schuckit, 1993; Schuckit, 1994). Additionally, Harrington et al. (1990) followed 80 adolescents who had demonstrated significant major depressive episodes until age 30 and found that they were no more likely than controls to develop alcohol or other drug dependencies. Nonetheless, some individuals with depression may increase their alcohol use when they are depressed (Wood et al., 1977).

If depression leads to substance use, then it would be expected that the onset of depression would precede the onset of substance use disorders. Schuckit et al. (1997a, 1997b) examined lifetime rates of major depression in 2,713 alcohol-dependent subjects and found that only 5 percent had the onset of depression before the onset of alcohol dependence, 12 percent developed major depression after the onset of alcohol dependence but during a period of abstinence, and 32 percent had major depression only in the context of an active phase of their alcohol dependence. Other studies have found that 8–31 percent of patients with co-occurring alcohol use disorders and depression have the onset of depression before the onset of alcohol abuse (Hasegawa et al., 1991; Powell et al., 1987; Woodruff et al., 1973). Christie et al. (1988) evaluated patients with substance use and depressive or anxiety disorders. Depression or anxiety preceded the substance abuse disorder 74 percent of the time. Additionally, Henry and colleagues (1993) found that depression in boys at age 11 predicted later marijuana/glue and multiple drug use. Halikas, Goodwin, and Guze (1972) found that

50 percent of marijuana users with depression began using marijuana after their first depressive episode. Taken together, these studies suggest that depression precedes alcohol use approximately 30 percent of the time, leaving a large majority of patients in whom alcohol use occurs before the onset of depression. However, the effect of drugs other than alcohol may be different (Paton et al., 1977). Studies are conflicting, probably because of methodological limitations, including varying definitions of age of onset and the failure to distinguish between individual drug effects. Additionally, most studies did not differentiate among substance use, abuse, and dependence. This distinction is important because substance dependence disorders may account for a large portion of the high co-occurrence of substance use and affective disorders.

If major depression leads to substance use in some people but not others, then subjects with depression and substance use may have higher familial rates of substance use than those who are depressed without co-occurring substance use. In general, the studies that have examined familial rates of substance use in depressed probands have not reported elevated familial rates of substance use (table 2.3). However, the studies that examined familial rates of alcohol use in depressed probands with alcohol use as compared to depressed probands without alcohol use report conflicting results. Hasegawa et al. (1991) assessed familial rates of alcoholism and depression in 136 patients divided into three groups — those with primary depression, secondary depression, and nondepressive alcoholism. No statistically significant differences were noted in rates of family history of alcoholism and depression among the three groups. Maier, Lichterman, and Minges (1994) and Maier and Merikangas (1996) found no difference in familial rates of alcoholism among family members of probands with major depression with and without alcoholism and with alcoholism without major depression. In contrast, Merikangas et al. (1985a, 1985b) found offspring of probands with depression and secondary alcoholism to have a threefold greater risk of alcoholism than offspring of probands with depression alone. The NIMH Collaborative Study reported higher familial rates of alcoholism in probands with secondary depression (depression that occurs after alcohol use) than in depressed probands without alcohol use (Katz et al., 1979). Other studies have also found higher familial risk of alcoholism in probands with alcoholism and depression as compared with alcoholic probands (Aneshensel and Huba, 1983; Coryell et al., 1992; Grant and Pickering, 1997; Leibenluft et al., 1993). Grant and Pickering (1997) found familial rates of alcoholism to be greater in patients with primary depression as compared to probands with only depression, in patients with secondary depression as compared to probands with only depression, and in patients with concurrent depression and alcoholism as compared to probands with depression (however, there was no difference when all four groups were compared). In general, there may be an increased familial risk for "alcoholism" in depressed probands with co-occurring alcohol use as compared with probands with depression alone or alcoholism alone. However, the conflicting results may be due to failure to differentiate among alcohol use, abuse, and dependence; failure to account for substances other than alcohol; and inconsistent definitions of primary and secondary depression.

Table 2.3. Rates of Major Depression and Substance Abuse in Relatives of Depressed Probands

Study	Total No. of Probands	Major Depression (%)	Substance Use Disorder (%)
Winokur and Clayton, 1967[i]	426	17[j]	3[b]
Winokur et al., 1971	100	16	6[b,h]
Winokur et al., 1973[c]	225	12[j]	10[b,d]
Gershon et al., 1982[h]	30	17	7[e]
Weissman et al., 1984[a]	335	18	7[b,e]
Spring and Rothgery, 1984[a]	22	32	14[b]
Merikangas et al., 1985a[f]	114	16	9[b]
Merikangas et al., 1985b[a]	114	15	14[b]
Andreasen et al., 1987	330	26	19
Kupfer et al., 1988[k]	188	21	16[b]
Puig-Antich et al., 1989[g]	48	34	26
Coryell et al., 1992	153	28	22[b]
Leibenluft et al., 1993	33	23	17
Goldstein et al., 1994[a]	41	35	22[b]
Maier and Merikangas, 1996[a]	160	19	9[b]

[a]Percentage is frequency of first-degree relatives.
[b]Alcohol abuse only.
[c]Percentage is morbid risk in parents.
[d]Percentage is morbid risk in fathers.
[e]Includes patients with substance abuse only (i.e., does not include patients with substance abuse plus another psychiatric disorder, e.g., bipolar disorder).
[f]Offspring only.
[g]Percentage is morbid risk in first-degree relatives age 18+ of child probands.
[h]Percentage is morbid risk in first-degree relatives.
[i]Percentage is morbid risk in siblings.
[j]Percentage includes all affective illnesses.
[k]Percentage is morbid risk in parents and siblings.

Based on the above research, there may be a subset of patients with affective illnesses in whom the affective illness leads to substance use disorders. Therefore, it is essential to prevent the onset of substance use in these patients by educating them about the effects of substance use during their initial treatment for and throughout the course of their affective illness. Since these patients often have family members who use substances, education of family members should be included in the treatment plan. Additionally, since some patients with affective illnesses increase their substance use when they are in depressed or manic states, mood stabilization and medication compliance should be primary treatment goals.

Hypothesis 2: Substance Dependence May Initiate Affective Illnesses

A second explanation for why substance dependence is so common in affective disorders is that the affective illness occurs as a sequela of the substance use disorder. It is well known that most substances of abuse can produce affective symptoms in users that mimic primary affective disorders (Goodwin and Jamison, 1990). Therefore, substance dependence may either directly cause symptoms that resemble those of primary affective disorders or precipitate affective illness in vulnerable individuals (Post, 1992). To explain the excess of substance dependence in bipolar disorder and unipolar depression, substance use would have to precipitate affective illness in people who otherwise would not have become ill, thereby selectively increasing the number of bipolar and unipolar patients with concurrent substance use disorders. If this occurs, then (1) substance dependence should begin before the onset of bipolar and unipolar disorders, (2) affective episodes should occur during periods of substance dependence and not after periods of sobriety, and (3) patients with substance dependence should have lower familial rates of unipolar or bipolar disorder than patients without.

Bipolar Disorder

As previously reviewed, approximately 60 percent of patients develop substance abuse before the onset of their bipolar illness (Strakowski and DelBello, 2000). Moreover, several investigators reported that bipolar patients with antecedent alcohol abuse have a later age of bipolar onset than do those without antecedent alcohol abuse (Morrison, 1975; Strakowski et al., 1996, 1998b; Winokur et al., 1995). This observation led Winokur et al. (1995) to suggest that several years of alcohol use may be necessary to precipitate bipolar illness in some patients who might not otherwise have developed affective illness.

If substance dependence initiates a bipolar syndrome, then patients using drugs or alcohol would be expected to have frequent affective episodes, which would occur much less often, if at all, when the patient achieved sobriety. Unfortunately, few studies have examined the longitudinal courses of bipolar and substance use disorders in patients with both. Winokur et al. (1995) reported that, at five years of follow-up, only 5 percent of the patients with bipolar disorder continued to exhibit alcoholism, compared with 37 percent at intake. Those patients for whom alcohol abuse preceded the onset of the bipolar illness were more likely to recover and had fewer affective relapses than patients in whom affective illness predated the onset of the alcoholism. These findings indirectly suggest that some bipolar patients with antecedent alcoholism may require alcohol abuse to maintain affective symptoms. Young, Patel, and Keeler (1981) followed 15 bipolar patients with alcohol abuse for 1 year. They found that symptoms of alcoholism tended to appear before affective symptoms in those patients with affective relapses. We recently examined the temporal relationships of the courses of bipolar and co-occurring substance use disorders during a 12-month follow-up period (Strakowski et al., 1998b). During follow-up, 54 percent of the patients with a history of alcohol abuse experienced ongoing affective episodes in the absence of alcohol abuse, although alcohol abuse always occurred concurrently with an affective syndrome. These data suggest that affective symptoms do not necessarily initiate drinking in patients with a history of alcohol abuse, but when alcohol abuse does occur, it is associated with affective symptoms. In contrast, 21 percent of patients with drug abuse experienced resolution of their bipolar disorder while continuing to abuse drugs (cannabis in all cases). Thus, some patients are not simply using cannabis for symptom modulation, nor is cannabis abuse directly inducing affective and psychotic symptoms in many patients. Together, these studies suggest that a subgroup of bipolar patients with substance dependence exhibit a course of illness consistent with the hypothesis that substance dependence precipitates affective episodes.

To address these relationships in more detail, we have incorporated week-by-week longitudinal assessments based directly on the methodology of the NIMH Collaborative Depression Study (Katz et al., 1979; Mueller et al., 1994) in an ongoing longitudinal study of first-episode mania. In this study, substance use and affective illness are independently rated over time. In a small sample of 18 patients with histories of alcohol or cannabis dependence, we examined these data for associations between the courses of bipolar disorder and of alcohol and cannabis dependence for up to 68 weeks of follow-up. We classified patients according to the relative courses of affective and substance use disorders. Seven patients (39%) developed most interval affective episodes after increases in or continuous alcohol or cannabis abuse, and in 6 of these, substance dependence had begun at least 1 year before the onset of the affective illness. This subgroup fits our hypothesis that bipolar illness is precipitated by substance dependence in some patients. Four other subjects (22% of the total group) who exhibited substance dependence that began before the onset of bipolar illness may also belong in this subgroup. One of these demonstrated continuous affective episodes and substance dependence throughout a 16-week follow-up. The other 3 patients experienced, concurrently, complete resolution of both substance dependence and affective symptoms. In contrast, only a single subject (6%) demonstrated exacerbations of cannabis dependence (that was not antecedent) in apparent response to new affective episodes, consistent with the hypothesis that substance dependence occurs in response to bipolar symptoms. Additionally, 3 subjects demonstrated new affective episodes in the absence of substance abuse during follow-up, and the final 2 subjects continued to abuse cannabis and alcohol after recovering from their index manic episode, thereby not obviously fitting any of the hypothesized associations. However, with additional course data and longer follow-up periods, many of these patients may declare or develop different associations between the courses of substance use and bipolar disorders.

If substance dependence causes bipolar disorder in patients who would not otherwise develop bipolar illness, then those patients should demonstrate a lower familial risk for bipolar disorder than patients with no substance abuse history. As noted, several studies examined rates of familial affective illness in bipolar patients with or without alcohol abuse and reported few differences between the two groups. However, the investigators did not separately identify patients in whom alcohol abuse began before the onset of bipolar disorder (Dunner, Hensel, and Fieve, 1979; Miller et al., 1996a, 1996b; Morrison 1975; Winokur et al., 1995). We recently examined familial rates of affective illness in first-episode manic patients with antecedent alcohol abuse (DelBello et al., 1999). We found that affective illness was significantly less common in the relatives of probands with both antecedent alcohol abuse and bipolar disorder than those of probands with bipolar disorder alone. These results again suggest that, in subgroups of patients (e.g., those with antecedent alcohol abuse), different associations may be found between bipolar and substance use disorders than when studying patients more generally.

Unipolar Depression

As discussed previously, the few studies that have examined relationships between age at onset of substance use and depression have provided conflicting results. Based on these studies, however, the effects of alcohol may be different from those of cocaine. Specifically, in the majority of cases (possibly up to 70%), the onset of alcoholism precedes that of depression. In contrast, the onset of cocaine use usually follows the onset of depression. Grant, Hasin, and Dawson (1996) examined age at onset of alcoholism and depression in primary (depression before alcoholism) depressives versus secondary depressives and found similar ages at onset of alcoholism but a significantly later onset of depression in secondary depressives, suggesting that, in these patients, alcohol use may have been necessary to initiate the depression.

Additional support for the hypothesis that substance dependence precipitates affective illnesses is provided by several studies reporting that longer duration of alcohol consumption is associated with greater prevalence of depression. For this reason, Schuckit (1986, 1994) describes the importance of differentiating between primary and secondary affective disorders. Schuckit suggests that patients with episodes of major depression only in the context of substance abuse should be considered as having a secondary affective disorder and patients with major depression antedating severe alcohol problems should be considered to have a primary affective disorder. The potential relevance of this distinction is justified in that only 5 percent of alcoholic men and 15 percent of alcoholic women demonstrate major depressive episodes independent of heavy drinking. Therefore, 85–95 percent of alcoholic persons have depression only during periods of heavy alcohol use. In contrast, Moscato et al. (1997) found that depressive symptoms in women predicted later alcohol use (at 3–7 years follow-up) but alcohol problems did not predict later depressive symptoms in men, supporting the hypothesis that affective illness initiated substance dependence. However, others have found a reciprocal relationship where alcohol use in the long term (12 months) leads to increases in depression and depression in the short term (4–8 months) leads to increase in alcohol use (Dawson and Grant, 1998). A meta-analysis of eight longitudinal studies revealed a positive relationship between earlier depression and later quantity of alcohol consumption and quantity of alcohol consumption and later alcohol use in women (Hartka et al., 1991; Miller et al., 1996a, 1996b). To our knowledge, no studies have examined the longitudinal relationship between substance use and depression in patients already diagnosed with these co-occurring disorders.

With the exception of Leibenluft and colleagues (1993), who did not use direct family interviews, family history studies, in general, have reported no differences in familial rates of unipolar depression between depressed probands with and without alcohol use (Grant and Pickering, 1997; Maier, Lichterman, and Minges, 1994; Merikangas et al., 1985a, 1985b; Musty and Kaback, 1995; Schuckit et al., 1997b). Future investigations examining familial rates of depression need to better define substance use disorders, examine the effects of substances other than alcohol, and examine whether substance use was antecedent to the onset of affective disorder in probands.

In general, patients who come to clinical attention for substance use disorders need to be carefully evaluated for symptoms and signs of affective disorders, which if severe enough should be treated accordingly. Additionally, patients with substance abuse disorders should be educated about the potential risk of precipitating the onset of an affective disorder with continued use of substances.

Hypothesis 3: Affective and Substance Use Disorders Share a Risk Factor

In addition to one disorder precipitating the other, the elevated rates of substance dependence in affective illnesses could result from a shared risk factor for both conditions. One proposed risk factor is that the gene or genes causing affective disorders also contribute to the development of substance abuse (Goodwin and Jamison, 1990). In general, family studies have not supported this hypothesis (see tables 2.2 and 2.3). An alternative risk factor that may be common to both disorders is psychosocial stress. Post (1992) proposed that recurrent affective illnesses may be initiated by stressful life events through a sensitization or kindling mechanism. Specifically, he suggested that stressors are more common at the onset of the affective disorder and that these stressors precipitate the first few affective episodes in vulnerable individuals. As the illness progresses, episodes occur after increasingly milder stressors, thereby becoming more frequent. Over time, permanent changes in gene expression in the brain lead to spontaneous affective episodes. Some but not all clinical studies have supported this hypothesis (Ambelas, 1979, 1987; Ellicott et al., 1990; Ezquiaga, Gutierrez, and Lopez, 1987; Hammen et al., 1989; Hunt, Bruce-Jones, and Silverstone, 1992; McPherson, Herbison, and Romans, 1993). Other studies have suggested that, even in the absence of clinical evidence for sensitization or kindling, stressors may precipitate affective episodes in bipolar patients throughout the course of illness (Hammen et al., 1989; Hunt, Bruce-Jones, and Silverstone, 1992).

Similarly, alcohol and drug dependence may be initiated after life stressors, and stressors have been associated with relapse from sobriety (Abbey, Smith, and Scott, 1993; Brown et al., 1990; Kreuger 1981; Smith, Abbey, and Scott, 1993), although this has not been observed universally (Johnson and Pandina, 1993; Miller et al., 1996a, 1996b). This disagreement, plus other findings, has led investigators to propose a "stress-vulnerability" model of alcohol relapse, in which stressful life events interact with other environmental and psychological factors leading to relapse (Brown et al., 1995a, 1995b). It is possible that these same vulnerabilities interact with stressful life events in affective disorders, also contributing to the initiation of affective episodes. Unfortunately, to our knowledge, no study has examined associations among stressful life events, substance dependence, and affective episodes in bipolar patients.

Although we have not specifically examined associations between life events and the course of illness in our outcome studies, we did prospectively study associations between posttraumatic stress disorder (PTSD) and bipolar disorder in patients with both conditions (Strakowski et al., 1998b). We observed that PTSD (and the trauma causing it) typically developed more than one year before the onset of the affective illness. The course of PTSD was distinct from that of the bipolar disorder in most patients with both syndromes and was not significantly associated with the development of substance abuse syndromes. However, PTSD was far more prevalent in these patients than expected by chance. These data suggest that there may be a subgroup of bipolar patients who experience severe life stressors and develop both PTSD and bipolar disorder that then progress independently.

The few studies that have examined the relationship between unipolar depression, stressful life events, PTSD, and substance use disorders have found these variables to be related. Boyd (1993) examined 105 African American women who used crack cocaine for histories of sexual abuse and depression. She found that 61 percent of the women reported at least one episode of sexual abuse, 70 percent met DSM-III criteria for lifetime major depression, and the mean age of first sexual abuse was younger than the mean age of first illicit drug use and the mean age of first depressive symptoms. However, subjects were not assessed for symptoms of PTSD, and sexual abuse was not limited to childhood sexual abuse. Despite these limitations, this study does provide evidence for the high co-occurrence of sexual abuse, substance use disorders, and major depression and possibly that sexual abuse may precede the latter two in most cases. Buckner and Mandell (1990) found that stressful life events and low self-esteem predicted symptoms of depression in methaqualone users, suggesting a multifactorial nature of depressive symptoms in drug abusers.

Treatment Considerations

Although there are still insufficient data to decide whether any one hypothesis is correct, there may be evidence to support all three hypotheses, suggesting that the relationship between substance use and affective disorders is heterogeneous. Therefore, when evaluating patients with both conditions it would be prudent to attempt to identify the manner in which the courses of the disorders occur relative to each other. If substance use leads to affective episodes, then substance abuse should be treated as primary, with aggressive treatment of the substance use disorder and education about the psychiatric complications of substance use. However, depressive or bipolar symptoms should be aggressively treated if they are severe or persist despite abstinence. Some authors recommend 2–4 weeks of abstinence before treating depression, based on the studies of depressed alcoholic persons (Anthenelli and Schuckit, 1993; Brown and Schuckit, 1988; Wood et al., 1977). However, waiting that long in patients with acute mania may not be possible. In general, inquiring about mood symptoms during a significant period of abstinence may help differentiate a primary substance use disorder from a primary affective disorder. Additionally, in each patient, establishing the chronology of the appearance of the disorders and gathering family history may provide helpful information as to whether affective illness led to substance use disorders or vice versa (Harrington et al., 1990).

　　If the affective illness seems to lead to a substance use disorder, then the affective illness should be treated as primary. However, alcohol and drug use prevention should begin at the onset of the affective illness, even with patients who have been sober, as new affective symptoms and signs may increase the risk of substance use disorder relapse. Patients should be educated that drinking and substance use are likely to exacerbate the course of affective illness (Schuckit, 1986). They should also be advised that affective symptoms may exacerbate the course of substance use disorders.

An alternative to this sequential approach, which incorporates a more integrated treatment of both disorders, has been increasing in clinical practice. To our knowledge, there have yet to be studies that have found one method of treatment superior to the other. Most investigators advocate the use of pharmacotherapy to treat the affective illness in hope of reducing patients' symptoms and making them able to participate in substance abuse treatment programs. Although alcohol use does not increase relapse rates in patients with depression, previous studies suggest that treating depressed substance users with antidepressants may decrease depressive symptoms, but few studies have examined their effects on substance use (Merikangas and Gelernter, 1990; Weiss, Greenfield, and Najavits, 1995). Further studies are needed to investigate the benefits of pharmacotherapy, particularly using the new antidepressants in the treatment of depressed substance abusers. Studies of mood stabilizers in the treatment of bipolar disorder and substance abuse have provided conflicting results and are limited because of their small sample sizes (Gawin and Kleber, 1984; Greeley, Swift, and Heather, 1992; Nunes et al., 1993).

If a common risk factor seems to be precipitating both affective and substance use disorders (i.e., sexual abuse, trauma, and PTSD), then treatment should be tailored to minimize the effect of the stressor and decrease the specific symptoms. Research is needed to identify these risk factors and develop prevention and early intervention strategies for those at risk. Clearly, the relationships between substance use and affective disorders warrant further clinical study. As studies advance our understanding about how these disorders interact, effective treatment options for specific clinical situations will become clearer.

Conclusion

Three proposed mechanisms for understanding the high co-occurrence between affective and substance use disorders are that (1) affective illness initiates substance dependence, (2) substance dependence initiates affective disorders in patients who would not otherwise develop affective illness, and (3) both conditions occur as a result of a common risk factor. From the evidence presented, it seems that the relationship between substance use and affective disorders is heterogeneous, as there may be subsets of patients in which each of the above mechanisms may help to explain the relationship between co-morbid substance use and affective disorders. Diagnostic evaluations should be aimed at understanding relevant clinical and demographic characteristics, the family history of affective and substance use disorders, and the longitudinal relationship between the co-occurring illnesses. This approach may help to elucidate which of the proposed mechanisms may be applicable to an individual patient. Based on the few existing data, we suggest treatment strategies. However, further studies of relatively homogeneous subsets of patients (possibly based on mechanism of comorbidity) are necessary.

ACKNOWLEDGMENTS
The research for this chapter was supported in part by NIMH awards MH54317 and MH/DA58170.

REFERENCES
Abbey, A., M. J. Smith, and R. O. Scott. 1993. The relationship between reasons for drinking alcohol and alcohol consumption: An interaction approach. *Addictive Behaviors* 18:659–70.
Ablon, S. L., and F. K. Goodwin. 1974. High frequency of dysphoric reactions to tetrahydrocannabinol among depressed patients. *American Journal of Psychiatry* 131:448–53.
Ambelas, A. 1979. Psychologically stressful events in the precipitation of manic episodes. *British Journal of Psychiatry* 135:15–21.
———. 1987. Life events and mania: A special relationship. *British Journal of Psychiatry* 150:235–40.
Andreasen, N. C., J. Rice, J. Endicott, W. Coryell, W. M. Grove, and T. Reich. 1987. Familial rates of affective disorders. *Archives of General Psychiatry* 44:461–69.
Aneshensel, C. S., and G. J. Huba. 1983. Depression, alcohol use and smoking over one year: A four-wave longitudinal causal model. *Journal of Abnormal Psychology* 92:134–50.
Anthenelli, R. M., and M. A. Schuckit. 1993. Affective and anxiety disorders and alcohol and drug dependence: Diagnosis and treatment. In *Comorbidity of Addictive and Psychiatric Disorders*, edited by N. S. Miller and B. Stimmel, 73–87. New York: Haworth Press.
Anthony, J. C., and J. E. Helzer. 1991. Syndromes of drug abuse and dependence. In *Psychiatric Disorders in America: The Epidemiologic Catchment Area Study*, edited by D. A. Regier and L. N. Robins, 116–54. New York: Free Press.

Bernadt, M. W., and R. M. Murray. 1986. Psychiatric disorder, drinking and alcoholism: What are the links? *British Journal of Psychiatry* 148:393–400.

Boyd, C. J. 1993. The antecedents of women's crack cocaine abuse: Family substance abuse, sexual abuse, depression and illicit drug use. *Journal of Substance Abuse Treatment* 107:433–38.

Brown, S. A., and M. A. Schuckit. 1988. Changes in depression among abstinent alcoholics. *Journal of Studies on Alcohol* 49:412–17.

Brown, S. A., P. W. Vik, J. R. McQuaid, T. L. Patterson, M. R. Irwin, and I. Grant. 1990. Severity of psychosocial stress and outcome of alcoholism treatment. *Journal of Abnormal Psychology* 99:344–48.

Brown, S. A., R. K. Inaba, J. C. Gillin, M. A. Schuckit, M. A. Stewart, and M. R. Irwin. 1995a. Alcoholism and affective disorder: Clinical course of depressive symptoms. *American Journal of Psychiatry* 152:45–52.

Brown, S. A., P. W. Vik, T. L. Patterson, I. Grant, and M. A. Schuckit. 1995b. Stress, vulnerability, and adult alcohol relapse. *Journal of Studies on Alcohol* 56:538–45.

Buckner, J. C., and W. Mandell. 1990. Risk factors for depressive symptomatology in a drug using population. *American Journal of Public Health* 80:580–85.

Christie, K. A., J. D. Burke, D. A. Regier, D. S. Rae, J. H. Boyd, and B. Z. Locke. 1988. Epidemiologic evidence for early onset of mental disorder and higher risk of drug abuse in young adults. *American Journal of Psychiatry* 145:971–75.

Coryell, W., G. Winokur, M. Keller, W. Scheftner, and J. Endicott. 1992. Alcoholism and primary major depression: A family study approach to co-existing disorders. *Journal of Affective Disorders* 24:93–99.

Davidson, K. M. 1995. Diagnosis of depression in alcohol dependence: Changes in prevalence with drinking status. *British Journal of Psychiatry* 166:199–204.

Dawson, D. A., and B. F. Grant. 1998. Family history of alcoholism and gender: Their combined effects on DSM-IV alcohol dependence and major depression. *Journal of Studies on Alcohol* 59:97–106.

DelBello, M. P., S. M. Strakowski, K. W. Sax, S. L. McElroy, P. E. Keck Jr., S. A. West, and G. F. Kmetz. 1999. Familial rates of affective and substance use disorders in patients with first-episode mania. *Journal of Affective Disorders* 56:55–60.

Diaz, M. A., T. N. Wise, and G. O. Semchyshyn. 1979. Self-medication with pseudoephedrine in a chronically depressed patient. *American Journal of Psychiatry* 136:1217–18.

Dunner, D. L., B. M. Hensel, and R. R. Fieve. 1979. Bipolar illness: Factors in drinking behavior. *American Journal of Psychiatry* 136:583–85.

Dwyer, J. T., and G. R. DeLong. 1987. A family history study of twenty probands with childhood manic-depressive illness. *Journal of the American Academy of Child and Adolescent Psychiatry* 26:176–80.

Ellicott, A., C. Hammen, M. Gitlin, G. Brown, and D. Jamison. 1990. Life events and the course of bipolar disorder. *American Journal of Psychiatry* 147:1194–98.

Ezquiaga, E., J. L. A. Gutierrez, and A. G. Lopez. 1987. Psychosocial factors and episode number in depression. *Journal of Affective Disorders* 12:135–38.

Feinman, J. A., and D. L. Dunner. 1996. The effect of alcohol and substance abuse on the course of bipolar affective disorder. *Journal of Affective Disorders* 37:43–49.

Gawin, F. H., and H. D. Kleber. 1984. Cocaine abuse treatment: An open pilot trial with desipramine and lithium carbonate. *Archives of General Psychiatry* 41:903–9.

———. 1986. Abstinence symptomatology and psychiatric diagnosis in cocaine abusers. *Archives of General Psychiatry* 43:107–13.

Gershon, E. S., J. Hamovit, J. J. Guroff, E. Dibble, J. F. Leckman, W. Sceery, S. D. Targun, J. I. Nurnberger, L. R. Goldin, and W. E. Bunney. 1982. A family study of schizoaffective, bipolar I, bipolar II, unipolar, and normal control probands. *Archives of General Psychiatry* 39:1157–67.

Goldstein, R. B., M. M. Weissman, P. B. Adams, E. Horwath, J. D. Lish, D. Charney, S. W. Woods, C. Sobin, and P. J. Wickramaratne. 1994. Psychiatric disorders in relatives of probands with panic disorder and/or major depression. *Archives of General Psychiatry* 51:383–94.

Goodwin, F. K., and K. R. Jamison. 1990. *Manic-Depressive Illness*. New York: Oxford University Press.

Grant, B. F. 1995. Comorbidity between DSM-IV drug use disorders and major depression: Results of a national survey of adults. *Journal of Substance Abuse* 7:481–97.

Grant, B. F., and R. P. Pickering. 1997. Familial aggregation of DSM-IV alcohol use disorders: Examination of the primary-secondary distinction in a general population sample. *Journal of Nervous and Mental Disease* 185:335–43.

Grant, B. F., D. S. Hasin, and D. A. Dawson. 1996. The relationship between DSM-IV alcohol use disorders and DSM-IV major depression: Examination of the primary-secondary distinction in a general population sample. *Journal of Affective Disorders* 38:113–28.

Greeley, J., W. Swift, and N. Heather. 1992. Depressed affect as a predictor of increased desire for alcohol in current drinkers of alcohol. *British Journal of Addiction* 87:1005–12.

Halikas, J. A., D. W. Goodwin, and S. B. Guze. 1972. Marihuana use and psychiatric illness. *Archives of General Psychiatry* 27:162–65.

Hammen, C., A. Ellicott, M. Gitlin, and K. R. Jamison. 1989. Sociotropy/autonomy and vulnerability to specific life events in patients with unipolar depression and bipolar disorders. *Journal of Abnormal Psychology* 98:154–60.

Harrington, R., H. Fudge, M. Rutter, A. Pickles, and J. Hill. 1990. Adult outcomes of childhood and adolescent depression. *Archives of General Psychiatry* 47:465–73.

Hartka, E., B. Johnstone, E. V. Leino, M. Motoyoshi, M. T. Temple, and K. M. Filmore. 1991. A meta-analysis of depressive symptomatology and alcohol consumption over time. *British Journal of Addiction* 86:1269–81.

Hasegawa, K., H. Mulkasa, Y. Nakazawa, H. Kodama, and K. Nakamura. 1991. Primary and secondary depression in alcoholism — clinical features and family history. *Drug and Alcohol Dependence* 27:275–81.

Helzer, J. E., A. Burnam, and L. T. McEvoy. 1991. Alcohol abuse and dependence. In

Psychiatric Disorders in America: The Epidemiologic Catchment Area Study, edited by D. A. Regier and L. N. Robins, 81–115. New York: Free Press.

Henry, B., M. Feehan, R. Mcgee, W. Stanton, T. E. Moffitt, and P. Silva. 1993. The importance of conduct problems and depressive symptoms in predicting adolescent substance use. *Journal of Abnormal Child Psychology* 21:469–80.

Hensel, B., D. L. Dunner, and R. R. Fieve. 1979. The relationship of family history of alcoholism to primary affective disorder. *Journal of Affective Disorders* 1:105–13.

Hirschfeld, R. M. A., T. Kosier, M. B. Keller, P. W. Lavori, and J. Endicott. 1989. The influence of alcoholism on the course of depression. *Journal of Affective Disorders* 16:151–58.

Hunt, N., W. Bruce-Jones, and T. Silverstone. 1992. Life events and relapse in bipolar affective disorder. *Journal of Affective Disorders* 25:13–20.

Johnson, V., and R. J. Pandina. 1993. A longitudinal examination of the relationships among stress, coping strategies, and problems associated with alcohol use. *Alcoholism, Clinical and Experimental Research* 17:696–702.

Katz, M. M., S. K. Secunda, R. M. A. Hirschfeld, and S. H. Koslow. 1979. NIMH Clinical Research Branch Collaborative Program on Psychobiology of Depression. *Archives of General Psychiatry* 36:765–71.

Keck, P. E., Jr., S. L. McElroy, S. M. Strakowski, S. A. West, K. W. Sax, J. M. Hawkins, M. L. Bourne, and P. Haggard. 1998. Twelve-month outcome of bipolar patients following hospitalization for a manic or mixed episode. *American Journal of Psychiatry* 155:646–52.

Kessler, R. C., R. M. Crum, L. A. Warner, C. B. Nelson, J. Schulenberg, and J. C. Anthony. 1997. Lifetime co-occurrence of DSM-III-R alcohol abuse and dependence with other psychiatric disorders in the National Comorbidity Survey. *Archives of General Psychiatry* 54:313–21.

Khantzian, E. J. 1997. The self-medication hypothesis of substance use disorders: A reconsideration and recent applications. *Harvard Review of Psychiatry* 4:231–44.

Kreuger, D. W. 1981. Stressful life events and the return to heroin use. *Journal of Human Stress* 7:3–8.

Kupfer, D. J., L. L. Carpenter, and E. Frank. 1988. Is bipolar II a unique disorder? *Comprehensive Psychiatry* 29:228–36.

Leibenluft, E., P. A. Madden, S. E. Dick, and N. E. Rosenthal. 1993. Primary depression with secondary alcoholism compared with alcoholics and depressives. *Comprehensive Psychiatry* 34:83–86.

Lish, J. D., L. Gyulai, S. M. Resnick, A. Kirtland, J. D. Amsterdam, P. C. Whybrow, and R. A. Price. 1993. A family history study of rapid-cycling bipolar disorder. *Psychiatry Research* 48:37–45.

Maier, W., and K. Merikangas. 1996. Co-occurrence and co-transmission of affective disorders and alcoholism in families. *British Journal of Psychiatry* 168:93–100.

Maier, W., D. Lichterman, and J. Minges. 1994. The relationship between alcoholism and unipolar depression: A controlled family history study. *Journal of Psychiatric Research* 28:303–17.

Mayfield, D. G. 1968. Psychopharmacology of alcohol: Affective change with intoxication, drinking behavior, and affective state. *Journal of Nervous and Mental Disease* 146:314–21.

Mayfield, D. G., and L. L. Coleman. 1968. Alcohol use and affective disorder. *Diseases of the Nervous System* 29:467–74.

McLellan, A. T., G. E. Woody, and C. P. O'Brien. 1979. Development of psychiatric illness in drug abusers. *New England Journal of Medicine* 301:1310–14.

McPherson, H., P. Herbison, and S. Romans. 1993. Life events and relapse in established bipolar affective disorder. *British Journal of Psychiatry* 163:381–85.

Merikangas, K. R., and C. S. Gelernter. 1990. Comorbidity for alcoholism and depression. *Psychiatric Clinics of North America* 13:613–32.

Merikangas, K. R., J. F. Leckman, B. A. Prusoff, D. L. Pauls, and M. M. Weissman. 1985a. Familial transmission of depression and alcoholism. *Archives of General Psychiatry* 42:367–72.

Merikangas, K. R., M. M. Weissman, B. A. Prusoff, D. L. Pauls, and J. F. Leckman. 1985b. Depressives with secondary alcoholism: Psychiatric disorders in offspring. *Journal of Studies on Alcohol* 46:199–204.

Miller, N. S., and J. Fine. 1993. Current epidemiology of comorbidity of psychiatric and addictive disorders. *Psychiatric Clinics of North America* 16:1–10.

Miller, N. S., D. Klamen, N. G. Hoffmann, and J. A. Flaherty. 1996a. Prevalence of depression and alcohol and other drug dependence in addictions treatment populations. *Journal of Psychoactive Drugs* 28:111–24.

Miller, W. R., V. S. Westerberg, R. J. Harris, and J. S. Tonigan. 1996b. What predicts relapse? Prospective testing of antecedent models. *Addiction* 91(suppl):155–72.

Morrison, J. R. 1975. The family histories of manic-depressive patients with and without alcoholism. *Journal of Nervous and Mental Disease* 160:227–29.

Moscato, B. S., M. Russel, M. Zielezny, E. Bromet, G. Egri, P. Mudar, and J. R. Marshall. 1997. Gender differences in the relation between depressive symptoms and alcohol problems: A longitudinal perspective. *American Journal of Epidemiology* 146:966–74.

Mueller, T. I., P. W. Lavori, M. B. Keller, A. Swart, M. Warshaw, D. Hasin, W. Coryell, J. Endicott, J. Rice, and H. Akiskal. 1994. Prognostic effect of the variable course of alcoholism on the 10-year course of depression. *American Journal of Psychiatry* 151:701–6.

Musty, R. E., and L. Kaback. 1995. Relationship between motivation and depression in chronic marijuana users. *Life Sciences* 56:2151–58.

Nunes, E. V., P. J. McGrath, S. Wager, and F. M. Quitkin. 1993. Lithium treatment for cocaine abusers with bipolar spectrum disorders. *American Journal of Psychiatry* 150:963–65.

Paton, S., R. Kessler, and D. Kandel. 1977. Depressive mood and adolescent illicit drug use: A longitudinal analysis. *Journal of Genetic Psychology* 131:267–89.

Penick, E. C., B. J. Powell, B. L. Liskow, J. O. Jackson, and E. J. Nickel. 1988. The stability of coexisting psychiatric syndromes in alcoholic men after one year. *Journal of Studies on Alcohol* 49:395–405.

Post, R. M. 1992. Transduction of psychosocial stress into the neurobiology of recurrent affective disorder. *American Journal of Psychiatry* 149:999–1010.

Post, R. M., J. Kotin, and F. K. Goodwin. 1974. The effects of cocaine on depressed patients. *American Journal of Psychiatry* 131:511–17.

Powell, B. J., M. R. Read, E. C. Penick, N. S. Miller, and S. F. Bingham. 1987. Primary and secondary depression in alcoholic men: An important distinction. *Journal of Clinical Psychiatry* 48:98–101.

Puig-Antich, J., D. Goetz, M. Davies, T. Kaplan, S. Davies, L. Ostrow, L. Asnis, J. Twomey, S. Iyengar, and N. Ryan. 1989. A controlled family history study of prepubertal major depressive disorder. *Archives of General Psychiatry* 46:406–18.

Regier, D. A., M. E. Farmer, D. S. Rae, B. Z. Locke, S. J. Keith, L. L. Judd, and F. K. Goodwin. 1990. Comorbidity of mental disorders with alcohol and other drug abuse: Results from the Epidemiologic Catchment Area (ECA) Study. *Journal of the American Medical Association* 264:2511–18.

Reich, L. H., R. K. Davies, and J. M. Himmelhoch. 1974. Excessive alcohol use in manic-depressive illness. *American Journal of Psychiatry* 131:83–86.

Rosenberg, P. B., I. Ahmed, and S. Hurwitz. 1991. Methylphenidate in depressed medically ill patients. *Journal of Clinical Psychiatry* 52:263–67.

Rosenfeld, A. A. 1979. Depression and psychotic regression following prolonged methylphenidate use and withdrawal: Case report. *American Journal of Psychiatry* 136:226–28.

Schuckit, M. A. 1986. Genetic and clinical implications of alcoholism and affective disorder. *American Journal of Psychiatry* 143:140–47.

———. 1994. Alcohol and depression: A clinical perspective. *Acta Psychiatrica Scandinavica* 377(suppl):28–32.

Schuckit, M. A., and M. G. Monteiro. 1988. Alcoholism, anxiety and depression. *British Journal of Addiction* 83:1373–80.

Schuckit, M. A., J. E. Tipp, M. Bergman, W. Reich, V. M. Hesselbrock, and T. L. Smith. 1997a. Comparison of induced and independent major depressive disorders in 2,945 alcoholics. *American Journal of Psychiatry* 154:948–57.

Schuckit, M. A., J. E. Tipp, K. K. Bucholz, J. I. Nurnberger, V. M. Hesselbrock, R. R. Crowe, and J. Kramer. 1997b. The life-time rates of three major mood disorders and four major anxiety disorders in alcoholics and controls. *Addiction* 92:1289–1304.

Smith, M. J., A. Abbey, and R. O. Scott. 1993. Reasons for drinking alcohol: Their relationship to psychosocial variables and alcohol consumption. *International Journal of Addictions* 28:881–908.

Sonne, S. C., K. T. Brady, and W. A. Morton. 1994. Substance abuse and bipolar affective disorder. *Journal of Nervous and Mental Disorders* 182:349–52.

Spring, G. K., and J. M. Rothgery. 1984. The link between alcoholism and affective disorders. *Hospital and Community Psychiatry* 35:820–23.

Strakowski, S. M., and M. P. DelBello. 2000. The co-occurrence of bipolar and substance use disorders. *Clinical Psychology Review* 20:191–206.

Strakowski, S. M., M. Tohen, A. L. Stoll, G. L. Faedda, and D. C. Goodwin. 1992.

Comorbidity in mania at first hospitalization. *American Journal of Psychiatry* 149:554–56.

Strakowski, S. M., M. Tohen, A. L. Stoll, G. L. Faedda, P. V. Mayer, M. L. Kolbrener, and D. C. Goodwin. 1993. Comorbidity in psychosis at first hospitalization. *American Journal of Psychiatry* 150:752–57.

Strakowski, S. M., S. L. McElroy, P. E. Keck Jr., and S. A. West. 1994. The co-occurrence of mania with medical and other psychiatric disorders. *International Journal of Psychiatry in Medicine* 24:305–28.

Strakowski, S. M., P. E. Keck Jr., S. L. McElroy, H. S. Lonczak, K. L. Tugrul, and S. A. West. 1995. Chronology of comorbid and principal syndromes in first-episode psychosis. *Comprehensive Psychiatry* 36:1–8.

Strakowski, S. M., S. L. McElroy, P. E. Keck Jr., and S. A. West. 1996. The effects of antecedent substance abuse on the development of first-episode mania. *Journal of Psychiatric Research* 30:59–68.

Strakowski, S. M., P. E. Keck Jr., S. L. McElroy, K. W. Sax, J. M. Hawkins, G. F. Kmetz, V. H. Upadhyaya, K. C. Tugrul, and M. L. Bourne. 1998a. Twelve-month outcome following a first hospitalization for affective psychosis. *Archives of General Psychiatry* 55:49–55.

Strakowski, S. M., K. W. Sax, S. L. McElroy, P. E. Keck Jr., J. M. Hawkins, and S. A. West. 1998b. Psychiatric and substance abuse syndrome co-occurrence in bipolar disorder following a first psychiatric hospitalization. *Journal of Clinical Psychiatry* 59:465–71.

Strober, M., W. Morrell, J. Burroughs, C. Lampert, H. Danforth, and R. Freeman. 1988. A family study of bipolar I disorder in adolescence: Early onset of symptoms linked to increased familial loading and lithium resistance. *Journal of Affective Disorders* 15:255–68.

Taylor, M. A., and R. Abrams. 1981. Early- and late-onset bipolar illness. *Archives of General Psychiatry* 38:58–61.

Tohen, M., C. M. Waternaux, and M. T. Tsuang. 1990. Outcome in mania: A four-year prospective follow up of 75 patients utilizing survival analysis. *Archives of General Psychiatry* 47:1106–11.

Verdoux, H., M. Mury, G. Besancon, and M. Bourgeois. 1996. Comparative study of substance dependence comorbidity in bipolar, schizophrenic and schizoaffective disorders. *Encephale* 22:95–101.

Wallace, A. E., L. L. Kofoed, and A. N. West. 1992. Double-blind, placebo-controlled trial of methylphenidate in older, depressed medically ill patients. *American Journal of Psychiatry* 152:929–31.

Weiss, R. D., and S. M. Mirin. 1987. Substance abuse as an attempt at self-medication. *Psychiatric Medicine* 3:357–67.

Weiss, R. D., M. L. Griffin, and S. M. Mirin. 1992. Drug abuse as self-medication for depression: An empirical study. *American Journal of Drug and Alcohol Abuse* 18:121–29.

Weiss, R. D., S. F. Greenfield, and L. M. Najavits. 1995. Integrating psychological and pharmacological treatment of dually diagnosed patients. *National Institute on Drug Abuse Research Monograph* 150:110–28.

Weissman, M. M., J. K. Myers, and P. S. Harding. 1980. Prevalence and psychiatric heterogeneity of alcoholism in a United States urban community. *Journal of Studies on Alcohol* 41:672–81.

Weissman, M. M., E. S. Gershon, K. K. Kidd, B. A. Prusoff, J. F. Leckman, E. Dibble, J. Hamovit, W. D. Thompson, D. L. Pauls, and J. J. Guroff. 1984. Psychiatric disorders in the relatives of probands with affective disorders. *Archives of General Psychiatry* 41:13–21.

Weller, R. A., E. Aberger, and S. L. Goldberg. 1989. Marijuana use and abuse in psychiatric outpatients. *Annals of Clinical Psychiatry* 1:87–91.

Winokur, G., and P. Clayton. 1967. Family history studies: II. Sex differences and alcoholism in primary affective illness. *British Journal of Psychiatry* 113:973–79.

Winokur, G., P. J. Clayton, and T. Reich. 1969. *Manic Depressive Illness*. St. Louis: C. V. Mosby.

Winokur, G., R. Cadoret, J. Dorzab, and M. Baker. 1971. Depressive disease. *Archives of General Psychiatry* 24:135–44.

Winokur, G., J. Morrison, J. Clancy, and R. Crowe. 1973. The Iowa 500: Familial and clinical findings favor two kinds of depressive illness. *Comprehensive Psychiatry* 14:96–106.

Winokur, G., W. Coryell, H. S. Akiskal, J. Endicott, M. Keller, and T. Mueller. 1994. Manic-depressive (bipolar) disorder: The course in light of a prospective ten-year follow-up of 131 patients. *Acta Psychiatrica Scandinavica* 89:102–10.

Winokur, G., W. Coryell, H. Akiskal, J. D. Maser, M. B. Keller, J. Endicott, and T. Mueller. 1995. Alcoholism in manic-depressive (bipolar) illness: Familial illness, course of illness and the primary-secondary distinction. *American Journal of Psychiatry* 152:365–72.

Wood, D., S. Othmer, T. Reich, J. Viesselman, and C. Rutt. 1977. Primary and secondary affective disorder 1: Past social history and current episodes in 92 depressed inpatients. *Comprehensive Psychiatry* 18:201–10.

Woodruff, R. A., S. B. Guze, P. J. Clayton, and D. Carr. 1973. Alcoholism and depression. *Archives of General Psychiatry* 28:97–100.

Young, L. D., M. Patel, and M. H. Keeler. 1981. The effect of lithium carbonate on alcoholism in 20 male patients with concurrent major affective disorder. *Currents in Alcoholism* 8:175–81.

Ziedonis, D. M., and T. R. Kosten. 1991. Depression as a prognostic factor for pharmacological treatment of cocaine dependence. *Psychopharmacology Bulletin* 27:337–43.

3

The Assessment of Mood and Substance Use Disorders

Shelly F. Greenfield, M.D., M.P.H.

The clinical assessment of patients with mood and substance use disorders is important because (1) mood and substance use disorders commonly co-occur, (2) the presence of either disorder increases the risk of onset of the other disorder, and (3) the co-occurrence of either disorder has negative prognostic implications for the course of the other disorder.

Substance use disorders and mood disorders (i.e., depressive disorders, bipolar disorder, and dysthymia) commonly co-occur in both community and treatment-seeking populations. According to an early epidemiological study, 44 percent of individuals in the community who had a lifetime diagnosis of alcohol dependence had also experienced a lifetime history of major depression (Weissman and Myers, 1980). In fact, individuals with substance use disorders have an increased risk of developing a mood disorder. According to the Epidemiological Catchment Area (ECA) Study, conducted with a community population in the early 1980s, those with a lifetime history of any alcohol abuse or dependence were almost twice as likely as those without this history to have a mood disorder; those with any other drug abuse or dependence were almost five times as likely as those without this history to have a lifetime diagnosis of mood disorder (Regier et al., 1990).

In addition to the increased risk of mood disorders among those with substance abuse or dependence, individuals with mood disorders have an increased risk of developing a substance use disorder. The ECA Study found that those with any mood disorder were nearly three times as likely to have a lifetime diagnosis of substance abuse or dependence as individuals without a mood disorder. Individuals with a lifetime history of bipolar disorder were nearly seven times as likely to have substance abuse or dependence in their lifetime as those without bipolar disorder. Compared to those without major depression and dysthymia, those with unipolar major depression had almost twice the likelihood and those with dysthymia had 2.4 times the likelihood of having a co-occurring substance use disorder (Regier et al., 1990). Although it was long assumed that substance use disorders were more likely to precede mood disorders in dually diagnosed individuals, community-based epidemiological studies have demonstrated that it is more likely for mood disorders to precede the onset of a substance use disorder (Kessler et al., 1997).

A growing body of research indicates a worse outcome for substance use disorders in individuals with co-occurring mood disorders than in those without a mood disorder. For example, one prospective study of 101 men and women hospitalized for alcohol dependence showed that those with a diagnosis of current major depression were more likely both to initiate drinking and to relapse to heavy drinking after discharge from the hospital, regardless of whether the depression was diagnosed as primary or secondary (Greenfield et al., 1998). Coryell and colleagues (1992) found that subjects diagnosed with depression and comorbid substance use disorders had more suicide attempts and longer episodes of depression than did those without substance use disorders. In fact, one study has shown that co-occurring major depression in individuals with substance use disorder is associated with an increased risk of suicidal ideation, suicide attempts, and completed suicide (Weiss and Hufford, 1999). Other studies of individuals with major depressive disorder and co-occurring alcohol use disorders have had similar findings (Hasin, Endicott, and Lewis, 1985; Mueller et al., 1994). In addition, a review of the literature on comorbid substance use and bipolar disorders (Tohen et al., 1998) concluded that individuals with bipolar disorder and co-occurring substance use disorders have more lifetime psychiatric hospitalizations, worse psychosocial outcomes, and more rapid mood relapses than those without substance use disorders.

Importantly, although patients with coexisting psychiatric illness and substance use disorders have traditionally had poor outcomes (McLellan, 1986), studies of concurrent treatment of both disorders have demonstrated more favorable outcomes (Cornelius et al., 1997; Mason et al., 1996; McGrath et al., 1996; Weiss, Najavits, and Mirin, 1998). For example, the study by McGrath and collaborators (1996) demonstrated that, among 69 actively drinking alcoholic persons who had a coexisting primary depressive disorder, those who were treated with imipramine rather than placebo had a modest improvement in depressive symptoms as well as decreased alcohol consumption. Mason and colleagues (1996) found that, among 71 patients with primary alcohol dependence and secondary depression, those receiving desipramine rather than placebo experienced decreased depressive symptoms as well as a longer period of alcohol abstinence. Similar results have been demonstrated with fluoxetine-treated patients with coexisting alcohol dependence and major depressive disorder (Cornelius et al., 1997).

Along with these studies of antidepressant treatment among individuals with coexisting alcohol dependence and depressive disorder, a naturalistic outcome study of depression and alcohol dependence by our group at McLean Hospital and Harvard Medical School (Greenfield et al., 1998) showed the negative consequences of not treating co-occurring depressive disorder among alcohol-dependent individuals. This prospective study of 101 men and women who were hospitalized for alcohol dependence followed patients monthly for 1 year after discharge. The study demonstrated that, among individuals who relapsed to drinking, those with coexisting major depression had shorter periods of abstinence after discharge (an average of 38 days after hospital discharge) than did those without co-occurring major depression (an average of 125 days of abstinence following discharge). Among individuals with major depression, 20 percent of those who received antidepressants at discharge remained abstinent from alcohol 1 year later, while all of those who did not receive antidepressant treatment had relapsed by 100 days after discharge.

One of the most significant findings of this longitudinal study was the importance of making a formal diagnosis of depression. As most clinicians are aware, many people experience depressive symptoms when they are drinking. However, the presence of depressive symptoms alone does not constitute a diagnosis of depression. The diagnosis of depression requires a constellation of symptoms to be present every day for a discrete time period (e.g., at least 14 days). In our study, individuals who met the criteria for a *diagnosis* of major depression at any time in the 6 months before hospitalization, *regardless of their drinking status when they met those criteria*, relapsed to alcohol more quickly than those without depression. However, when depression was measured symptomatically (e.g., the presence or absence of symptoms of depression at the time of admission), there was no relationship between this symptom measure and the length of abstinent time after hospitalization. Thus, it is important for prognosis and treatment to establish the existence of a *diagnosis* of depressive disorder and not just the presence or absence of depressive symptoms among those with alcohol dependence (Greenfield et al., 1998). Successful concurrent treatment of mood and substance use disorders, therefore, depends on a careful, accurate assessment and diagnosis.

Definitions of Substance Use and Mood Disorders

Diagnosing Substance Use Disorders

According to the fourth edition of the American Psychiatric Association's *Diagnostic and Statistical Manual of Mental Disorders* (DSM-IV) (1994), a diagnosis of *substance dependence* is made when there has been a maladaptive pattern of substance use leading to clinically significant impairment or distress, as manifested by at least three of seven symptoms or behaviors occurring within the same 12-month period. These symptoms or behaviors are

1. tolerance to the substance, as defined by either a need for markedly increased amounts of the substance to achieve intoxication or desired effect or diminished effect with continued use of the same amount of the substance

2. withdrawal, as manifested by the characteristic withdrawal syndrome for a particular substance or by the taking of the same or a related substance to relieve or avoid withdrawal symptoms

3. taking of the substance in larger amounts or over a longer period than was intended

4. a persistent desire or unsuccessful efforts to cut down or control substance use

5. a great deal of time spent in activities necessary to obtain the substance, use the substance, or recover from its effects

6. the giving up or reducing of important social, occupational, or recreational activities because of substance use

7. continuation of substance use despite knowledge of having a persistent or recurrent physical or psychological problem that is likely to have been caused or exacerbated by the substance

A diagnosis of *substance abuse* is made when the individual has never before met the criteria for dependence and exhibits a maladaptive pattern of substance use leading to significant impairment or distress as manifested by any one or more of four behaviors occurring within a 12-month period:

1. recurrent substance use resulting in a failure to fulfill major role obligations at work, school, or home
2. recurrent substance use in situations in which it is physically hazardous
3. recurrent substance-related legal problems
4. continued substance use despite having persistent or recurrent social or interpersonal problems caused or exacerbated by the effects of the substance

Importantly, the criteria for substance abuse and dependence are the same regardless of the specific substance or substances of abuse. The assessment for the presence or absence of substance abuse or dependence in any individual should thus aim to elicit the presence or absence of the behaviors and symptoms listed above in the 12 months before the interview (current diagnosis) or in any 12-month period earlier in the individual's life (past diagnosis). The criteria for these disorders are the same regardless of whether the individual has a mood disorder. At times, clinicians can be led away from the diagnosis of a substance use disorder by such thoughts as "the increase in this patient's daily alcohol consumption occurred because of her depression," or "this patient began heavy marijuana smoking only after his first manic episode," or "this patient uses cocaine only when she is depressed." Strict adherence to the criteria listed above is essential to accurate diagnosis.

Diagnosing Mood Disorders

According to DSM-IV, mood disorders include major depressive disorder (either single episode or recurrent), dysthymic disorder, depressive disorder not otherwise specified, bipolar disorder (types I, II, and not otherwise specified), cyclothymic disorder, and substance-induced mood disorder. It is not possible to review each of these in detail, but a brief review of the diagnosis of major depressive disorder, dysthymic disorder, and bipolar disorder and of ways to differentiate these from substance-induced mood disorders is warranted.

Major depressive disorder is diagnosed when five or more of nine possible symptoms have been present during the same 2-week period and represent a change from previous functioning. Of the symptoms, at least one must be either

1. the presence of depressed mood most of the day, nearly every day either by the person's self-report or by the observation made by others or

2. loss of interest or pleasure in all or almost all activities most of the day, nearly every day

The other symptoms are

3. significant weight change that was not purposeful
4. too little or too much sleep, nearly every day
5. psychomotor agitation or retardation (observable by others)
6. fatigue or loss of energy nearly every day
7. feelings of worthlessness or excessive or inappropriate guilt
8. diminished ability to think or concentrate or indecisiveness nearly every day
9. recurrent thoughts of death, recurrent suicidal ideation with or without a plan, or a suicide attempt

In addition to the requirement that five or more of these criteria be met within a 2-week period, the symptoms must not meet criteria for a mixed episode of depression and must cause clinically significant distress or impairment in social, occupational, or other important areas of functioning. To meet the criteria for major depressive episode, the symptoms cannot be better accounted for by bereavement and cannot be due to the direct physiological effects of a general medical condition (e.g., hypothyroidism). Moreover, the symptoms cannot be attributable to the use of drugs or alcohol.

According to the DSM-IV, there are six separate sets of criteria for bipolar I disorder as well as separate criteria for bipolar II disorder, bipolar disorder not otherwise specified, and cyclothymic disorder. Bipolar I disorder can be diagnosed if the individual ever had symptoms that met the criteria for a manic episode. A manic episode is defined by the DSM-IV as "a distinct period of abnormally and persistently elevated, expansive, or irritable mood, lasting at least one week" or lasting even less time if hospitalization was required. During this period of mood disturbance, three or more of seven possible symptoms must be present (four or more if mood was irritable and not elevated): inflated self-esteem or grandiosity, decreased need for sleep, pressured speech, flight of ideas or sense that thoughts are racing, distractibility, increase in goal-directed activity, or excessive involvement in pleasurable activities. The mood disturbance must be sufficiently severe to cause marked impairment in functioning, must not meet the criteria for a mixed episode, and must not be due to the direct physiological effects of a substance (drugs of abuse or a medication) or a general medical condition (e.g., hyperthyroidism).

Dysthymic disorder is diagnosed when a person has had depressed mood for most of the day, for more days than not, for at least 2 years. During periods of depression, the person must have also had at least two of the following six symptoms: poor appetite or overeating, too little or too much sleep, low energy or fatigue, low self-esteem, poor concentration or difficulty making decisions, or feelings of hopelessness. Importantly, no major depressive episode can have occurred during the first 2 years of the disorder. However, a major depressive episode may have occurred after 2 years duration of dysthymic disorder; this superimposed major depressive episode on a chronic dysthymia is sometimes referred to as "double depression." Like the mood disorders described above, dysthymic symptoms are not supposed to be due to the direct physiological effects of a substance or a general medical condition. In childhood and adolescence, dysthymia is considered to be equally prevalent in males and females, but dysthymia is two to three times as prevalent in adult women as in men (American Psychiatric Association, 1994).

One of the important criteria for each of the mood disorders as described in the DSM-IV is that the mood symptoms cannot be better accounted for by another general medical condition. Certain medical illnesses can cause mood disturbance (e.g., hypothyroidism, hyperthyroidism, tumors) (Kirch, 1989). For any first episode of mood disorder, it is especially important that concurrent medical illness be excluded as a cause of depressive symptoms.

A substance-induced mood disorder is a prominent and persistent disturbance in mood judged to be due to the direct effects of a substance such as a medication, exposure to a toxicant, other somatic treatment of depression, or substance of abuse. It is, therefore, quite important to be aware of medications that can produce symptoms of depression (e.g., beta blockers, such as propranolol for cardiac illness or alpha-methyldopa for hypertension) or symptoms of mania (e.g., steroids, such as prednisone for inflammatory illness). A history of symptoms (especially in a first episode) with an onset that is concurrent with the start of any of these medications warrants investigation.

With respect to alcohol or drug use, mood symptoms that may be considered more likely to be substance-induced rather than accounted for by a primary mood disorder (1) are likely to occur only in the context of intoxication or withdrawal, (2) are generally transient in duration (perhaps less than 2 to 4 weeks), (3) have generally not occurred before the onset of substance use or problems with substances, and (4) have not occurred during periods of abstinence. The following sections will address more specifically the typical presentations of individuals with co-occurring mood and substance use disorders, case examples, and methods of history taking and evaluation to disentangle the web of symptoms and arrive at appropriate diagnosis.

Typical Presentations

Although each individual patient will present to the clinician with a history and symptoms that are unique to that person, four general types of presentation are most typical:

1. prominent substance use disorder, with mood disorders that are more difficult to detect
2. prominent mood disorder, with more subtle symptoms of substance use disorder
3. prominent symptoms of both substance use and mood disorder
4. mood disorder after remission from substance use disorder

How the patient initially presents will probably fit into one of these four categories depending on a combination of several factors, including the severity of symptoms, the help-seeking behavior of the individual (Chrisman, 1977), how the patient views his or her illness(es) (Kleinman, 1980), and the sector of the health care system to which the person comes for help (Weisner, 1993). Patients often differ from one another, as well as from their treating clinicians, in the way that they explain to themselves and understand the nature of the problem from which they are suffering. Such personal explanations are often referred to as explanatory models of illness (Kleinman, 1980).

With respect to substance use disorders, there is often a gender difference in the way in which individuals understand their illness (Greenfield and O'Leary, 2002). Women are more likely to perceive their substance abuse problem as being caused by depression or marital or family troubles, and men are more likely to ascribe their difficulties to their drinking or drug use. It is, therefore, more common for women with co-occurring mood and substance use disorders to seek help from mental health and primary care clinicians, describing symptoms of depression or life stress (Weisner and Schmidt, 1992). Often their histories of alcohol or drug abuse are not elicited by the evaluating clinician, and the substance use disorder may go undiagnosed. By comparison, men are more likely to seek help for their alcohol or drug use disorder and may not complain of their depressive symptoms. Therefore, given the high co-occurrence of mood and substance use disorders, differences in the ways in which patients may understand and label their illnesses, and different patterns of help seeking, it is important for clinicians carefully to elicit histories and symptoms of both mood and substance use disorders in all patients presenting for treatment.

Patients with co-occurring mood and substance use disorders will often present to clinicians with one of four general patterns of illness, which are described below and illustrated by case examples.

The Presentation of Prominent Substance Use Disorder, with Mood Disorders That Are More Difficult to Detect

Some patients will present to the clinician complaining primarily of their use of alcohol or other drugs. Patients may discuss the effect their substance use has on their family, work life, physical health, or another area of functioning. They may report the physical effect of substances during either intoxication or withdrawal states or may report that substances seem to contribute to diminished energy, lower mood, feelings of anxiety, or disruptions in sleep or appetite. Although the prominent behaviors and symptoms reported by the patient center on the negative consequences of alcohol or drug use, reports of diminished energy, lower mood, and other possible symptoms of mood disorder should be pursued in detail by the clinician to identify whether there is a co-occurring mood disorder. Individuals who present in this way are more likely to be seen in an alcohol or substance abuse treatment setting. In general, this presentation is more prevalent among men.

Cases 1 and 2 illustrate presentation with prominent symptoms of substance use disorder. Careful psychiatric assessment revealed concurrent mood disorder, and the patients received subsequent treatment for both disorders.

Case 1. Mr. A. is a 20-year-old man who was admitted to a substance abuse treatment program because he reported to his family that he had been snorting heroin, smoking marijuana, and misusing prescription antidepressants given to him by a classmate. Psychiatric assessment on admission revealed that the patient had had diminished sleep for 3 weeks and no sleep for 48 hours, as well as increasing energy, pressured speech, diminished concentration, and loose associations. The patient also reported an initial inflation of mood and gradual onset of irritability, which he had tried to diminish by snorting heroin, smoking marijuana, and using his classmate's antidepressant medication. He was diagnosed with bipolar disorder, first manic episode and polysubstance abuse and was admitted to the hospital for acute treatment of mania. Further history taking in the hospital revealed that, from age 16 to 20, the patient had sporadically experienced brief episodes of increased energy, decreased sleep, diminished concentration, and irritability lasting 2–3 days at a time. During those episodes, he reported "chain-smoking" marijuana because it seemed to diminish his irritability and help with concentration. His marijuana use was otherwise intermittent during that period. In retrospect, the treating clinician concluded that the patient had experienced brief, untreated and undiagnosed hypomanic episodes between ages 16 and 20 and most recently had experienced his first full manic episode. His polysubstance abuse initially occurred secondary to his mood symptoms but had increased over time as the mood symptoms became more frequent and severe. The patient's bipolar disorder responded to lithium and antidepressant treatment. With treatment of the mood disorder and provision of education and supportive therapy regarding the negative effects of substance use on the stability of his bipolar disorder, the patient experienced full remission of his polysubstance abuse.

Case 2. Ms. B. is a 29-year-old married woman who entered an outpatient substance abuse treatment program after her husband found her using cocaine in their attic and insisted that she receive treatment for her cocaine use. Early in treatment, Ms. B. explored her initiation of cocaine use in college and her continued use in spite of promises to her husband that she would no longer use after they were married. Ms. B.'s therapist wondered about past and current depression and referred Ms. B. to a psychiatrist for evaluation. The history gathered by the therapist and the evaluating psychiatrist revealed that Ms. B. had felt depressed "as long as I can remember, but certainly since I was 10 or 11." She reported feeling "blah" most of the time through junior high and high school but did well in school, earning mostly A's "because I pushed myself and it was important in our family." She reported that, when she used cocaine in college, her mood felt almost normal when she was intoxicated but that she did not use it often because "it wasn't around that much and I didn't have that much money, but I would have used it if I could have." After college graduation and her marriage, she occasionally used cocaine at parties when other people had it. However, approximately 6 months before her recent treatment, she reported that she felt the gradual onset of diminished energy, low mood, difficulty getting out of bed, and negative and guilty thoughts. During this time she began to think more about cocaine use and an acquaintance of hers was willing to help her obtain it. She reported that she wanted to use the cocaine "because I liked it, but also to help me feel better." The psychiatrist diagnosed Ms. B. with "double depression" (dysthymia with recent major depression). Ms. B. subsequently received simultaneous treatment for her mood disorder and cocaine dependence in the form of group and individual therapy as well as pharmacotherapy with sertraline. She and her husband attended mutual help groups together and separately. Ms. B. experienced remission from her dysthymia and depression. She had a brief relapse to cocaine use 11 months after her initiation of treatment but has since experienced a 3-year period of abstinence.

The Presentation of Prominent Mood Disorder, with More Subtle Symptoms of Substance Use Disorder

Some patients will present to the clinician reporting severe symptoms of mood disorder, which may be limited to depressive symptoms or may include intermittent periods of decreased need for sleep and/or inflated mood. Such individuals may clearly and cogently report symptoms consistent with mood disorder and may offer no information about their use of substances unless asked. Careful history taking may then reveal that, in addition to the symptoms consistent with mood disorder, the individual has patterns of use of alcohol or other drugs that are consistent with abuse or dependence. Thus, for example, a woman who has given a history of major depression may report, when a careful history is taken, that she drinks two to four glasses of wine each night until she passes out. Similarly, a man presenting with a history of dysthymia may drink a six-pack of beer each evening and more on the weekends to help him "get through the day." Another individual may say that, during the times she "requires less sleep and is in a good mood," she smokes a lot of marijuana just "to calm down." Individuals who present in this way have identified their difficulties as problems with their mood, and they are more likely to seek care in a general medical setting, in their primary care clinicians' offices, or in a general mental health setting; they are unlikely to present to a substance abuse specialist. Individuals with co-occurring mood and substance use disorders who identify depression as their most prominent difficulty are more likely to be female.

Case 3. Ms. C. is a 32-year-old married mother of two small children who had recently moved to the area from a different state. She visited her primary care physician for a routine examination and noted that she had felt some depression over the previous 6 months. Her physician elicited additional symptoms of weight loss and hypersomnia, and after laboratory tests and physical examination revealed no abnormality, referred her to a therapist for further evaluation. The history elicited by the therapist revealed that Ms. C.'s mother had recently received treatment for depression. Ms. C. complained that she had felt isolated caring for her two young children, having left friends and part-time employment in her previous community when her husband's job was relocated. Gradually she noted she had more difficulty getting out of bed in the morning and had a hard time falling asleep. She had begun to worry that she wasn't attentive enough to her children because her concentration seemed diminished, and she had lost pleasure in many of the things she usually enjoyed doing. She noted an eight-pound unintentional weight loss because "I just don't really feel like eating." She reported that her husband had expressed some concern about her low mood and had encouraged her to see her doctor.

When her therapist initially asked her about her use of alcohol, the patient acknowledged being a "social drinker." During a subsequent session, the patient again complained of her trouble getting to sleep, and the therapist asked her if there was anything that helped. The patient acknowledged that "some alcohol" worked, but "I don't really think it is a problem." On further questioning, the patient revealed that she had been a heavy binge drinker in college but had stopped drinking after college; she subsequently drank only when she went out to dinner (about once each week) and abstained during her pregnancies and when nursing. She noted that, after their move 6 months before, she occasionally poured herself a glass of wine at dinnertime to "help me get through the evening." As her mood worsened and she experienced difficulty getting to sleep, she frequently would get up from bed after her husband had fallen asleep and would drink another glass of wine to help put her to sleep. Over the past 2 months, she noted the need for more wine and most recently was drinking two or three glasses of wine before falling asleep. She felt that this resulted in her having difficulty getting up in the morning. The patient also revealed during this discussion that her father had had a drinking problem when she was a little girl but had stopped "cold turkey" when she was 11 and had been abstinent since then. The therapist diagnosed worsening alcohol abuse and major depression. The patient was eventually treated with fluoxetine with excellent response. In addition to her therapy, she attended a small women's Alcoholics Anonymous (AA) group for 3 months and remained abstinent from alcohol. Although the patient subsequently reported that she wanted to return to "social drinking" sometime in the future, she agreed with her therapist that alcohol might worsen her depression and interfere with her medication treatment. She also realized that, in light of her family history, she might be at risk for further drinking problems. She, therefore, agreed that for the "near future" she would continue to abstain from alcohol.

Case 4. Ms. D. is a 50-year-old widowed woman with recurrent major depression. For 4 years Ms. D. had been seen by a psychiatrist who had treated her with psychotherapy and antidepressants, with only modest and temporary improvements in her depressive symptoms. Ms. D.'s psychiatrist noted that she was severely depressed with decreased spontaneous movements, diminished appetite, increased sleep, persistent guilt, and depressive, self-denigrating ruminative thoughts in spite of maximum doses of antidepressants. He therefore referred her for outpatient electroconvulsive therapy (ECT). After a brief course of ECT, she improved markedly and was started on an antidepressant.

During the ECT, Ms. D.'s daughter (who lived in another state) expressed some concern that her mother's drinking might be worsening her depression. On further exploration with her psychiatrist, Ms. D. asserted that alcohol was "not a problem," in that she drank only one or two glasses of wine with dinner. She agreed that she should remain abstinent from alcohol while she was being treated for her depression but declined any additional alcohol treatment.

Although she initially responded to ECT, Ms. D.'s depression did not resolve. She continued in psychotherapy, and a variety of pharmacotherapies were tried. During this period, she denied using alcohol. One year later, Ms. D. was admitted to the hospital because she was severely depressed and her daughter had found her in a state of clear intoxication from alcohol. Ms. D. said that she had recently begun to drink more heavily but denied that she had been drinking for very long, and she discussed her prominent mood symptoms and the need for the alcohol when she felt desperate from depression. Ms. D. completed inpatient detoxification and was eventually discharged to an outpatient program to address continued depression and relapse prevention. Ms. D. remained depressed but said that she was abstinent from alcohol and agreed to take disulfiram (Antabuse).

Three months later, on another visit, Ms. D.'s daughter found many empty wine bottles in her home. Her psychiatrist had a family meeting with the patient and her daughter. During this meeting, the patient reported drinking continuously throughout the time of treatment and not actually using the prescribed disulfiram. She reported no clear abstinent period during her outpatient treatment. Ms. D. was admitted to a longer-term alcohol treatment facility. After discharge, she reported abstinence at 3 months and felt that a new regimen of medications had improved her mood considerably.

These two cases illustrate clinical presentations of two women with prominent depressive symptoms and substance abuse that is more difficult to detect. In case 3, the patient defined her problem as depression and isolation and initially presented to her primary care physician. The diagnosis of depression was made readily. Her drinking history was later elicited, leading to an additional diagnosis of worsening alcohol abuse and the added treatment recommendations of alcohol abstinence and relapse prevention through psychotherapy, pharmacotherapy, and AA attendance. In case 4, the patient defined her main problem as depression and minimized her use of alcohol (when she was not frankly denying it) as only necessary to control depressive symptoms that had not responded to medication. It eventually became apparent that the patient clearly had two independent but related disorders requiring simultaneous treatment. The continued use of alcohol had diminished the effectiveness of her depression treatment, and the patient's depression, therefore, seemed to be resistant to treatment.

The Presentation of Symptoms of Both Substance Use Disorder and Mood Disorder

Individuals who present with prominent symptoms of both disorders most often have experienced relatively severe symptoms of both disorders over time and often present more acutely or in more intensive settings (e.g., a hospital or an emergency room) than do persons with more prominent symptoms of one disorder or the other. Such individuals often have an early onset and may have had an extensive history of previous treatments for both disorders. Case 5 illustrates presentation of symptoms of both disorders concurrently.

Case 5. Mr. E. is a 33-year-old single sales representative who presented to a therapist complaining of depression and daily marijuana use. Mr. E. reported smoking marijuana daily since age 16 but noted that, in the past year, he had begun smoking it in the morning and evening instead of just the morning. In the previous 3 months, he had been tempted to leave work to smoke but hadn't yet done so. He thought marijuana was starting to interfere with his work because he was distracted by his desire to use it, but he didn't wish to become totally abstinent. In addition, he said that he had felt depressed for "a long time" but in the past year felt that he "was really depressed." He described becoming less social because his mood was low, and he had negative thoughts about himself, felt guilty about small things he did or interactions he had with friends, was very self-critical, and had difficulty getting out of bed. He thought these symptoms had been worse for about 1 month. He was presenting to the therapist because of his worsening mood and because he had tried snorting heroin the previous week for the first time and "liked it" and felt "scared I might get hooked on it and I don't have enough money for that." The therapist diagnosed Mr. E. as having major depressive disorder as well as marijuana dependence and recent heroin use. Mr. E. agreed that his marijuana use was a problem but did not wish to stop. He was most eager to have his depression improve. He and his therapist agreed on an 8-week course of treatment for his depression with individual therapy and pharmacotherapy and that they would continue to discuss his feelings about marijuana and the advantages and disadvantages of his continued use. The patient experienced some mood improvement on paroxetine, but his marijuana use increased over the next 8 weeks and he used heroin again by nasal insufflation. Eventually, Mr. E. agreed with his therapist that he would not feel the full effects of his antidepressant if he did not stop his drug use; he also recognized that his salary was not supporting his spending on drugs, and he was accruing more financial debt. He agreed to go to Narcotics Anonymous to try to cut back his use and eventually stop.

The Presentation of Mood Disorder after Remission from Substance Use Disorder

It is not uncommon for a person with a prominent substance use disorder to experience prominent mood symptoms after achieving a period of abstinence. This happens most often when major depressive disorder or bipolar disorder have co-occurred with a severe substance use disorder with very few or very brief periods of abstinence. In such a case, the substance use disorder has produced symptoms of disordered behavior and cycles of intoxication and withdrawal of sufficient severity that it has been impossible to detect co-occurring mood symptoms or cycles. It is then only during a period of abstinence that it becomes clear that the individual also suffers from mood symptoms that are consistent with another co-occurring disorder such as major depression or bipolar disorder. Cases 6 and 7 illustrate the presentation of mood disorders after the achievement of abstinence.

> *Case 6.* Mr. F. is a 40-year-old man with a history of progressive alcohol dependence. Eventually, Mr. F.'s drinking interfered with his marriage and his job performance, and he agreed to an inpatient admission for detoxification. After detoxification, Mr. F. decided he could no longer subject his wife and daughter to the negative consequences of his drinking, and he engaged in an outpatient rehabilitation program and became stably abstinent from alcohol. Approximately 6 months after his detoxification, Mr. F. became increasingly depressed and he noted decreased energy, difficulty concentrating, difficulty getting up in the morning, and trouble falling asleep at night. He also had guilty ruminations about "ruining" his family's lives and had passive suicidal ideation about "being better off dead." His wife brought him to an admissions department of a psychiatric hospital for evaluation, and he was diagnosed with depressive disorder as well as alcohol dependence in remission. Mr. F.'s history revealed probable episodes of depression in his early adulthood that were generally obscured by drinking and drug use. Mr. F.'s mood was eventually stabilized with an antidepressant, and he continued to remain abstinent from alcohol.

Case 7. Mr. L. is a 30-year-old married man who presented for treatment of depression. The patient gave a clear history consistent with dysthymia since age 15 and currently described low mood, low energy, irritability, difficulty falling asleep, and awakening in the middle of the night. He reported being completely abstinent from alcohol and used no other drugs. Further history revealed that the patient had symptoms consistent with alcohol dependence from age 20–25 and then decided to stop drinking "cold turkey" on his own at age 25. Mr. L. reported remaining abstinent since that time.

In addition to the depressive symptoms reported by Mr. L. before the onset of his drinking problem, he said that since discontinuing alcohol he had experienced low mood and low energy, irritability, difficulty with his temper in interactions with coworkers, poor sleep, and a negative self-image. He had been in individual psychotherapy for 2 years and had just begun couples treatment. He had never had any trial of pharmacotherapy and had never had a diagnosis of major depression made by a clinician. He had been unwilling to consider medication treatment because of his experience with alcohol and his reluctance to use any "substance." The patient, however, was tired of feeling down and irritable and receiving negative feedback from coworkers and his wife about his irritability. The evaluating clinician made a diagnosis of major depression as well as alcohol dependence in remission. The patient was treated with a serotonergic antidepressant, and all symptoms of depression remitted. He remained abstinent from alcohol and continued on an antidepressant as well as in couples and individual psychotherapy to address marital issues and issues of self-esteem.

These cases illustrate the presentation of prominent mood disorders after remission from substance use disorder. In case 7, the symptoms of major depressive disorder did not come to the attention of a clinician until long after alcohol dependence was in remission. In case 6, the clear presentation of depression occurred approximately 6 months after cessation of drinking. In both cases, history reveals that mood disorders were present during the period of substance abuse but were much more difficult to detect because of the effects of the substances. In addition, it seems likely that mood disorders in each of these cases preceded the onset of alcohol or drug use. These clinical histories are consistent with population-based studies demonstrating that the mood disorder more frequently precedes the substance use disorder than vice versa (Kessler et al., 1997).

General Points Illustrated by the Cases

The clinical cases presented above illustrate the potential difficulties in diagnosing and assessing one disorder in the presence of the other. For example, cases 6 and 7 show two individuals with prominent alcohol dependence who each had longstanding mood disorders that were obscured by the persistent use of alcohol. After achieving abstinence, the co-occurring mood disorder gained prominence and was diagnosed and treated. Cases 1 and 2 show two individuals who presented with more prominent substance abuse problems but for whom additional history taking revealed coexisting mood disorder. In case 2, family members were concerned about the patient's drug use, and they helped secure treatment for him on that basis. However, full evaluation revealed symptoms consistent with mania. In the course of treatment, the patient's mania resolved and his prominent substance abuse remitted. The patient continued to struggle with mood instability but did not relapse to drug use. The woman in case 2 had prominent symptoms of cocaine dependence and presented for treatment of this. Additional assessment revealed past episodes of probable depressive disorder since late adolescence. This patient required simultaneous treatment for her cocaine dependence and depressive disorder.

Given the often-confusing symptom picture presented by patients with concurrent mood and substance use disorders, it is important to have some guidelines and fundamental assessment strategies that will aid careful and accurate diagnoses in these cases.

The Fundamentals of Assessment and Disentangling the Web of Symptoms

The case examples illustrate the way in which symptoms of mood and substance use disorders can be entangled and how difficult it can be to diagnose accurately individuals with both disorders. This difficulty can arise (1) from the patient's own self-report, in which the patient describes symptoms of one disorder and not the other (because the patient is unaware that the other disorder exists or because the patient may not wish to disclose symptoms of the disorder, especially substance use); (2) because the symptoms themselves may be caused by either disorder (e.g., psychotic symptoms that might be substance induced or part of mania or psychotic depression) or by both (e.g., depressed mood may be part of major depressive disorder and may be worsened by heavy drinking); or (3) from the temporal relationship between the disorders (e.g., if the onset of a substance use disorder precedes that of a mood disorder, it may be difficult to detect the onset of the mood disorder, and one might only see worsening substance abuse).

In attempting to disentangle the web, the clinician can use several important tools and guidelines to arrive at an accurate diagnostic assessment and treatment plan. These include (1) the diagnostic interview, (2) interview of family members or significant others, (3) use of drug screening, (4) blood tests, and (5) screening tests and symptom rating scales.

The Diagnostic Interview

The first major step in disentangling the web of symptoms is to be alert to the high likelihood of co-occurrence of mood and substance use disorders in any patient who presents with symptoms and a history consistent with one disorder or the other. This will prompt the taking of a complete history of symptoms that might be diagnostic of either or both disorders.

Taking the History of the Substance Use Disorder. A full history of the onset, duration, and development of the substance use disorder is important. It is often helpful to ask patients to go back in time and tell you when they first started using the substance, first had a problem, and first had treatment. For multiple substances, this history should be taken for each substance. As patients relate the problems they had, it is helpful to document the type of problems and when they occurred. For example, it is useful to document chronologically the onset of loss of control over amount of substance used, onset and progression of tolerance, attempts to cut back or stop, first and subsequent blackouts, withdrawal symptoms, seizures, and legal, physical, familial, or employment difficulties. It is also helpful to document the history of treatments and the patient's view of what was and was not helpful in maintaining abstinence. With respect to diagnosis and prognosis, it is helpful to know if there is a family history of alcohol or drug abuse or dependence in any primary relative (parents, siblings, children). A paternal or maternal history of alcohol dependence will confer a risk of developing alcohol dependence that is three to five times the risk for an individual without that family history.

Taking the History of the Mood Disorder. A full history of the onset and progression of the mood disorder is important. It is helpful again, here, to explore the history in chronological order from the first time the patient felt depressed or had manic symptoms, the duration of the episodes, the severity and characteristic symptoms, whether the patient received treatment, the types of treatment as well as patient's perception of what was or wasn't helpful, and interepisode recovery or remission from symptoms. In trying to disentangle symptoms of depression that may be substance induced or may be part of a mood disorder, it is helpful to know whether there is a family history of depression or bipolar disorder. A strong family history of mood disorder (especially in either parent) raises the likelihood that a pattern of mood symptoms in an individual with substance use disorder is more likely to be part of an independent mood disorder.

In addition, taking the history of the mood disorder should be directed toward understanding whether the pattern, duration, and number of mood symptoms meets diagnostic criteria. It is not unusual to find, for example, that someone who is either intoxicated from alcohol or has recently withdrawn from alcohol complains of lowered mood and energy or reports feeling guilty about their drinking. However, when these feelings and thoughts are part of substance use disorders and not consistent with coexisting mood disorder, they are not accompanied by some of the other symptoms of mood disorder (e.g., weight loss, difficulty sleeping), are more transient, and do not fit the characteristic time course of an independent mood disorder.

Relating the History and Symptoms of the Two Disorders through Time. In the face of long-term active substance dependence, it is often difficult for the clinician to distinguish between substance-induced mood symptoms and those of an independent mood disorder. For example, Jaffe and Ciraulo (1986) pointed out that, in assessing an individual with a long history of alcohol dependence and depressive symptoms, it can be difficult to determine whether the depression is due to the direct effects of the alcohol itself, is a response to the numerous losses that can occur in the lives of some with substance dependence, is part of feeling desperate and discouraged about being unable to stop drinking, is the result of previous head trauma (e.g., as a sequelae of falling when intoxicated) or metabolic disturbance, or is an independent mood disorder. This difficulty can also be true of psychotic symptoms and sleeplessness that occur in the setting of active cocaine use. It can be difficult to say whether this is a result of cocaine intoxication, a manifestation of mania as part of bipolar disorder, or both.

Several guidelines can be helpful in this process. When taking a history of both the mood and substance use disorder through time, it is most important to note times when the disorders overlap and times when they do not. Which disorder came first? Were mood symptoms ever present during periods when substances were not used? The presence of mood disorder symptoms before substance use or during periods of abstinence is helpful in making the diagnosis of mood disorder. Often this chronologically based history taking will help disentangle the onset and development of the two disorders.

According to the DSM-IV, clinicians can use a guideline of 4 weeks of abstinence before diagnosing an independent mood disorder rather than a substance-induced mood disorder. However, this is meant only to be a *guideline* and not a strict rule. In fact, the DSM-IV provides the caveat that a mood disorder should be diagnosed if the symptoms present are neither qualitatively nor quantitatively what would be expected from the amount and duration of the substances used. Thus, it is important to relate the symptoms the patient reports to the symptoms one might expect either during intoxication or upon cessation of the substance(s) the patient has been using. If there is significant overlap, it might be prudent to wait for up to 4 weeks of abstinence to see if the symptoms improve. If, however, after the patient stops substance use, the mood symptoms continue to worsen rather than slowly improving, this probably indicates an independent mood disorder. Finally, if the patient has met criteria for mood disorder before the onset of substance use or during a previous period of abstinence, it is more persuasive to expect the symptoms to be part of an independent mood disorder. Initiating treatment of the mood disorder is thus likely to be the more prudent course.

Interview of Family Members or Significant Others

In addition to interviewing the patient and taking a careful history, it is often helpful to interview a family member or a significant other. Such individuals can provide additional observations of behavior and of the temporal relationships of symptoms that can be quite helpful in formulating a diagnosis. This may be especially helpful when a clinician is trying to diagnose a substance use disorder in a patient with prominent mood disorder symptoms, but it may prove just as useful when trying to establish a time course for the onset and progression of mood symptoms in a patient who has a prominent substance use disorder. For example, a significant other may provide information about a patient's behaviors during a possible manic episode that the patient minimizes.

The Use of Drug Screening

Accurate detection of substance use in a patient with a mood disorder is often facilitated if the clinician uses multiple sources of data. Thus, in addition to the patient interview and interview of a significant other, the clinician may also wish to obtain urine toxicologic screens. Urine toxicology has almost no utility in detecting alcohol abuse or dependence because of the rapidity with which excreted alcohol metabolites disappear from urine. Urine toxicology is also insufficient on its own in detecting drug abuse or dependence because it is generally most accurate in detecting recent drug use. Thus, for example, alcohol metabolites may be detected in urine only within 12 hours of consumption, and cocaine metabolites may be detected in urine only within 72 hours of use. Therefore, a negative urine screen for these substances may be a "false negative" result if these substances were used several days earlier than the requisite time frame for a positive urine result. On the other hand, some substances may be detected in urine for weeks after substance use. Thus, marijuana metabolites as well as metabolites of some long-acting benzodiazepines may be found in urine for as much as 1 month after use. Therefore, an individual may not have used one of these substances for weeks while his or her urine will be positive, thus yielding a "false positive" for recent substance use.

However, if a patient knows that a urine drug test will be part of the assessment, he or she might be more willing to be forthcoming in reporting substance abuse. On the other hand, some data indicate that self-reports are as accurate as urine drug screens if an individual does not anticipate negative consequences based on self-reporting of his or her drug use (Weiss, Najavits, and Mirin, 1998). Therefore, the utility of urine drug screening may be influenced by the setting of the assessment (e.g., a patient may be more willing to accurately self-report drug use in an outpatient treatment program where there are no clear negative consequences and there is a therapeutic alliance with the treater than in an emergency room where there may be concern about reporting of the information and where the patient has only this brief, single contact with the evaluating clinician).

Blood Tests

Blood tests have limited utility in the diagnosis of coexisting mood and substance use disorders. In suspected alcohol use disorders, liver function tests are often evaluated to determine the potential effect of chronic alcohol consumption on the liver. In diagnosis, these tests are not necessarily informative unless they are positive. In other words, a person may have alcohol dependence in spite of normal liver enzymes. However, elevated liver enzymes should heighten suspicion of problematic alcohol use, or another potential cause of this elevation should be sought. Only one liver enzyme is thought to be specific for alcohol-induced liver inflammation, and that is gamma-glutamyl-transferase (GGT). Elevation of GGT would provide additional evidence of an alcohol use disorder. Research has indicated that measuring levels of carbohydrate-deficient transferrin (CDT) may be useful in detecting recent heavy drinking; CDT was found to be superior to GGT in detecting relapse in men with alcoholism (Schmidt et al., 1997), and a combination of GGT and CDT may increase sensitivity for detection of heavy drinking, especially in young women (Anton and Moak, 1994). Finally, an elevation of the mean corpuscular volume (MCV) can be indicative of folic acid deficiency, which is sometimes seen in chronic alcoholism.

With respect to suspected mood disorders, especially depression, a suspected first episode of depression ought to prompt the exclusion of other medical causes (e.g., hypothyroidism, diabetes, concurrent medications). When indicated, an evaluation for this may include physical examination and the ordering of appropriate blood chemistries.

Screening Tests and Symptom Rating Scales

Screening tests and symptom rating scales cannot take the place of a careful diagnostic interview in making accurate diagnoses. However, screening tests may be useful in some practice settings in which clinicians are trying to gain a rapid appreciation for the likelihood that a disorder may exist in a patient. Thus, for example, in a setting that primarily provides assessment and treatment for individuals with mood disorders, rapid screening tools such as the CAGE (Mayfield, McLeod, and Hall, 1974), the Michigan Alcoholism Screening Test (MAST) (Favazza and Pines, 1974), or the Drug Abuse Screening Test (DAST) (Skinner, 1982) may provide clinicians with an indication of which patients need to have more in-depth assessment of their alcohol and drug use. Similarly, in settings that primarily provide assessment and treatment for individuals with substance use disorders, a symptom rating scale such as the Beck Depression Inventory (BDI) (Beck et al., 1961) or the Hamilton Depression Rating Scale (HAM-D) (Hamilton, 1960) may help identify individuals with high scores who should have a complete diagnostic interview regarding depression and other possible coexisting mood disorders.

Conclusion

Mood and substance use disorders commonly co-occur, and concurrent treatment for both disorders can enhance prognosis and outcome for each. Patients may most typically present with prominent symptoms of substance use disorder and more difficult to detect mood disorder, with prominent mood symptoms and more subtle substance abuse symptoms, with symptoms of both disorders, or with mood symptoms that have had their prominent onset after cessation of substance use. When a patient presents with symptoms that are consistent with either a substance use disorder or a mood disorder, it is important that the clinician take a complete and detailed history of the onset and progression of symptoms of both types of disorders. Interviews with family members or significant others, urine toxicologic screens, and blood tests may have utility in some clinical circumstances. Most important is a complete and detailed history that includes the times of onset, progression of symptoms, temporal relationship between symptoms of the two types of disorders, and family history of either or both disorders, which will provide key information to help disentangle the web of symptoms and arrive at an accurate diagnostic assessment.

ACKNOWLEDGMENTS
This work was supported by grants DA00407 and DA09400 from the National Institute of Drug Abuse, grant AA11756 from the National Institute on Alcohol Abuse and Alcoholism, and a grant from the Dr. Ralph and Marian Falk Medical Research Trust.

REFERENCES
American Psychiatric Association. 1994. *Diagnostic and Statistical Manual of Mental Disorders*, 4th ed. Washington, D.C.: American Psychiatric Press.
Anton, R. F., and D. H. Moak. 1994. Carbohydrate-deficient transferrin and g-glutamyltransferase as markers of heavy alcohol consumption: Gender differences. *Alcoholism, Clinical Experimental Research* 18:747–54.

Beck, A. T., C. H. Ward, M. Mendelson, J. Mock, and J. Erbaugh. 1961. An inventory for measuring depression. *Archives of General Psychiatry* 4:561–71.

Chrisman, N. J. 1977. The health seeking process: An approach to the natural history of illness. *Culture, Medicine and Psychiatry* 4:351–77.

Cornelius, J. R., I. M. Salloum, J. G. Ehler, et al. 1997. Fluoxetine in depressed alcoholics. *Archives of General Psychiatry* 54:700–705.

Coryell, W., J. Endicott, and G. Winokur. 1992. Anxiety syndromes as epiphenomena of primary major depression: Outcome and familial psychopathology. *American Journal of Psychiatry* 149:100–107.

Favazza, A. R., and J. Pines. 1974. The Michigan alcoholism screening test. *Quarterly Journal of Studies on Alcohol* 35:925–29.

Greenfield, S. F., and G. O'Leary. 2002. Gender differences in substance use disorders. In *Gender Issues in Psychiatry*, edited by J. Herrerra. Washington, D.C.: American Psychiatric Press.

Greenfield, S. F., R. D. Weiss, L. R. Muenz, L. M. Vagge, J. F. Kelly, L. R. Bello, and J. Michael. 1998. The effect of depression on return to drinking. *Archives of General Psychiatry* 55:259–65.

Hamilton, M. 1960. A rating scale for depression. *Journal of Neurology, Neurosurgery and Psychiatry* 23:56–62.

Hasin, D., J. Endicott, and C. Lewis. 1985. Alcohol and drug abuse in patients with affective syndromes. *Comprehensive Psychiatry* 26:283–95.

Jaffe, J. H., and D. A. Ciraulo. 1986. Alcoholism and depression. In *Psychopathology and Addictive Disorders*, edited by R. Meyer. New York: Guilford Press.

Kessler, R. C., R. M. Crum, L. A. Warner, C. B. Nelson, J. Schulenberg, and J. C. Anthony. 1997. Lifetime co-occurrence of DSM-III-R alcohol abuse and dependence with other psychiatric disorders in the National Comorbidity Survey. *Archives of General Psychiatry* 54:313–21.

Kirch, D. G. 1989. Medical assessment and laboratory testing in psychiatry. In *Comprehensive Textbook of Psychiatry*, edited by H. Kaplan and B. Sadock. Baltimore: Williams & Wilkins.

Kleinman, A. 1980. *Patients and Healers in the Context of Culture*, 71–118. Berkeley and Los Angeles: University of California Press.

Mason, B. J., J. H. Kocsis, E. C. Ritvo, et al. 1996. A double-blind placebo-controlled trial of desipramine for primary alcohol dependence stratified on the presence or absence of major depression. *Journal of the American Medical Association* 275:761–67.

Mayfield, D., G. McLeod, and P. Hall. 1974. The CAGE questionnaire: Validation of a new alcoholism screening instrument. *American Journal of Psychiatry* 131:1121–23.

McGrath, P. J., E. V. Nunes, J. W. Stewart, et al. 1996. Imipramine treatment of alcoholics with primary depression. *Archives of General Psychiatry* 53:232–40.

McLellan, A. T. 1986. "Psychiatric severity" as a predictor of outcome from substance abuse treatments. In *Psychopathology and Addictive Disorders*, edited by R. E. Meyer. New York: Guilford Press.

Mueller, I. T., P. W. Lavori, M. B. Keller, A. Swartz, M. Warshaw, D. Hasin, et al. 1994.

Prognostic effect of the variable course of alcoholism on the 10-year course of depression. *American Journal of Psychiatry* 151:701–6.

Regier, D. A., M. E. Farmer, D. S. Rae, B. Z. Locke, D. Keith, L. L. Judd, and F. K. Goodwin. 1990. Comorbidity of mental disorders with alcohol and other drug abuse. *Journal of the American Medical Association* 264:2511–18.

Schmidt, L. G., K. Schmidt, P. Dufeu, A. Ohse, H. Rommelspacher, and C. Miller. 1997. Superiority of carbohydrate-deficient transferrin to g-glutamyltransferase in detecting relapse in alcoholism. *American Journal of Psychiatry* 154:75–80.

Skinner, H. A. 1982. The drug abuse screening test. *Addictive Behaviors* 7:363–71.

Tohen, M., S. F. Greenfield, R. D. Weiss, C. A. Zarate, and L. M. Vagge. 1998. The effect of comorbid substance use disorders on the course of bipolar disorder: A review. *Harvard Review of Psychiatry* 6:133–41.

Weisner, C. 1993. Toward an alcohol treatment entry model: A comparison of problem drinkers in the general population and in treatment. *Alcoholism, Clinical and Experimental Research* 17:746–52.

Weisner, C., and L. Schmidt. 1992. Gender disparities in treatment for alcohol problems. *Journal of the American Medical Association* 268:1872–76.

Weiss, R. D., and M. R. Hufford. 1999. Substance abuse and suicide. In *The Harvard Medical School Guide to Suicide Assessment and Intervention*, edited by D. Jacobs, 300–310. San Francisco: Jossey-Bass Publishers.

Weiss, R. D., L. M. Najavits, and S. M. Mirin. 1998. Substance abuse and psychiatric disorders. In *Clinical Textbook of Addictive Disorders*, 2d ed., edited by R. J. Frances and S. I. Miller, 291–318. New York: Guilford Press.

Weissman, M. M., and J. K. Myers. 1980. Clinical depression in alcoholism. *American Journal of Psychiatry* 137:372–73.

4

Integrated Treatment Using a Recovery-Oriented Approach

Dennis C. Daley, Ph.D., Ihsan M. Salloum, M.D., M.P.H., and Michael E. Thase, M.D.

Our focus on recovery-oriented therapy for the dual disorders of depression or bipolar illness combined with a substance use disorder begins with a brief discussion of an integrated dual disorders model of treatment, the concept of recovery, factors mediating recovery, the continuum of care for dual disorders, and stages of change and phases of recovery. The major thrust of this chapter is discussing the biopsychosocial issues in recovery associated with mood and substance use disorders, substance use lapse and relapse, mood disorder relapse, and the ongoing use of recovery tools. Numerous clinical issues and strategies face patients and families experiencing dual disorders.

Our model of integrated dual disorders recovery therapy (DDRT) draws on clinical strategies used in addiction counseling (Daley and Marlatt, 1997a, 1997b), cognitive therapy (Beck, 1995), behavioral skills training (Liberman, DeRisi, and Mueser, 1989), interpersonal psychotherapies (Frank and Kupfer, 1994; Weissman, Markowitz, and Klerman, 2000), motivational interviewing (Miller and Rollnick, 2002), and relapse prevention (Daley and Marlatt, 1997c). DDRT assumes that there are several possible relationships between substance use and mood disorders: (1) mood disorders are a risk factor for substance use disorders, (2) substance use disorders are a risk factor for mood disorders, (3) a mood disorder can complicate recovery from addiction or contribute to a substance use lapse or relapse, (4) a substance use disorder can complicate recovery from a mood disorder and contribute to relapse or recurrence, and (5) these disorders can develop at different points in time and not be meaningfully linked. Our recovery-oriented model posits that there are different phases of treatment for dual disorders, and each phase has therapeutic issues and interventions associated with it as well as criteria with which clinicians can determine the progress of a patient. DDRT uses both individual and group modalities to educate patients, teach coping skills, and help resolve personal problems contributing to or resulting from the disorders. More background information leading to the development of this recovery-oriented treatment model and the description of clinical applications can be found in other publications (Daley and Moss, 2002; Daley and Thase, 2000). In addition, given that many dual disordered patients, especially those with persistent and chronic forms of mental illness, have severe levels of psychopathology with numerous psychosocial problems (e.g., homelessness, unemployment, and limited income) and deficits (e.g., lack of vocational skills), they often benefit from referral to ancillary or social services such as vocational training, public assistance, food banks, or shelters.

Recovery from Mood and Substance Disorders

The Concept of Recovery

Recovery is a concept widely accepted in the field of chemical dependency treatment, and more recently it has been used with psychiatric disorders and dual disorders. *Recovery* generally refers to the process of managing both the mood and substance use disorders and making positive changes in self and lifestyle. Although treatment aids the patient in the initiation of recovery and the process of change, much of it occurs in the context of the patient's life outside of treatment. Recovery-oriented treatment is an interactive process in which the clinician engages the patient as an active collaborator in identifying problems and issues and exploring strategies to cope effectively with these. In addition to traditional talk therapy, clinicians use active techniques with patients such as behavioral rehearsals, structured workbook activities, bibliotherapy assignments, written techniques (e.g., recording and rating moods, automatic thoughts and counter statements, cravings to engage in substance use, completing daily and weekly schedules of activities), and educational audio- tapes or videotapes (see suggested patient and family educational resources at the end of the chapter for specific examples).

Recovery is best viewed as an active process in which the patient

• acquires information about the mood disorder and the substance use dis- order, the interaction of the dual disorders, the process of recovery, the role of professional treatment and medications, and the process of relapse

• increases awareness related to the effect of the dual disorders on self and others, ways in which he or she copes with problems and symptoms, level of motivation to change, and personal barriers to making changes

• stabilizes from the acute effects of substance use or major psychiatric symptoms

• develops behavioral, cognitive, and interpersonal strategies and coping skills to effectively manage specific symptoms of the substance use disorder (e.g., cravings to use, social pressures to engage in use, early signs of relapse) or the mood disorder (e.g., changes in mood, persistent mood symptoms, early signs of relapse) and makes goal-directed behavioral and interpersonal changes

• includes the family or significant others in treatment and the recovery process

Factors Mediating Recovery

Although there are many similar elements to recovery despite the specific types and combinations of disorders, the actual recovery process will vary among pa- tients. Recovery and the ability to manage the disorders and make positive per- sonal or lifestyle changes will be mediated by a variety of illness, client, family, and social system factors.

The Type and Severity of the Mood Disorder. Patients with more chronic and severe manifestations of psychiatric symptoms require more extensive profes- sional treatment. They also experience more complications in the recovery process because of suicidal or homicidal thoughts or severely impaired judg- ment. For example, a patient with recurrent major depression with residual mood symptoms and fewer internal (psychological) and external (e.g., social support) resources may not recover as easily as a patient experiencing a first episode of major depression who functions well once mood symptoms are in remission. Or a patient in a mixed state of mania and depression may, as a result of denial, poor judgment, or grandiosity, resist psychiatric hospitalization despite the clear objective need to stabilize acute symptoms.

The Type and Severity of the Substance Use Disorder. Patients with addiction often experience difficulty initiating and maintaining abstinence from substances. They frequently enter an abstinence-withdrawal pattern with good intentions but backslide when the distress associated with abstinence overwhelms their motivation and limited coping repertoire. For example, a heroin addict with a long history of intravenous drug use can experience postacute withdrawal symptoms in the early weeks of abstinence, which can adversely affect motivation to remain drug-free.

The Level of Social Anxiety. Many patients evidence symptoms of social anxiety or social phobias as well as avoidance behaviors. For example, a patient highly anxious about self-disclosing thoughts, feelings, or problems in groups may avoid the anticipated humiliation or embarrassment by refusing to attend group treatment sessions or self-help programs and hence not benefit from group-oriented programs that facilitate positive attitudes about recovery or teach specific recovery skills.

The Effects of Disorders on Current Functioning. Patients with multiple psychosocial problems often struggle in their recovery because of the adverse effects of these multiple problems on their mood and their level of motivation to change. For example, a patient who loses a job as a result of impairment caused by either or both of the disorders and who experiences an additional threat of loss of family stability may become demoralized and feel less confident about managing the disorders. Or a patient who is homeless may have trouble complying with the medication regime or therapy program.

The Effects of Disorders on Family and Significant Relationships. Patients with serious interpersonal problems who have minimal support or are involved in relationships that have an adverse effect on mood or the ability to stay sober often struggle in their recovery. For example, if the family of the dual disordered patient is critical and nonsupportive, the risk of relapse increases.

Demographic Characteristics (age, gender, employment status, ethnicity).
Unemployed patients and those from lower socioeconomic backgrounds often
experience problems with housing, money, childcare, and transportation that
affect their ability to comply with professional treatment and self-help group
attendance. As a result, they may not gain optimum benefits and may experience more difficulties in recovery.

The Level of Acceptance of Disorders and the Motivation to Change. Patients
who do not believe they have a mood disorder, substance use disorder, or both
will have little or no motivation to change or engage in treatment or the process
of recovery. Denial is common among patients with substance use disorders as
well as bipolar disorders. Although external pressure to change from family, the
court system, or an employer may facilitate involvement in treatment or a recovery program and lead to short-term change, longer-term recovery and more
permanent change require the patient to accept the dual disorders and have a
reasonable level of motivation to make changes. For example, if a patient accepts the mood disorder but minimizes the alcoholism, he is more likely to
continue drinking excessively. Mood, motivation, and efficacy of medications
all may be adversely affected by the ingestion of alcohol, leading to complications in the recovery process.

Personality Factors. Many patients with mood and substance use disorders
have additional personality disorders or traits that interfere with recovery. For
example, a patient who is stubborn and resists professional advice on the need
to change, how to change, or the need for involvement in a recovery program
is more likely to struggle compared to the patient open to accepting help and
support from others.

Cognitive Factors. Cognitive impairment interferes with the patient's ability to learn information and recovery skills needed to cope with mood or substance use disorders. Some patients with mood disorders experience psychotic
features that, if not treated, adversely affect their ability to manage their illnesses and engage appropriately in a recovery program. In addition, some patients have beliefs that make their recovery more difficult. For example, the patient with bipolar disorder who expects an uncomplicated course of recovery
but experiences periods of mood instability or only partial response to treatment may feel demoralized during periods when symptoms flare up.

Current Family and Social Supports. Patients with supportive family and so-cial support systems tend to function better than those lacking support or those involved in negative social networks. For example, an addicted patient lacking sober or drug-free friends often feels more pressure to engage in substance use and is more prone to relapse compared to the patient with sober friends or fam-ily members who promote recovery and support efforts to change.

Therapeutic Alliance. Patients who develop a stronger working alliance with their therapist or treatment team have better collaboration, adherence, and completion rates and hence better clinical outcomes than patients who do not like or trust their caregiver. A positive alliance is one in which the patient feels accepted, understood, and not judged for his behaviors or mistakes. This is characterized by a sense of working collaboratively as a team to address the pa-tient's problems.

The Appropriateness of the Treatment Regimen. A patient's ability to change is also affected by the specific clinical services provided and their appropriate-ness. If, for example, an intense level of structured care such as detoxification, partial hospitalization, or an intensive outpatient program is needed but not available, the patient may not get sufficient help in stabilizing from the acute symptoms of the disorder. This, in turn, will make it difficult to engage in the recovery process. Or, if a patient with severe, incapacitating mood syndrome does not respond to various medications used alone or in combination, he may benefit from electroconvulsive treatment (ECT). However, if this treatment is not available or offered, the patient will not experience the potential benefits. Similarly, if an alcoholic patient struggles with recovery and needs a pharma-cological adjunct such as ReVia (naltrexone) or Antabuse (disulfiram), but these are not available, the chances of a good recovery may decrease.

Recovery Issues and Treatment Interventions

The Continuum of Care

Effective treatment of mood disorders combined with substance use disorders requires that the clinician be able to access a range of clinical services within the continuum of care. Patients will move along the continuum of care as needed, based on symptoms and problems. Critical transitions include mov-ing from one type of treatment or level of care to another. Often, patients fail to follow through with treatment when they move between levels of care. Therefore, close attention to strategies that can enhance compliance is important in improving the odds of the patient successfully moving from one level of care to the next.

Since clinical services for substance abuse are dictated by medical necessity, the clinician should be familiar with the dimensions and levels of care delineated by the American Society on Addiction Medicine (ASAM). Dimensions of care refer to current clinical symptoms and related medical, psychiatric, psychological, motivational, or social sequelae that affect the patient's specific treatment needs and ability to engage in recovery. The six dimensions of care are (1) intoxication and withdrawal potential, (2) biomedical conditions and complications, (3) behavioral conditions and complications, (4) treatment acceptance or resistance, (5) relapse potential, and (6) recovery environment.

The Phases of Recovery

Clinicians and researchers have written about stages of change for or phases of recovery from substance use (Marlatt and Gordon, 1985), depressive disorders (Thase and Sullivan, 1995), bipolar disorders (Frank and Kupfer, 1994), dual disorders, and psychological problems (Prochaska, Norcross, and DiClemente, 1994). For example, treatment of mood disorders involves acute, continuation, and maintenance phases of treatment (Thase, 1992). Our work on dual disorders led us to develop a model with six phases of treatment: engagement, stabilization, early recovery, middle recovery, late recovery, and maintenance (Daley and Thase, 2000). During the engagement and stabilization phases, diagnoses are established, acute symptoms of either disorder are addressed, and ambivalence, denial, substance use cravings, and the need for social support are addressed as needed. Early recovery focuses on helping the patient identify and manage triggers for substance use, negative affects, cognitive distortions, effects of illness on the family, and persistent psychiatric symptoms. Middle recovery focuses on specific relationship problems or interpersonal deficits, relapse issues, and spirituality. Late recovery continues on the work of previous stages, revisits specific issues or problems as needed, and focuses on lifestyle balance, personality issues (referred to as "character defects" in 12-step programs), and exploration of significant developmental experiences that are unresolved. Maintenance focuses on continued work on self and personal growth.

Since recovery is seldom a linear path and patients often have setbacks, issues related to developing and using family and recovery support systems such as self-help programs, changes in motivation, compliance with treatment goals and plans, substance abuse relapses, and exacerbation of psychiatric symptoms are addressed as needed during the course of treatment. Given the influence of managed care in reducing the number of treatment sessions, clinicians have to be realistic in helping patients set goals and determining the focus on treatment. Many patients use therapy for a limited time and continue working on recovery issues by using the support of self-help programs such as Alcoholics Anonymous (AA), Narcotics Anonymous (NA), or mental health–related programs (such as Recovery, Inc., or Emotions Anonymous). In addition, many patients seek help for discrete episodes of illness and terminate treatment once their symptoms are controlled or remitted.

In determining treatment goals and suggesting recovery strategies for individual patients, the clinician can assess the patient's current level of motivation and decide where the patient fits in terms of phases of recovery. For example, if the patient is struggling with acceptance of one or both of the disorders and is very ambivalent about changing, the clinician should focus on motivational issues rather than on issues pertinent to relapse or the maintenance phase of treatment. Or, if the patient is just beginning recovery and has only recently initiated sobriety, yet wants to focus treatment on marital issues, the clinician should attempt to redirect the focus of treatment to early recovery issues.

Physical Issues in Recovery

Patients should be encouraged to get a thorough physical examination to rule out medical problems that could contribute to their mood disorder. Many patients have medical problems or disorders that can interfere with recovery if not properly assessed or treated. Some medications for physical disorders can have potentially adverse interactions with medications used to treat mood or other psychiatric disorders, so the clinician should be aware of medications the patient is taking.

Patients with substance dependence disorders need to focus on strategies to initiate and maintain abstinence. In more severe cases, this will require detoxification in a hospital, residential, or ambulatory setting. Substance-dependent patients need help monitoring and managing cravings to use substances, particularly in the early weeks and months of recovery when cravings are common, persistent, and intense.

Exercise, diet, sleep, and relaxation habits all may affect mood symptoms or substance use and should be addressed as part of the overall treatment plan. Sleep hygiene strategies can help patients improve mood or energy level. However, it is not unusual for patients to take several months or longer after they quit using substances to develop regular sleep patterns.

Patients on mood-stabilizing medications and certain antidepressants should be monitored with regular blood-level determinations to ensure that medication levels are in the therapeutic range. This also helps to establish whether the patient is compliant with taking the medication as prescribed. Some patients may not spontaneously report poor medication compliance or admit to it when asked.

Urine drug screens can be used as an external motivator to stop using substances and as a way of measuring whether substances are being used by the patient. Patients mandated by employers or the legal system often are required to submit regular urine samples. However, even patients not required to give samples often report that they benefit from them because knowing that they will be checked for substance use sometimes provides an extra incentive for them to abstain.

Achieving Psychiatric Stability

For the patient to achieve psychiatric stability, the clinician must assess and address safety issues for patients who are suicidal or homicidal or are involved in interpersonal violence. Substance abuse is often a risk factor for violence, and patients may display violent behaviors or be victimized by violence (e.g., domestic violence).

Other major symptoms of the psychiatric disorder, such as severe mood disturbance or instability or sleep disturbance, may require medications before therapy can be optimally effective. Clinicians should monitor medication compliance, since poor compliance often contributes to a lack of or partial response to medications and patients do not always report such poor compliance. Poor compliance can also be a factor in clinical deterioration, substance use relapse, and subsequent hospitalization. Since all patients do not respond the same to psychiatric medications, if psychiatric symptoms persist in the abstinent patient who complies with medication, the nonphysician clinician may arrange for the patient to be assessed for augmentation therapy. Patients with chronic mood disorders often need more than one mood-stabilizing or anti-depressant medication to experience optimum benefits from pharmacotherapy.

Dual disordered patients sometimes experience pressure from family members or members of self-help groups to stop taking psychiatric medications because of the erroneous belief that one is not truly sober if medicines are being used or the belief that one should be able to handle problems without relying on "crutches" such as medication. Some patients will need help anticipating and preparing to deal with such pressures so that medications are not stopped prematurely.

Managing Persistent Psychiatric Symptoms

Some patients will experience persistent symptoms of their mood disorder. The clinician can focus on helping the patient to accept the persistent nature of these symptoms and to learn when a change in the level of the symptom requires a different clinical intervention, such as a change in medication or increased therapy sessions. On the other hand, the clinician should avoid the trap of arranging a medication re-evaluation every time that a patient experiences symptom changes. Some patients, for example, constantly seek medication changes whenever their symptoms wax or wane. Some of these patients resist psychotherapy and self-help groups and perceive the doctor and the medicines as the only form of treatment.

Psychological Issues in Recovery

Identifying feelings, discriminating moods, and managing negative affect are potential areas of clinical focus among mood and substance use disorders. Anger, anxiety, boredom, depression, loneliness, guilt, and shame are common issues in recovery. Many patients are angry and resentful that they have a mood or substance use disorder. Some resent the fact that they cannot drink alcohol safely or in moderation. Patients often feel guilty for having one or more disorders. Some feel bad about the possibility (or reality) of offspring developing similar disorders.

Many patients have trouble managing or tolerating distress and use substances as a quick fix for painful affects. They need to learn new coping strategies to manage their uncomfortable mood states. Clinicians can help patients by teaching them how to monitor their moods, understand the connection between thoughts and feelings, learn to identify and address problems, beliefs, and thoughts contributing to negative affect, and learn assertive and appropriate expression of feelings. If, for example, a patient reports involvement in an interpersonal relationship that clearly has a major adverse effect on the patient's mood, the clinician can initiate a discussion of this issue and attempt to help the client determine how to address the issues involved in this interpersonal problem.

Patients sometimes have difficulty discriminating between normal fluctuations of moods and signs that their mood disorder is significantly worsening. They need help in monitoring mood changes and knowing when changes represent a movement toward relapse.

Interpersonal, job, financial, and other actual or symbolic losses are common with mood and substance use disorders. These losses often contribute to significant grief in the patient. In addition, some patients experience a loss of potential or dreams as a result of the disability associated with more severe manifestations of illness. For example, a bipolar patient who once functioned as a professional and now can barely hold a nonprofessional job has many losses with which to deal — the profession, a way of supporting self or family, status, self-esteem, and the "healthy side of self." Recovery from substance dependence also contributes to grief as patients "lose" the euphoria or other feelings that substances provide, a way of living, and, in some instances, the sense of excitement associated with a lifestyle of "living on the edge."

Fear of recurrence of illness after a period of remission is another psychological issue for patients with bipolar disorder or recurrent major depression. Patients also worry about their offspring developing a mood or substance use disorder, since many of these run in families. When a child of a patient develops a psychiatric or substance use disorder, the parent often feels guilty and responsible and thus will need help addressing this important issue.

Cognitive Issues in Recovery

Negative thinking and cognitive distortions are common with dual disordered patients. In 12-step programs, the term *stinking thinking* is used to connote negative or self-sabotaging thoughts that may lead to relapse or contribute to unhappiness of the recovering individual. The clinician can encourage the patient to discuss thoughts and beliefs about the illnesses, medications, and participation in treatment and recovery. Patients can be taught to keep thought records in which they record negative thinking or cognitive distortions and to practice countering these. Cognitive therapy provides a rich array of clinical strategies to help patients change thoughts and core beliefs that contribute to depressed or anxious moods or substance use (Beck, 1995; Beck et al., 1993).

Other Psychiatric Comorbidity

Patients with mood and substance use disorders also experience anxiety and psychotic and other types of psychiatric symptoms or disorders in the course of their recovery. Patients need help understanding and managing these symptoms, particularly because the risk of suicide is higher in complicated cases of mood disorders, such as those with psychotic features. Although psychotherapy can be useful in helping the patient manage symptoms, additional medications or ECT may also be needed, particularly in cases involving more severe and persistent mood symptoms that do not respond to a single medication.

Family Issues in Recovery

Families are often adversely affected by dual disorders (Daley, Moss, and Campbell, 1993; Daley and Thase, 2000). The clinician can help the patient understand and accept the effects of his disorders on the family. Although anxiety provoking, this can help the patient become more motivated to comply with treatment and change, as well as more sensitive to the suffering experienced by the family.

Involving the family in treatment gives family members an opportunity to learn about the dual disorders, gain support, and deal with their emotional reactions. It also provides family members with an opportunity to learn behaviors that support recovery and those that are less helpful or potentially have an adverse effect on the patient's recovery. For example, family conflicts or high expressed emotion are associated with recurrence of mood disorder or relapse to substance abuse. Making family members aware of this and helping them accept the need to regulate their emotional response can be quite helpful. Referring families to ongoing family therapy or self-help groups may be helpful. Clinicians can help families regardless of whether they are trained in family therapy. In-person sessions or telephone conversations asking for the family's input or providing information or support to them can be positive. In some instances, family members will have disorders of their own that require treatment, so the clinician can make referrals when needed. For example, a wife of a depressed alcoholic man attended several outpatient sessions during the course of her husband's treatment. During this time, she experienced an episode of major depression and was referred for an evaluation and treatment.

In the 12-step program of recovery, steps 8 and 9 deal with "making amends." Early founders of 12-step programs knew that recovering individuals had to address the pain inflicted on their families for recovery to progress. Even if the clinician does not use a 12-step approach to treatment, the process of making amends can be discussed with the patient relevant to either of the disorders.

Interpersonal and Social Issues in Recovery

The clinician can help the patient examine the effects of the dual disorders on interpersonal relationships and social functioning. Negative social networks are common with addiction, regardless of type or psychiatric comorbidity. Patients need help establishing sober relationships and developing a supportive recovery network. Patients can be helped by facilitating their attendance at self-help meetings and recovery clubs and their building of positive social supports.

Individuals with depressive or bipolar disorders often have problems with social or work relationships. Unsatisfying or unhealthy relationships can contribute to mood symptoms as well as dissatisfaction with life. These patients sometimes have problems with their interpersonal style that cause significant deficits in their ability to relate effectively with others. Treatment can help by identifying and addressing interpersonal problems, conflicts, and deficits. Some patients benefit from assertiveness training and learning of skills such as how to ask for help or support and how to be supportive to others so that there is a sense of reciprocity in interpersonal relationships. Interpersonal disputes and deficits are two of the main areas of clinical intervention of treatments such as interpersonal psychotherapy used with depression or addiction and interpersonal and social rhythm therapy used for bipolar disorder (Frank and Kupfer, 1994; Miklowitz, Frank, and George, 1996).

Mood and substance use disorders often have an adverse effect on occupational functioning. The clinician can help by discussing any relevant issues for a particular patient and by facilitating vocational assessment, counseling, or training, if needed. Being employed often has a positive influence on mood as well as sobriety status. Patients with legal problems in relation to substance use disorder or bizarre behaviors associated with bipolar illness may require help in addressing their legal problems as well as their emotional reactions to these difficulties.

The more persistently and chronically impaired mood-disordered addicted patients who receive disability checks can benefit from help addressing check-day stresses. Others in the community, particularly drug dealers or substance abusers, know when these patients receive their government checks and often prey on these patients to get them to buy drugs or give them money.

Role Transitions

The interpersonally oriented psychotherapies put much emphasis on address-ing role transitions as part of therapy. Role transitions, such as having a child, launching an adolescent, getting married, separated, or divorced, or losing a job, become an area of clinical focus when such events cause major changes in roles or stresses in the lifestyle of a patient.

Structured Time and Pleasant Activities

Patients often need help creating and maintaining structure in their daily lives. Structuring the day and week aids recovery by providing a sense of discipline and regularity. The clinician can help with predictable changes in the patient's routine, such as going on vacation or a business trip. It is important for bipo-lar patients to try to maintain regularity of meals and sleeping and prevent overstimulation or understimulation while away from home. For substance abusers, maintaining recovery disciplines while on vacation or business trips may involve making sure to attend self-help meetings, read recovery literature, or follow their plan for daily meditation or prayer.

These patients often benefit from help in identifying and engaging in pleas-ant activities. Involvement in pleasant activities can have a positive effect on de-pressed mood and provide stimulation and motivation. Such activities can also help decrease feelings of boredom that often precede substance abuse relapse.

Spiritual Issues in Recovery

Spirituality has long been recognized as an important issue in recovery from addiction. Interventions include helping the patient reduce shameful feelings and find meaning in life, introducing the patient to the 12-step program of re-covery, and encouraging the patient to use a "Higher Power" and participate in spiritual activities such as attending services, praying, or reading. Many find spirituality a source of strength and inspiration, especially during difficult times. The importance of spirituality is evident in many of the 12 steps of AA, NA, and Cocaine Anonymous (steps 2, 3, 5, 6, 7, 11, and 12). Persons with al-coholic and/or drug addiction frequently report that spiritual suffering far ex-ceeded any physical suffering associated with physical dependency and that spirituality is necessary for a healthy, long-term recovery.

Substance Use Lapse and Relapse

Most people who quit drinking or using other drugs experience one or more lapses or relapses (Daley and Marlatt, 1997c). A *lapse* refers to an initial period of substance use after a period of recovery. The patient's emotional and cog-nitive reaction to a lapse determines whether this will lead to a full-blown re-lapse. The clinician can help the patient to understand relapse as a process and an event and to identify and manage both obvious and subtle relapse warning signs. These relapse warning signs usually are changes in the patient's think-ing or attitudes, emotions, or behaviors before the ingestion of substances. A microanalysis of past lapses or relapses is an excellent way to help patients learn from past experiences.

Another intervention is to help the patient identify and manage high-risk situations that increase relapse risk. The most common high-risk situations across a range of addictions include negative emotional states, social pressures to engage in substance use, interpersonal conflicts, urges and temptations, pos-itive emotional states, and testing of personal control. Helping the patient learn to intervene early in the lapse or relapse process is another intervention that can lead to minimizing the damage when the patient returns to substance use. Finally, the clinician should help the patient understand the potential conse-quences of substance use on psychiatric symptoms because addiction relapse often contributes to psychiatric relapse.

Mood Disorder Relapse

Many patients with mood disorder have recurrent episodes of depression or mania and should be educated about and prepared for the possibility of relapse

(Craighead et al., 1998). Clinicians can teach patients general and illness-specific warning signs of relapse or recurrence as well as strategies to manage these warning signs. General warning signs may include a decrease in compliance with medications or in attendance at therapy sessions or self-help groups; an increase in pessimism or negative thoughts about self or recovery; or changes in habits, daily routines, sleep, emotional sensitivity, or behavior. Illness-specific warning signs include experiencing symptoms of the depression or mania after a period of partial or full remission. For bipolar disorder, common warning signs of relapse include less need for sleep, a significant increase in activities or projects, a significant increase in irritability or grandiosity, racing thoughts, and difficulty relaxing. Common early signs of depression relapse include a marked increase in problems related to sleeping or in the amount of time spent sleeping, decreased motivation, reduced libido, increased feelings of tiredness or lethargy, decreased efficiency at performing tasks, and increase in pessimistic, hopeless, or suicidal thinking. Another major clinical strategy is helping the patient deal with high-risk factors associated with recurrence of the mood disorder. High-risk factors include relapse to alcohol or other drug use, severe or prolonged stress at home or work or in interpersonal relationships, major disruptions to daily routines, and noncompliance with treatment.

Since some patients will experience more than one episode of mania, depression, or both over time or experience an episode after a significant period of remission, the clinician should prepare the patient for the possibility of a setback. Early intervention in a relapse can often prevent serious damage or the need for psychiatric hospitalization. In some instances of serious relapse in which the patient is at risk for suicide, the family will need help in knowing when and how to intervene with the patient. This may require initiation of an involuntary commitment. Patients often need help understanding and dealing with mood disorder relapses, as these can be psychologically devastating, particularly after a period of remission during which the patient functioned well.

The Ongoing Use of Recovery Tools

Recovery tools refer to all of the various cognitive, behavioral, and interpersonal strategies that a patient uses to help manage the mood and substance use disorders; make positive changes in self, relationships, and lifestyle; and maintain gains made in the course of recovery (Miklowitz, Frank, and George, 1996). Clinicians can help identify those tools most suitable for the individual patient and help the patient learn to use these on an ongoing basis. Although some patients will remain in maintenance treatment for years because of the chronicity of their disorders, others will receive professional treatment for a short period. Helping patients learn to use various recovery tools can reduce relapse risk in the future.

The following two cases illustrate different levels of severity of illness, motivation to engage in self-help groups, and response to professional treatment. The first case involves a man with a long-term and extensive substance dependence disorder, bipolar disorder, and personality disorder who had a partial yet significant response to treatment. This patient had been treated numerous times in acute care and long-term psychiatric facilities, addiction rehabilitation facilities, and outpatient programs. He represents the type of patient with chronic and severe psychiatric and addictive disorders who receives multiple services over time and often resists recommendations of professionals. The second case involves a woman with alcohol dependence and major depression who had an excellent response to her first involvement in professional treatment over a period of 6 months. This patient had 12 sessions with an outpatient therapist and 4 sessions with a psychiatrist, who initiated antidepressant therapy. This patient continued pharmacotherapy and AA attendance after completion of treatment. These two cases also illustrate some recovery issues in outpatient treatment.

Case 1. Larry is a 49-year-old, unemployed, divorced father of two sons with a lifelong history of problems with alcohol, cocaine, and marijuana. He also has a significant history of interpersonal violence and has been arrested for several assaults. Larry has been diagnosed with a bipolar disorder and antisocial personality disorder and has been hospitalized on four occasions for severe mood symptoms and homicidal feelings. He also completed a several-month residential treatment program for addiction. In addition, Larry has received outpatient treatment on several occasions and has been prescribed mood stabilizers and antidepressants. He has refused partial hospital and intensive outpatient treatment and self-help meetings such as NA and AA. The focus of his outpatient treatment has been on maintaining abstinence from substances, controlling aggressive impulses to avoid violent altercations, resolving conflicts between him and his sons, complying with mood-stabilizing medications, managing persistent mood symptoms (especially irritability and depression), and implementing some structure in his week. Although Larry's attendance at outpatient treatment has been erratic, he has been able to maintain total abstinence from substances for long periods (up to several years), drastically reduced the frequency of interpersonal violent episodes, established relatively good relationships with his sons, maintained a relationship with a live-in partner, and sought help from his outpatient treatment team during periods when homicidal feelings were strong.

Although not an ideal candidate for psychotherapy, Larry established a trusting alliance with his outpatient therapist and periodically engaged in sessions for several months or called for help during serious crises. While he still has problems with mood symptoms and interpersonal relationships and experiences periods of increased rage, relative to his baseline symptoms Larry has made moderate improvements. In terms of phases of recovery, Larry typically deals with issues pertinent to stabilizing acute symptoms and to the early and middle phases of recovery. His pattern is to stabilize acute symptoms, use outpatient treatment for several months, and then drop out. He also occasionally uses inpatient hospital stays to gain control over aggressive feelings.

Case 2. Marie is a 36-year-old, married mother of one son and one daughter who works as a health care professional. She has a several-year history of untreated episodes of major depression and alcohol dependence. Marie sought treatment for the first time at the advice of a friend. During the initial phase of outpatient treatment, she focused on establishing and maintaining abstinence from alcohol, learning how to manage cravings and thoughts of wanting to use, dealing with work- and family-related stresses that increased her desires to drink alcohol, and reducing her feelings of guilt and shame related to having both an alcohol problem and a mood disorder. Despite the persistence of her depression and limited response to psychotherapy, she initially refused to consider an evaluation for medication, insisting that her mood would improve as she gained more time sober from alcohol.

Treatment focused on helping her accept her mood disorder and on exploring her beliefs that she should be able to resolve her depression without the use of medicine and that taking psychiatric medications was not a good idea because she was alcoholic and had a propensity to use substances to excess. She altered her beliefs and finally agreed to an evaluation, and her mood improved markedly after starting an antidepressant. As a result of improved mood, Marie was then able to address a problem in her marital relationship and her dissatisfaction with her career. Her marital problems improved moderately, and she took a new job. After several months of continued sobriety and stable mood, she terminated outpatient therapy but continued taking medications because of the recurrent nature of her depression. Marie also continued in AA as part of her efforts to maintain sobriety and prevent relapse to alcohol use.

The Use of Medication

Medications are important in the treatment of mood disorders (American Psychiatric Association, 1993, 1994; Goodwin and Jamison, 1990; Hilty, Brady, and Hales, 1999), substance use disorders, and dual disorders (American Psychiatric Association, 1995; Cornelius et al., 1997; Salloum et al., 1998). The nonpsychiatrist clinician must be prepared to deal with a variety of medication-related issues. These include persuading a reluctant patient to consider a medication evaluation, facilitating medication evaluations and collaborating with the treating psychiatrist, monitoring medication compliance and side effects, and helping the patient address concerns about medications or side effects with the treating physician. The clinician may have to help the patient deal with the perception of taking psychiatric medications while being in recovery from a substance use disorder or deal with pressures from others (e.g., family members or members of self-help programs) to stop taking psychotropic medications. In addition, the clinician has to deal with patients who resist using psychotherapy or who expect any problems or changes in symptoms to be addressed primarily through the use of pharmacotherapy.

Self-Help Groups

The clinician can educate and prepare the patient to attend self-help groups related to addiction (e.g., Alcoholics Anonymous, Narcotics Anonymous, Cocaine Anonymous [CA], Rational Recovery, SMART Recovery, Women for Sobriety), mood or other psychiatric disorders (e.g., manic-depression support group, Recovery, Inc., Emotions Anonymous), and/or dual disorders (e.g., Dual Recovery Anonymous, Double Trouble). This involves providing information, answering questions, addressing the patient's beliefs about self-help programs, discussing previous experiences, identifying resistances to participating in support groups, discussing benefits of self-help programs, and facilitating entry into these. The clinician should be flexible in the approach taken in using self-help groups, as not all patients respond in the same way. Although the majority of our patients find AA, NA, or CA helpful, some don't find these beneficial at all and prefer attending Rational Recovery, SMART Recovery, Double Trouble, or other mental health support groups. Encouraging patients to seek sponsors and work the 12-step program may be helpful. In some instances, introducing the patient to others in recovery facilitates entry into a self-help program.

Measuring Outcome

Outcome of treatment can be measured in a variety of ways related to clinical symptoms, functioning, and participation in treatment. With substance use disorders, outcome can be measured in terms of cessation or reduction in the amount and frequency of substance use, reductions in high-risk behaviors (e.g., using needles to ingest drugs, engaging in unprotected or promiscuous sex), reduction of severity of lapses or relapses, resolution of family or psychosocial problems, and improvement in functioning and overall quality of life. Outcome for mood disorders can be measured in terms of remission of specific symptoms, reduction of severity of symptoms, reduced severity of relapses or recurrences, resolution of family or life problems caused or exacerbated by the mood disorder, and improvement in overall functioning and quality of life. Outcome can also be measured in terms of the process of treatment (e.g., compliance with medications, therapy attendance, self-help program attendance, or completion of an episode of treatment). Measuring outcome allows clinicians, patients, and family members to see progress (or lack of it) over time. It is not unusual for patients to improve but maintain the belief that they are not getting better.

Conclusion

Mood and substance use disorders are common clinical conditions affecting large numbers of patients seeking help in substance abuse or mental health treatment systems. Although a variety of specific treatment models or approaches have been demonstrated to be successful with alcoholism, drug dependency, and bipolar or depressive illness, the challenge for the clinician is to provide an integrated approach to treatment that takes into account problems and issues relevant to both the mood and the substance use disorder. Since relapse to one disorder often affects relapse to the other disorder, integrated treatment is all the more important. In working with these dual disordered patients, the clinician must also be sensitive to issues and needs of the family and be aware of how the patient affects the family and how the family influences the patient.

Treatment of mood and substance use disorders often involves psychosocial treatments (individual, group, or family therapy), medications, and self-help program attendance. Depending on the unique clinical presentation and needs of each patient, the clinician can address a range of physical, psychological, family, social and interpersonal, and spiritual issues in recovery. Given the realities of addiction relapse and recurrence of psychiatric illness, the clinician also needs to focus on relapse prevention and intervention strategies to minimize the adverse effects of setbacks.

ACKNOWLEDGMENTS
This work was supported in part by USPHS grants AA-10523 and AA-11929 from the National Institute on Alcohol Abuse and Alcoholism, Rockville, Maryland.

REFERENCES
American Psychiatric Association. 1993. Practice guideline for major depressive disorder in adults. *American Journal of Psychiatry* 150(suppl 4):1–26.
———. 1994. Practice guideline for the treatment of patients with bipolar disorder. *American Journal of Psychiatry* 151(suppl 12):1–36.
———. 1995. Practice guideline for the treatment of substance use disorders. *American Journal of Psychiatry* 152(suppl 11):1–36.
Beck, A., F. Wright, B. Liese, and C. Newman. 1993. *Cognitive Therapy of Substance Abuse.* New York: Guilford Press.
Beck, J. S. 1995. *Cognitive Therapy: Basics and Beyond.* New York: Guilford Press.
Cornelius, J. R., I. M. Salloum, J. G. Ehler, et al. 1997. Fluoxetine in depressed alcoholics: A double-blind, placebo-controlled trial [see comments]. *Archives of General Psychiatry* 54:700–705.
Craighead, W. E., D. J. Miklowitz, F. C. Vajk, and E. Frank. 1998. Psychosocial treatments for bipolar disorder. In *A Guide to Treatments That Work*, edited by P. E. Nathan and J. M. Gorman, 240–48. New York: Oxford University Press.
Daley, D., and H. B. Moss. 2002. *Dual Disorders: Counseling Clients with Chemical Dependency and Mental Illness*, 3d ed. Center City, Minn.: Hazelden.
Daley, D. C., and G. A. Marlatt. 1997a. *Managing Your Alcohol or Drug Problem: Client Workbook.* San Antonio: Psychological Corp.
———. 1997b. *Therapist's Guide for Managing Your Alcohol or Drug Problem.* San Antonio, Tex.: Psychological Corp.
———. 1997c. Relapse prevention. In *Substance Abuse: A Comprehensive Textbook*, 3d ed., edited by J. H. Lowinson, P. Ruiz, R. B. Millman, and J. G. Langrod, 458–66. Baltimore: Williams & Wilkins.

Daley, D. C., and M. E. Thase. 2000. *Dual Disorders Recovery Counseling: A Biopsychosocial Approach to Addiction and Mental Health Disorders*, 2d ed. Independence, Mo.: Herald House / Independence Press.

Frank, E., and D. Kupfer. 1994. Interpersonal and social rhythm therapy for bipolar disorder: Integrating interpersonal and behavioral approaches. *AABT the Behavior Therapist* 17(7):143–49.

Goodwin, F. K., and K. R. Jamison. 1990. *Manic-Depressive Illness*. New York: Oxford University Press.

Hilty, D. M., K. T. Brady, and R. E. Hales. 1999. A review of bipolar disorder among adults. *Psychiatric Services* 50(2):201–13.

Liberman, R. P., W. J. DeRisi, and K. T. Mueser. 1989. *Social Skills Training for Psychiatric Patients*. New York: Pergamon Press.

Marlatt, G. A., and J.-R. Gordon. 1985. *Relapse Prevention*. New York: Guilford Press.

Miklowitz, D. J., E. Frank, and E. L. George. 1996. New psychosocial treatments for the outpatient management of bipolar disorder. *Psychopharmacology Bulletin* 32(4): 613–21.

Miller, W. R., and S. Rollnick. 2002. *Motivational Interviewing: Preparing People to Change Addictive Behavior*, 2d ed. New York: Guilford Press.

Prochaska, J. O., J. C. Norcross, and C. C. DiClemente. 1994. *Changing for Good: The Revolutionary Program That Explains the Six Stages of Change and Teaches You How to Free Yourself from Bad Habits*. New York: William Morrow.

Salloum, I. M., J. R. Cornelius, M. E. Thase, D. C. Daley, L. Kirisci, and C. Spotts. 1998. Naltrexone utility in depressed alcoholics. *Psychopharmacology Bulletin* 34: 111–15.

Thase, M. E. 1992. Long-term treatments of recurrent depressive disorders. *Journal of Clinical Psychiatry* 53(suppl 9):32–41.

Thase, M. E., and L. R. Sullivan. 1995. Relapse and recurrence of depression: A practical approach for prevention. *Journal of Nervous and Mental Disease* 181(8):261–77.

Weissman, M. M., J. C. Markowitz, and G. L. Klerman. 2000. *Comprehensive Guide to Interpersonal Psychotherapy*. New York: Basic Books.

5

Dual Recovery Therapy: Blending Psychotherapies for Depression and Addiction

Douglas M. Ziedonis, M.D., M.P.H., and Jonathan A. Krejci, Ph.D.

Psychosocial treatment continues to be the cornerstone of treatment for addictions and mood disorders, both with or without medications. Co-occurring addiction and mood disorders require an integrated clinical perspective by the clinician. Depending on several factors, including patient preference, the nature of the presenting problem, the referral or funding source, and expressed motivation to change his or her substance abuse, the patient may present for treatment in a mental health, addiction, or dual diagnosis treatment setting. Addiction treatment specialists can help patients with depression by learning and integrating the specific psychosocial treatments developed to treat depression.

The addiction treatment field is at an important point in building bridges between different treatment approaches and blending medical and recovery models. This trend parallels efforts at integration and the development of transtheoretical approaches in the mental health field about 15–20 years ago. Educators recognized that training and supervision were often unnecessarily fragmented and inconsistent and that apparently incompatible approaches could be reconciled at the level of both theory and practice.

This chapter is divided into two sections. The first section describes our dual recovery therapy approach to blending and modifying specific mental health and addiction psychotherapies. We present a treatment-matching approach to using motivational enhancement therapy, with several common case scenarios. In the second section, we outline the principles and techniques of three specific psychosocial treatments with demonstrated efficacy in the treatment of depression and suggest ways in which these approaches can be modified or adapted to the treatment of the depressed substance abuser.

Dual Recovery Therapy

Dual recovery therapy (DRT) blends modified traditional mental health and addiction psychotherapies into an integrated therapy approach (Ziedonis and Fisher, 1996; Ziedonis and Stern, 2001). DRT represents what we believe to be a unique contribution to the field, an attempt to integrate recovery language and concepts with more traditional mental health and substance abuse approaches. Addiction treatment psychotherapies that are blended include motivational enhancement therapy, relapse prevention, and recovery concepts drawn from 12-step facilitation. Depression treatment psychotherapies that are integrated include interpersonal, cognitive, and behavioral therapies for depression.

The skilled addiction therapist uniquely blends and tailors these approaches to the needs of the individual patient and decides which one of the three to emphasize at various times. Although the psychotherapy approaches for depression are described in this chapter as distinct entities, in practice therapists commonly use a synthesis of various approaches and strategies. These, in turn, are individually tailored to each patient on the basis of the particular clinical presentation and coping capacities. Content and process are inextricably intertwined, as both technique and the therapeutic relationship reciprocally evolve (American Psychiatric Association, 1993).

Dual recovery therapy takes into account the many ways in which psychiatric and addiction disorders interact. For example, individuals with clinical depression may exhibit low self-efficacy, low motivation and energy to make changes, maladaptive interpersonal styles of avoidance or antagonism, difficulties with managing affects, poor coping skills, and cognitive distortions.

Similarly, patients with substance use disorders often present with intense and frequent crises and chaotic lifestyles. They are likely to be inconsistent in their attendance at treatment and to present with multiple unexplained legal, vocational, medical, or social difficulties.

Patients may have different levels of motivation to address addictive and psychiatric disorders. Dual recovery therapy considers the patient's stage of recovery and motivation to address each problem. We have found that patients with low motivation to change their substance use respond best to a motivational enhancement therapy approach, while those with high motivation fare best with relapse prevention and 12-step facilitation. Similarly, motivational enhancement approaches are advisable for those reluctant to acknowledge their depression or to participate in psychosocial or medication treatments.

Psychosocial treatments target specific aspects of depression, including cognition, behavior, and affect. Depression might be related to grief, trauma, shame, alienation, loneliness, and low self-esteem. In general, targeted therapies are short-term and seek to alleviate the depressive condition per se, rather than to change character. We describe in detail interpersonal therapy, behavioral therapies, and cognitive therapy, while recognizing that psychodynamic therapies also may have an important role in the treatment of depression. For this chapter, we have limited our description of the psychodynamic approaches to a discussion of approaches with patients in stable recovery from addiction for at least 1 year who develop mild to moderate depression. Each therapy approach has a unique theoretical model of causes of depression that guides treatment, including the tone, perspective, and techniques. Books and therapy manuals have been developed for these approaches and are an excellent first step toward learning specific techniques and approaches (see under "Suggested Readings"). However, always remember that the development of rapport, empathy, and understanding is basic to all therapy.

Dual recovery therapy recognizes the need for hope, acceptance, and empowerment in the healing process of both disorders and embraces the recovery perspective for both addiction and depression (see chap. 4). Recovery is a powerful and meaningful word to those who have accepted their addiction and the need for change. There is no single agreed-upon method for defining or measuring recovery; it is simultaneously a process, an outlook, a vision, a guiding principle, and a symbol of a personal commitment to self-growth and self-discovery. Recovery is a complex and typically nonlinear process of transformation in which a patient's fundamental values and world view are gradually

Table 5.1. Dual Recovery Theory

Assumptions
    Based on biopsychosocial-spiritual model
    Need to modify treatment in response to co-occurring disorders
    Need to tailor treatment to stage of change and motivational level
    Importance of appropriate integration of medications and therapy
    Importance of engaging and motivating patients
    Central role of skill building and behavioral rehearsal/role playing
Role of the Therapist
    Engage patients using a positive, respectful, and active approach
    Promote and address mental health and addiction recovery (dual recovery) in all interactions
    Focus on structured learning and skill building
    Teach recovery concepts and relapse prevention
    Motivate using group support and positive reinforcement
    Blend spirituality and human values into treatment
    Engage significant others in treatment planning and support
Clinical Tools
    Breathing/relaxation exercises
    Relapse analysis
    Timeline for substance abuse and mood disorder
    Decisional balance
    Role plays

questioned and often radically changed. The overarching message is that hope and restoration of a meaningful life are possible, despite addiction or mental illness. Instead of focusing primarily on symptom relief, as the medical model dictates, recovery casts a much wider spotlight on restoring self-esteem and identity and attaining meaningful roles in society. Although recovery is often linked with 12-step recovery, many roads may converge on the same destination, and of late patients with a mental illness have adopted this word to describe their journey. This trend has been accelerated by the involvement of the dually diagnosed in 12-step recovery programs. Table 5.1 summarizes our dual recovery approach.

Treatment Matching

Despite the existence of many models of recovery, most describe a similar progression, and all agree that treatment must be stage-appropriate. Several models of dual recovery and dual recovery treatment have been described. The Boston University model (Anthony, 1991) suggests that patients go through stages of recovery that include shock, denial, depression, acceptance, hope, and empowerment. Another example (see chap. 4) posits initial stages of *engagement* and *stabilization*, followed by four recovery stages. In *early recovery*, skills specific to achieving abstinence and stabilizing psychiatric symptoms are emphasized. *Middle recovery* focuses on interpersonal and spiritual concerns. Achieving lifestyle balance and addressing longstanding personality problems are dominant themes in *late recovery*, while continued personal growth is the goal of *maintenance*. Similarly, Larsen (1985) distinguishes between stage I and stage II recovery, where the former entails achieving freedom from the primary substance and the latter involves changing deeply ingrained, self-defeating learned behaviors in relationships.

In addition to providing stage-specific interventions, effective treatment must integrate the biological, psychological, social, and spiritual, recognizing that the relative emphasis on these components changes with time. Neurobiological changes may be especially important during the early phase of recovery. The addicted brain changes from a pickle to a cucumber, and there are symptoms of acute withdrawal (days to weeks) and protracted withdrawal (weeks to months). During the initial phase there are characteristic symptoms of protracted abstinence syndrome, reversible cognitive impairments secondary to substance abuse, and reversible psychiatric symptoms induced by substance usage and dependence. Medications and cognitive-behavioral psychosocial treatment may be most crucial during this stage. After 6 to 12 months of abstinence, psychological symptoms are prominent and manifest as character defects or personality issues. Clinicians often begin to explore more emotionally charged issues that the patient was unable to address in earlier recovery stages. These can include problems with anger or histories of physical or sexual abuse. In stage II recovery (typically after 1 year of abstinence), deeply ingrained interpersonal issues begin to predominate, with patients now more able to deal with intimacy and stronger emotions related to close relationships. Interpersonally based treatments may be especially helpful at this stage. Table 5.2 summarizes these treatment-matching strategies.

The Role of Motivation in Dual Recovery Therapy and in the Stages of Recovery

Motivation to address both the addiction and the mood disorder often varies according to treatment setting. Dually diagnosed patients who enter the mental health treatment system often do not believe they have an addiction and en-

Table 5.2. Matching Recovery Stage with Substance Abuse Treatment Strategy

Stage of Recovery	Recommended Treatment
	Motivational Stages
Precontemplation or contemplation	Motivational enhancement therapy
	Psychoeducation
Preparation, action, maintenance	Relapse prevention; 12 steps
	Chronological Stages
Engagement and stabilization	Develop therapeutic alliance and engage
Early recovery (1–6 wk)	Achieving abstinence; stabilizing psychiatric symptoms; medication treatment of acute withdrawal
Middle recovery (6 wk–6 mo)	Resolution of protracted abstinence; stabilization
Late recovery (6–12 mo)	Emphasis on interpersonal concerns; early spiritual awareness
Maintenance (12 mo or more)	Continued personal and spiritual growth; achieving lifestyle balance; addressing longstanding personality problems

ter complaining of depressive symptoms. Those entering the addiction treatment system are often influenced quickly by the 12-step culture and led to believe that medications for depression are incompatible with recovery. Furthermore, addiction treatment professionals typically have not been trained to provide specific mental health treatment for depression. It is critical that both mental health and substance abuse clinicians understand how to organize treatment around phase of recovery, integrate mental health and addiction approaches, and assess and reassess stages of change and recovery.

Early in treatment, patients need to be engaged by increasing internal or external motivation to change and to accept their illnesses. These early stages of treatment focus on education about the illness, relapse prevention treatment, and 12-step facilitation to manage acute and protracted withdrawal symptoms. Later stages of recovery focus on addressing personality problems and interpersonal issues with spouse, family, and friends.

Our motivation-based treatment model was developed to help organize treatment planning and develop realistic treatment goals for the dually diagnosed at different motivational levels (Ziedonis and Fisher, 1996). This identifies patient motivation to stop using a particular substance, based on Prochaska's stages of change (Prochaska, DiClemente, and Norcross, 1992). It then matches each motivational stage (precontemplation, contemplation, preparation, action, and maintenance) to specific techniques from motivational enhancement therapy (Miller et al., 1995) and other mental health and addiction therapies. Our staging of dual recovery treatment recognizes that individuals can have varying levels of motivation for their mental health and substance abuse problems. When there is equal motivation for either problem, an integrated treatment that addresses both problems in parallel can occur. Unfortunately, often patients have high motivation for one problem and low motivation for another. The level of internal motivation determines a realistic treatment goal unless there is a powerful external motivator to force initial engagement and retention. For example, less-motivated patients often have harm reduction goals, while more-motivated patients have abstinence-oriented goals.

Motivational Enhancement Therapy during the Engagement Phase

As an introduction to the blending of psychosocial treatment, we discuss stages of dual recovery and issues related to increasing motivation and engaging people into treatment and acceptance of their illness through the use of motivational enhancement therapy (MET) (Miller et al., 1995). In contrast to traditional addiction approaches, MET assumes that motivation is a highly malleable state that is amenable to gentle and indirect means of persuasion. Essential to the approach is a respectful, compassionate, patient-centered attitude combined with a mixture of open-ended questioning and empathic listening. Rogerian reflective listening forms the cornerstone of MET. Patients are assumed to be ambivalent about their substance use, and the therapist is attentive to any patient statements indicating problem recognition or a desire for change. These statements are probed further, and the ambivalence is reflected back to the patient, with a particular emphasis on positive internal motivation. In addition, there are a variety of techniques to elicit self-motivational statements, summarize concerns, provide objective but personalized feedback, and elicit a commitment to change. Throughout, the patient is treated as an active collaborator in the treatment planning process. Significant others are also invited to collaborate in treatment planning and motivational enhancement and can provide important feedback to both the clinician and the patient (Miller and Rollnick, 2002).

Although considerable research remains to be done in this area, we believe that MET is ideal for a dually diagnosed population. First, it is most appropriate for patients in the precontemplation or contemplation stage of change, a category comprising approximately 77 percent of dually diagnosed patients

(Ziedonis and Fisher, 1996). Second, its nonconfrontational, empathic stance is likely to be more tolerable to the dually diagnosed than are traditional confrontational approaches. This stance is reflected in dual diagnosis models that emphasize the importance of engagement and the development of a trusting therapeutic relationship (e.g., chap. 4). Third, the empathic attitude of the therapist, combined with the recognition that few patients enter treatment in the action stage, is more compatible with principles of mental health treatment with which many patients will already be familiar.

It is vital that the MET practitioner shape interventions to the appropriate stage of change. This can be accomplished by a variety of formal instruments, including the University of Rhode Island Change Assessment (URICA; McConnaughy, Prochaska, and Velicer, 1983), the Readiness to Change Questionnaire (RCQ; Rollnick et al., 1992), and the Stages of Change Readiness and Treatment Eagerness Scale (SOCRATES; Miller and Tonigan, 1996). In addition, more informal strategies can be used. Patients should be asked in a direct but nonjudgmental manner about their desire to achieve abstinence and their willingness to commit to a quit date. Subjective perceptions of positive and negative aspects of continued substance use can be elicited, with an overvaluing of the former most typical of those in the precontemplation stage. Patients who are interpersonally disengaged in the interview or who are openly hostile, avoidant, or dismissive are most likely in the precontemplation stage, while those in the contemplation stage are more overtly ambivalent. These patients should not be confused with those in the action stage, who are openly and unambivalently requesting assistance with their substance abuse problem.

Treatment Matching Based on Motivational Levels to Change

Central to the effective treatment of the dually diagnosed is the recognition that interventions must be individually crafted. We have found it particularly important to attend carefully to three assessment domains. First, patients present with a vast array of substance use patterns, with considerable variability exhibited in terms of substances used, positive and negative consequences, and the effect of substance use on depressive symptoms. Second, as described by Greenfield (chap. 3), depressive symptoms similarly will vary in terms of prominence, reactivity to substance use, functional impairment, and subjective distress. Third, levels of motivation should be carefully assessed.

With regard to the last, we have found it crucial to recognize three basic truths regarding the wide variability in patient motivation. First, patients can be highly motivated to achieve abstinence from one substance but not from another. It is important that the clinician not dismiss these patients as unmotivated but rather work with them to achieve appropriate initial goals, with the understanding that total abstinence may be addressed later. Second, patients will exhibit varying levels of motivation toward their problems with mental health and substance abuse, as well as toward specific interventions within each problem domain. Third, it is vital always to cultivate a willingness to accept patients where they are and to interpret resistance as an invitation to shift strategies rather than a blanket refusal to accept help. We describe below three common clinical dilemmas as examples of these basic principles.

The "Low-Low" Patient

The "low-low" patient presents with minimal motivation to address either substance abuse or a mood disorder. These patients are frequently mandated to attend treatment, often as a result of legal problems stemming from substance abuse. They may present in a resistant or openly hostile manner or may simply appear resigned, apathetic, or reluctant to engage in treatment. Such patients can be a source of enormous frustration, and therapists often experience a variety of negative countertransferential reactions, including dismissing them as hopelessly uncooperative and unmotivated. While we acknowledge that the prognosis for such patients is often unfavorable, we have found several strategies to be useful. First, it is important to avoid confusing the patient's resistance to a particular intervention or diagnosis with an unwillingness to accept help. Many patients are more willing to acknowledge that substances have caused problems than they are to label themselves as an "addict" or an "alcoholic." Similarly, patients may not share their clinician's vision of an effective treatment plan, often for reasons that are not obvious. For example, suggesting assertiveness exercises as homework may elicit quiet resistance or noncompliance from an anxious patient, for whom relaxation training may be less threatening. Second, it is important to probe carefully for subjective distress linked with the mood or substance use disorder and to initiate treatment at the point of least resistance.

We find an MET approach invaluable with such patients. For the overtly resistant or rebellious patient, we like to explicitly avoid potential power struggles by emphasizing the freedom of the patient to embrace or refuse change.

For those who seem more reluctant or avoidant, a gentle, empathic approach is appropriate, with a strong emphasis on reflective listening and supporting self-efficacy. For both, the therapist should be highly attentive to patients' statements suggesting even a modicum of problem recognition. There are a variety of techniques to elicit self-motivational statements, including asking detailed questions about problematic incidents, asking the patient to envision the worst possible outcome of refusing to change, and inviting the patient to reflect on changes since the onset of substance use.

The Medication-Resistant Patient

Many recovering substance abusers are reluctant to take antidepressant medications. For some, this is attributable to the mistaken assumption that such medications are mood-altering substances with high potential for abuse and dependence. In such instances, psychoeducation about different classes of drugs and their effects will often suffice to allay concerns. Also helpful is a pamphlet written by physician members of Alcoholics Anonymous (AA) entitled *The AA Member: Medications and Other Drugs* (AA World Services, 1984), which endorses the importance of medications in treating recovering substance abusers with comorbid psychiatric disorders. Moreover, some patients express the realistic concern that they will be chastised in 12-step meetings for failing to be truly substance-free. For others, their resistance springs from a reluctance to acknowledge the presence of a bona fide depressive disorder.

For all such patients, we have found several interventions to be helpful. First, MET principles can be used to address clinical issues, including enhancing motivation to take medications. Areas of resistance should be acknowledged and explored rather than directly challenged, and specific concerns should be addressed in a respectful and empathic manner that emphasizes patient choice. Resistance can be reframed as a healthy desire to be involved in treatment decisions. Such an approach may serve to soften patient resistance and cultivate receptivity to information and education. Second, regardless of the clinician's belief in the importance of initiating medications, it is critical never to convey pessimism about treatment outcome. Rather, motivation for psychosocial treatments should be supported and praised, and specific interventions should be discussed. This serves to minimize the probability of fruitless power struggles while maximizing engagement and therapist credibility. As treatment progresses, motivation for medications can be periodically reassessed. For patients with sufficient motivation and cognitive functioning, cognitive or behavioral techniques can be taught and practiced. Helpful in this regard is *Feeling Good* (Burns, 1999), a detailed self-help manual that guides patients through a variety of cognitive techniques and principles, including cognitive distortions and dysfunctional thoughts, and that emphasizes practical, self-guided cognitive interventions. Third, engagement in ongoing addiction recovery should be supported. The clinician can then engage in periodic, collaborative reassessments of the quality of the patient's recovery program, with departures from the ideal reframed as further evidence of the need to consider other interventions.

Integrating the use of antidepressant medications into treatment may be important in treating delayed depression, as well as during the early abstinence phase. Medication treatment can only be effective if the patient accepts the need for the appropriate use of an antidepressant and maintains adherence to the medication prescription plan. Resistance to medication can also occur through AA sponsors, family members, and even staff. It is vital that staff share basic assumptions and knowledge about the pros and cons of antidepressant treatment. It is also important to keep the number of prescribing clinicians to a minimum and to assure that all parties involved in treatment maintain regular contact. The interested reader is referred to Riba and Balon's (1999) useful text about collaboration between psychotherapists and prescribing physicians.

Patients should play an active and collaborative role in the management of their medication. AA literature on the appropriate use of medications can be helpful in making medications more acceptable. Clinicians should also explain that, rather than being a magic bullet, medications are but one tool in the tool box of dual recovery, that antidepressants alone are not enough for most dually diagnosed patients, and that a recurrence of depressive symptoms can lead to addiction relapses.

Delayed Depression

In some instances, a depressive disorder will arise unexpectedly after several months of relatively uncomplicated abstinence. This requires a swift and compassionate response by the clinician, bearing in mind two important points. First, patients involved in 12-step recovery groups may have to cope with comments suggesting that depression is the result of failing to "work the program."

More than one vulnerable addict in early recovery has been driven from 12-step programs by the well-meaning but insensitive old-timer who sees their deteriorating mood as evidence of a "dry drunk." The sensitive clinician will reframe the depressive episode as an opportunity for further growth or as evidence for the need to address unfinished emotional business. Second, depressed mood represents a strong trigger for relapse and tends to generate hopelessness and a sense of futility about remaining abstinent in the face of continued suffering. It is crucial to avoid viewing or describing such concerns as "self-pity" but rather to empathize with the patient's plight while actively supporting her ability to survive a temporary setback.

In our experience, delayed depression occurs in two distinct patient subtypes, and distinguishing between the two is crucial. The first consists of those with longstanding interpersonal difficulties who are facing squarely for the first time the full implication of their quandary. For many women, the pain, fear and humiliation of an abusive or neglectful relationship is no longer tolerable without the palliative effect of the abused substance. Although many women with histories of abuse fare better with a female therapist, we've also found that an egalitarian male therapist who openly advocates for the patient's right to experience and express needs can have a powerful positive effect on women who mostly have experienced men as domineering or abusive. Nonetheless, care must be taken to avoid pressuring patients prematurely to enact changes that disrupt or dissolve long-term relationships. Alternatively, the clinician may become aware for the first time of an underlying antisocial, borderline, narcissistic, or avoidant personality disorder. Such a development should prepare the clinician for a more extended course of treatment with a higher probability of potential pitfalls. These include needless power struggles with the patient, impatience over slow progress and continued resistance, excessive caretaking, or a failure to sufficiently address self-endangering behaviors. It is essential that the clinician remain empathic but firm, as well as active, supportive, concerned, and engaging.

In other instances, the depressive episode is attributable to more acute stressors or traumas, often linked with socioeconomic deprivation. Financial difficulties, obstacles to obtaining work or day care, lingering problems with health or access to health care, and the death of family or friends can inspire feelings of hopelessness and futility. Such quandaries require a culturally sensitive clinician who can help the patient to develop and maintain reasons to carry on and to cultivate connections with recovering substance abusers from similar ethnic, cultural, and socioeconomic backgrounds. In addition, the clinician will enhance both credibility and treatment outcome by becoming involved in advocacy and case management, when appropriate.

In either instance, it is advisable to increase treatment intensity and to consider multiple treatment interventions and modalities. Specifically, supportive or therapeutic groups, as well as antidepressant medications, should be encouraged. Supportive significant others should be incorporated into treatment. In addition, concern about the patient's ability to maintain abstinence should be expressed in a forthright and nonjudgmental manner, and additional interventions should be discussed. These can include breathing exercises, relaxation training, assertiveness training, and concrete problem solving.

Psychodynamic Psychotherapy for Depression and Character Pathology

Psychodynamic therapies are based on psychodynamic theories regarding the origins of psychological vulnerability, personality development, and symptom formation as shaped by developmental deficit. Some of these theories focus predominantly on conflicts related to guilt, shame, interpersonal relationships, and the management of anxiety and repressed or unacceptable impulses. Others are more focused on developmental psychological deficits produced by problems in the relationship between the child and emotional caretakers, resulting in difficulties with self-esteem, psychological cohesiveness, and emotional self-regulation (American Psychiatric Association, 1993). A detailed description of the core principles, techniques, and adaptations of psychodynamic approaches is beyond the scope of the chapter. The interested reader is referred to Bean and Zimberg's (1981) work on dynamic approaches to the treatment of alcoholism or Bemporad's (1995) summary of dynamic formulations of depression.

Psychosocial Treatments for Depression

This section describes the core principles, techniques, and adaptations for substance abusers of three specific psychotherapies for treating depression. These treatments are based on specific theoretical models of depression. In our experience, all are compatible with initial interventions that include MET and psychoeducation for both the patient and concerned family members.

Cognitive therapy maintains that irrational beliefs and distorted attitudes toward the self, the environment, and the future perpetuate depressive affects. The goal of cognitive behavioral therapy is to reduce depressive symptoms by challenging and reversing these beliefs and attitudes. Cognitive distortions are like listening to "old tapes" with outmoded or self-destructive messages that reinforce all-or-nothing thinking and low self-esteem. We have found it helpful to use Burns's *Feeling Good* (1999) to educate patients about depression and the cognitive approach. Behavioral therapists appeal to learning theory in attempting to describe and explain the causes of depression. A change in the rate of reinforcement is believed to be a key factor in the origin, maintenance, and reversal of depression. Depression is caused by a loss of positive reinforcement, perhaps due to such events as separation, death, and sudden environmental change. The result is a reduction of coping skills, social withdrawal, and feelings of hopelessness and demoralization, which can lead to further reduction in positive reinforcement. Depression can also be the result of increased aversive consequences. In contrast, the perspective of interpersonal therapy focuses on the interpersonal context as both a cause and an effect of the depressive disorder. Significant disruptions in interpersonal functioning, such as major losses, role disputes, and transitions, as well as longstanding interpersonal deficits, may play an important role in the origin and maintenance of the depressive disorder.

Cognitive Therapy

Core Principles. Cognitive therapy is based on the assumption that depression and other negative feelings are the result of dysfunctional thoughts, beliefs, and assumptions about the self, the future, and the world. These can take the form of explicit, verbal self-statements or of background assumptions, which have been termed "silent assumptions" (Sacco and Beck, 1995). Depressed people tend to see themselves as deserving of failure or rejection and tend to expect that their efforts will result in disappointment, humiliation, or futility. They are more likely to exhibit *learned helplessness*, a condition in which those with histories of repeated failure are prone to demonstrate low task persistence and frustration tolerance. Similarly, their *attributional style* is likely to be pessimistic and dysfunctional. Several studies have demonstrated that depressive *attributions* (inferences about causation or ultimate responsibility, particularly in response to negative events) tend to follow a consistent pattern (Sweeney, Anderson, and Bailey, 1986). First, depressive attributions tend to be excessively *internal*, with depressed patients inappropriately blaming themselves. Second, they tend to be *global*, with the depressed patient generalizing from a single negative event to a more pervasive sense of failure and worthlessness. Third, depressed patients make more *stable* attributions, seeing their shortcomings as representing long-term character flaws.

Another concept central to cognitive theory is that of the *cognitive schema*. Schemas can be thought of as cognitive templates through which information is processed and interpreted. This interpretive process is typically automatic and operates outside of conscious awareness. Beck described systematic errors in interpretation that reflect dysfunctional cognitive schemas (cf. Sacco and Beck, 1995), including

- catastrophization: turning relatively minor disappointments into major catastrophes
- all-or-none thinking: viewing the world in absolute, mutually exclusive terms
- personalization: relating external events to oneself based on little or no evidence
- arbitrary inference: drawing inappropriate conclusions based on faulty, insufficient, or blatantly contradictory information
- disqualifying the positive: rejecting positive experiences by interpreting them as trivial or undeserved
- emotional reasoning: assuming that negative emotions invariably reflect the true state of the world

Core Techniques. Although negative thoughts, beliefs, and assumptions may find their origin in childhood experience, cognitive theory assumes that depression is more directly attributable to the ways in which patients repeatedly indoctrinate themselves with harsh, distorted, and dysfunctional misinterpretations. Consequently, while cognitive therapists exhibit an interest in earlier events that may give rise to maladaptive cognitive strategies, they typically maintain a steadfast focus on the depressed person's current cognitive distortions and attributional style. In addition, cognitive therapy demands that the practitioner be comfortable with an active, engaged, directive, and educational role. Treatment is typically highly focused and time limited, with a strong emphasis on the role of the patient in developing and maintaining the depressive disorder. Cognitive therapists typically present in clear, prosaic language the assumptions of the approach, mechanisms believed to underlie change, and the expected roles of the therapist and patient. A forthright and collaborative tone is cultivated, with the treatment provider sometimes portrayed as a consultant rather than a doctor.

A key intervention in the cognitive treatment of depression is helping the patient to become capable of identifying and altering problematic thoughts and assumptions. First, the therapist may ask the patient to explicitly examine the evidence available to support or refute the belief in question. Those with depression will typically present dreaded outcomes in a fatalistic and absolutist manner, and we have found it useful to ask particularly intransigent patients if there is "any chance, no matter how small" that they have the ability to exercise some positive influence on the outcome. Second, the therapist may introduce the concept of the *mental filter*, which refers to the tendency for automatic assumptions to screen out those external stimuli that contradict one's fundamental world view. We have found it useful to explain by analogy that the patient is "wearing depression glasses" that color both perception and interpretation by selecting some "wavelengths" and eliminating others.

Third, the therapist may invite the patient to examine negative, fatalistic, or self-critical attributions that lead to an exaggerated sense of blame and responsibility. For example, patients can be asked to keep a thought diary and to record connections between specific, negative thoughts and the emotions that follow. More informally, we have introduced the concept of "stories we tell ourselves" to highlight the basic principle that consciousness is narrative and that we are all constantly interpreting and explaining to ourselves the actions and motivations of ourselves and others.

Adaptations for Depressed Substance Abusers. Cognitive therapy has been adapted to treat substance abuse. Beck et al. (1993) provide a rich but accessible primer on the topic, and Marlatt and Gordon's (1985) work on relapse prevention draws heavily from the techniques and assumptions of cognitive therapy. However, the treatment of the depressed substance abuser presents specific challenges that call for modifications and integration.

First, for patients with an affinity for the disease model and a commitment to 12-step programs, both depression and its treatment can be reframed in terms that are compatible with their conceptualization of substance abuse recovery. Depression can be described as a parallel but interacting disease that both affects and is affected by other recovery efforts. It can be explained that it is not uncommon for patients to discover that their addiction has camouflaged a latent depression that only becomes apparent after a period of abstinence. Similarly, many patients are relieved to learn that one of the founders of AA, Bill W., had a depressive episode immediately before the spiritual experience that prompted him to reach out to another alcoholic for help (Nace, 1997).

Second, while AA and Narcotics Anonymous (NA) are typically described as spiritual programs, they incorporate an underlying cognitive component. From the wording of the second step ("Came to *believe*") to a variety of slogans (e.g., "Think!" "Stinking thinking"), members are exhorted to use overt cognitive processes as part of their efforts to maintain abstinence. Nowhere is this more apparent than in the concept of "stinking thinking" and in the oft-heard quip, "My best thinking got me into this program." These can serve as a springboard for the therapist to explain principles of cognitive treatment, draw parallels with 12-step recovery, and emphasize the importance of the simultaneous treatment of both disorders.

Specific cognitive techniques are also amenable to an integrative approach. For example, patients can be shown how dysfunctional cognitive processes (catastrophization, emotional reasoning, all-or-none thinking, etc.) can lead to both negative mood states and the justification of substance use. We have found it useful to explain that, by interpreting minor setbacks as catastrophes, they are unwittingly cultivating a doubly dangerous mindset. First, catastrophization leads to negative mood states, which have been shown to be very potent triggers for substance use (Cummings, Gordon, and Marlatt, 1980). Second, catastrophic thinking inspires a sense of futility, passivity, and pessimism that renders patients vulnerable to the conclusion that they have nothing further to lose by renewed substance use. Similarly, substance abusers often have difficulty with emotional reasoning, interpreting cravings as absolute imperatives to use. The savvy clinician can use this as an opportunity for a more general discussion of this process and its relationship to depressive symptoms, as well as to a more general tendency to interpret feelings of frustration as overwhelming, intolerable sensations demanding immediate gratification. Finally, all-or-none thinking is characteristic of depression. This can pose a particular danger for patients who are involved in 12-step recovery and who have recently experienced a return to substance use. Marlatt and Gordon (1985) describe the abstinence violation effect, a potentially paradoxical outcome of abstinence-based programs that view any substance use as disastrous. They suggest that patients' attributions and interpretations regarding a *lapse* (an initial return to substance use) determine whether they will experience a *relapse* (a return to habitual, destructive use). Those with a tendency toward internal, global, and stable attributions are more vulnerable to both depression and full-blown relapse, as are those who react with a relentlessly self-critical internal monologue.

Behavioral Therapy

Core Principles. By contrast with the cognitive school, behavioral approaches tend to downplay the importance of attributions, thoughts, and assumptions. Instead, they attempt to maximize the prediction and control of behavior by identifying external events that act to increase the probability of some behaviors at the expense of others. According to this view, the sadness, hopelessness, lethargy, and social isolation common to depression are the predictable result of an absence or withdrawal of *reinforcers*, defined as those positive events that follow and serve to maintain behaviors.

Alternatively, patients may be engaging in behaviors that others find *aversive* and that elicit *punishment* rather than positive reinforcement. In behaviorist terminology, punishment refers simply to negative events that serve to reduce the probability of a behavior rather than to deliberate attempts to punish or exact revenge. For example, Coyne (1976) contends that depression is maintained by the negative reactions of the patient's social circle. Initial expressions of concern and support give way to resentment, frustration, and anger as the depressed patient becomes more demanding. This creates mutual guilt and thinly veiled hostility, prompting greater social withdrawal, which in turn deprives the patient of those opportunities for social reinforcement that might serve to break the negative cycle.

Others have suggested *problem-solving deficits* as central to developing and maintaining a depressive disorder (e.g., Nezu, 1987), noting that several studies have demonstrated an association between depressive symptoms and poor problem-solving skills. Specifically, depressed patients appraise situations as threats rather than challenges, give up more easily, and see themselves as incapable of effecting positive change. They tend to define problems and generate solutions that are impoverished both in terms of quantity and quality. Consequently, they are prone to avoidance rather than coping, resulting in a gradually mounting number of life stressors.

In short, behavioral theories view depression as stemming from a paucity of rewarding events and coping skills. Confronted with multiple stressors, those vulnerable to depression may react with anxiety and fear, appraising the situation as fraught with danger or potential failure. In response, they react with avoidance and withdrawal. This strategy, while temporarily effective in shielding them from anxiety and failure, also serves to remove them from positive reinforcement and opportunities for success. As distress escalates, they make anxious and ambivalent efforts to elicit support from others. When these efforts prove fruitless, loved ones react with confusion and resentment, provoking the patient to further withdraw from his or her social circle. The patient plunges further into depression, fueled by a self-reinforcing cycle of anxiety, avoidance, and social isolation.

Core Techniques. Historically, cognitive and behavioral approaches derived from very different philosophical and conceptual origins and were for many years diametrically opposed. More recently, considerable rapprochement has been achieved, with cognitive-behavioral approaches integrating theory and techniques from both approaches. In addition, the role of the therapist in cognitive and behavioral therapies is similar. Behavior therapists tend to be active, engaged, and extremely present-centered, fostering a collaborative mindset. There is a strong emphasis on patient education and concrete problem solving, and treatment is generally time limited and highly structured. Completion of "homework" assignments is seen as crucial, and the successful behavior therapist devotes considerable time to discussing assignments and any obstacles or resistance that may arise.

A key component in both the assessment and treatment of depression is self-monitoring. Originally conceptualized primarily as a means of assessment and data collection, practitioners quickly realized that the very act of recording self-observations tended to increase the probability of desirable behaviors and hence could represent a potent intervention. One popular technique involves asking patients to rate both the anticipated effort and pleasure involved in performing a potentially reinforcing behavior (e.g., social interactions). This stems from the well-documented finding that depressed patients tend to overestimate the effort and underestimate the pleasure involved in activities. The therapist encourages the patient to record all instances of a target activity, as well as the *actual* effort and pleasure it entailed. Such an intervention can have the dual effect of increasing patients' exposure to potentially reinforcing events and making them more aware of the negative influence of their tendency toward avoidance and withdrawal.

Poor interpersonal skills and relationships can act as a potent force in the maintenance of a depressive disorder. Given the consistent finding that depressed patients have poor social skills, behavior therapists have developed interventions intended to provide opportunities to learn and practice specific prosocial behaviors. These interventions begin with therapist and patient observations of actual social interactions; proceed to therapist education, instruction, and modeling; and end with role plays in which the therapist shapes adaptive responses by gradually reinforcing with praise successive approximations of appropriate social behavior. Specific behaviors targeted can include maintaining eye contact, standing straight, using a firm but respectful tone of voice, asking questions, making appropriate self-disclosure, and ending conversations gracefully. Social skills training and role plays figure prominently in our DRT approach.

Based on the assumption that reinforcement can be derived from both internal and external sources, behavior therapists have stressed the importance of coaching patients to deliberately implement self-rewards as a means of shaping desired behavior. For those with a low activity level, rewards can be self-administered for small steps toward increased activity. It is crucial in this regard that reinforcers (1) be identified as rewarding by the patient, (2) be targeted to clearly identified behaviors, and (3) quickly and reliably follow the target behavior. In addition, patients should be encouraged to keep their expectations modest, with even small positive changes viewed as victories. Although some patients respond best to tangible rewards, they also can be coached to use self-praise as a form of self-reinforcement. This is particularly crucial for those who are inordinately self-critical and self-deprecating.

As mentioned above, depressed patients' attempts at problem solving tend to be half-hearted and impoverished. Several behavioral theorists have identified systematic training in problem-solving skills as a core intervention with depressed patients. One such approach (cf. D'Zurilla, 1988) identifies a five-stage model of adaptive problem solving. The first, *problem orientation*, reflects the assumptions, perceptions, appraisals, and attributions the patient brings to the problem. The second, *problem definition and formulation*, involves clarifying the nature of the problem and gathering relevant information. The third stage, the *generation of alternative solutions*, involves brainstorming as many potentially successful solutions as possible. *Decision making* follows naturally from the previous stage and entails appraising and selecting from among the alternatives generated. Finally, *solution implementation and verification* requires that the patient test the chosen solution in a real world setting, remaining attentive to feedback that refutes or verifies the success of the strategy.

Adaptations for Depressed Substance Abusers. Central to the behavioral approach is the assumption that changes in mood and self-concept will follow changes in behavior. This assumption, while counterintuitive to many, can be made more palatable to depressed patients in recovery by identifying parallels with drug and alcohol treatment programs. Slogans such as "Bring the body and the mind will follow" and "Just don't drink or drug and go to meetings" reflect strains of behavioral thought implicit in AA and NA, programs whose fundamental goal is the eradication of a specific, maladaptive pattern of behavior. Moreover, deliberate manipulation of reinforcers has been highly successful in a variety of substance abuse interventions (e.g., Higgins et al., 1991; Robles et al. 2002). Drawing such parallels can help to make this highly active and directive style of intervention more plausible to those patients who are accustomed to viewing therapy as a more leisurely, self-exploratory process. Patients can also be referred to Larsen's (1985) work on stage II recovery, in which he describes the role of deeply ingrained habits in perpetuating feelings and behaviors incompatible with recovery. Larsen offers a vision of stage II recovery as an opportunity to transcend simple abstinence, stating that recovery "demands that we literally go to war with ourselves, specifically with our own habits" (p. 36).

We have found it helpful to introduce a problem-solving approach by discussing drug and alcohol use as a "short-term solution to a long-term problem," pointing out that substance use is a highly effective reinforcer when it provides immediate and reliable escape from overwhelming feelings of sadness, guilt, or inadequacy. Patients also can be told that abstinence represents the loss of a primary source of reward and that failing to replace that source leaves them vulnerable to both depression and relapse. This can serve not only to reduce the stigma associated with substance abuse but also to highlight the importance of using some of the cognitive or behavioral strategies outlined thus far to develop more complex and adaptive strategies of mood management to replace the function previously served by drugs and alcohol. Similarly, tendencies toward impulsivity and low frustration tolerance can be reframed as deficient problem-solving skills, resulting in part from having been denied, through a long history of substance use, opportunities to develop more adaptive skills.

Social skills training can be initiated with patients new to treatment by role playing drug and alcohol refusal skills. The therapist can then explore more general instances of insufficient assertiveness or conflict avoidance that may render the patient vulnerable to depression. This can be particularly important with the female substance abuser, especially given findings suggesting that (1) a link exists between sexual trauma, depression, and substance abuse (Gomberg, 1999; Wilsnack and Wilsnack, 1993); (2) depressive symptoms may uniquely predispose women to subsequently developing a substance abuse disorder (Helzer, Burnham, and McEvoy, 1991); (3) compared both to men and to female controls, substance-abusing women are far more vulnerable to sexual exploitation, rape, and domestic violence (Stewart, 1996). It has been our experience that many women with alcohol use disorders will increase their drinking behavior to self-medicate internalized feelings of anger and shame stemming from interactions with partners who treat them in a condescending, aggressive, controlling, or belittling manner.

Interpersonal Psychotherapy

Core Principles. Developed in the late 1960s, interpersonal psychotherapy (IPT) (Klerman et al., 1984) has proven successful with depressed patients in a variety of clinical trials (Elkin et al., 1989). By contrast with cognitive and behavioral approaches, IPT focuses on the relationship between mood and interpersonal events. Compatible with a medical model, depression is conceptualized as a primary psychiatric disturbance, but one that can be strongly affected by the patient's most significant relationships. Interpersonal disturbances are described as falling into one of four problem areas. *Grief* is defined narrowly as a reaction to the loss of a loved one, with other significant losses categorized as role transitions. Bereavement becomes complicated and can lead to a major depression when the process of mourning becomes blocked as a result of avoiding thinking, talking, or experiencing emotion related to the loved one. *Role dispute* refers to conflict, tension, or friction with another. Common sources of role disputes include infidelity, loss of sexual appetite or functioning, impaired social and occupational functioning, and impaired communication. *Role transition* encompasses any significant change in social role, including both traumatic losses and desired transitions. These can include marriage or divorce, job losses or changes, the departure of a child from the home, the diagnosis of a significant medical illness, or loss of income, power, or status. Finally, the category of *interpersonal deficits* is reserved for patients with clear, longstanding interpersonal problems, frequently linked with an underlying personality disorder, to whom none of the other three problem areas apply.

Core Techniques. Like cognitive and behavioral therapies, IPT is time limited (typically consisting of 12–20 weekly sessions) and highly focused. However, of the three approaches discussed thus far, IPT is clearly the most compatible with psychodynamic thinking. Treatment is primarily conversational, with little emphasis on education, behavioral rehearsal, or homework assignments. Traditional psychodynamic techniques are common in IPT, including enhancing awareness and insight; encouraging intense emotional experience and expression; reviewing the contribution of early relationships to enduring, maladaptive interpersonal patterns; and exploring parallels between significant current relationships and the patient's negative and positive reactions to the therapist.

However, IPT departs radically from traditional psychodynamic approaches in its structured, sequential approach to treatment. As described by Markowitz and Weissman (1995), the initial stages of IPT progress in a predictable series of steps. First, symptoms are reviewed and a diagnosis given. Second, the patient is educated about depression, treatment options, and the sick role. The latter is unique among the approaches discussed thus far, as IPT emphasizes the importance of the patient accepting both the limitations that a psychiatric illness imposes and the responsibility for recovery that it implies. Third, the therapist explores the relationship history, including the capacity for intimacy and commitment, dysfunctional patterns, and the extent to which relationship expectations are unreasonable or unfulfilled. Fourth, the therapist decides which of the four problem areas is most relevant and begins to discuss the link between the identified problem area and depression. Finally, the IPT approach is discussed in detail, and specific treatment goals and options are discussed.

At this point, the interventions chosen differ according to the problem area identified. Those suffering with grief need help navigating the mourning process and resuming connections with other people and activities. Toward that end, the therapist explores feelings about the deceased, encouraging the expression of a range of feelings, including sadness, anger, guilt, and even relief. In addition, the therapist openly encourages the patient to begin to develop or re-establish other interests and activities, remaining sensitive to guilt, which may arise as the patient perceives that she is beginning to "replace" the loved one. Also crucial are repeated assurances that grieving, while agonizingly prolonged, is finite and that overwhelming and confusing emotions are normal and expected.

Treating the patient stuck in a role dispute often requires a more cognitive and behavioral approach. The therapist must assess the extent to which the dispute is the product of unrealistic expectations or beliefs about relationships and be willing gently to question underlying assumptions. In addition, the patient should be encouraged to engage in informal problem solving about the dispute, focusing on generating options, assessing their likelihood of success, and mobilizing outside resources in the implementation of a plan. In so doing, the therapist helps the patient to realize his role in the dispute and to become an active agent of change.

As with those experiencing grief, patients negotiating role transitions often require a period of mourning before they can fully accept the loss of the old role. Consequently, the therapist will facilitate emotional expression and an exploration of positive and negative effects of the transition. However, by contrast with deaths, role transitions are likely to result in less-profound grieving, with some patients puzzled that an eagerly awaited transition often entails loss and sadness. Also, compared with the loss of a loved one, a negative role transition may entail a greater injury to self-concept and self-esteem, as well as strong feelings of shame and failure.

It is in the treatment of those suffering primarily from enduring interpersonal deficits that the psychodynamic flavor of IPT is most evident. Whereas behavioral approaches stress the acquisition of concrete social skills through role plays and behavioral rehearsal, IPT focuses on reviewing the contribution of past relationships, identifying maladaptive interpersonal patterns, and drawing parallels between the patient's feeling about the therapist and other significant relationships. However, IPT retains a primary focus on the present, and the therapist will often explicitly encourage experimentation with new interpersonal behaviors.

Adaptations for Depressed Substance Abusers. As with cognitive and behavioral approaches, IPT themes consistent with 12-step principles can serve to make the approach palatable to depressed substance abusers in recovery. The NA big book states, "In the process of recovery we were restored to sanity and part of sanity is effectively relating to others" (Narcotics Anonymous, 1984, p. 37). Similarly, both the AA Big Book and the 12 steps discuss at length the importance of mending shattered relationships, eliminating self-centeredness and resentment toward others, and making amends to those harmed. Of the approaches discussed here, IPT is clearly the most compatible with a disease model and is therefore compatible with AA's and NA's characterization of addiction as an illness.

Historically, the literature on addiction treatment has been relatively silent on the issue of grief. With the advent of acquired immune deficiency syndrome (AIDS) and the growing recognition that substance-abusing patients are at a dramatically increased risk of suicide and premature mortality (Ziedonis, 1992), this silence has become untenable. It is our impression that substance-abusing patients are highly vulnerable to suffering from complicated bereavement. For many, an IPT approach may represent the first opportunity to discuss and fully experience the loss and to address the resulting guilt, sadness, anger, and fear. However, it is crucial that this work is done in a measured and balanced manner and that care is taken not to prematurely provoke overwhelming emotion. In most instances it is advisable to postpone grief work until several months of sustained and meaningful recovery has been attained.

Role disputes commonly center on betrayal and disappointment experienced by the patient's family members and loved ones. Many become resentful as they see the patient reaping the benefits of recovery while they suffer in silence with painful memories of past traumas and transgressions. For those with sufficient interpersonal skills and emotional resilience, conjoint sessions with significant others may be indicated. Unfortunately, it has been our experience that some family members, burdened with years of frustration and fruitless efforts at resolution, become highly critical and negative, thus effectively punishing the patient for opening the channels of communication. The clinician must balance the legitimate need for the patient to fully understand and accept the consequences of his actions with the equally legitimate need to protect the depression-prone patient from overwhelming guilt and self-loathing. In some instances, it is advisable to postpone conjoint sessions, maintaining an IPT focus by helping the patient to understand the central interpersonal issues and their relevance to the history of mood disorder, think constructively about future solutions rather than dwelling excessively on past transgressions, and become involved in making amends to those harmed.

Alternatively, the patient may become increasingly disillusioned with a long-term relationship. This is particularly likely for those involved in sustained and productive recovery, who may find that they have outgrown an addicted or psychiatrically impaired partner. Issues of guilt are particularly profound for those patients who have functioned as a caretaker for a very impaired partner. It is generally wise to avoid prematurely lobbying for the patient to dissolve the relationship, except in those instances in which the patient's basic safety may be at risk. For those involved in 12-step recovery, who may daily receive well-meaning advice to "change people, places, and things," the IPT therapist may represent the sole outlet for feelings of guilt, attachment, and ambivalence. In general, clinicians must remain extremely sensitive to the loss associated with any significant relationship, regardless of the level of dysfunction, and remain mindful that these relationships may serve a stabilizing function of which the clinician is unaware.

It is our impression that many substance-abusing patients experience problems with role transitions. Primary among these is the transition in identity from addict to recovering addict. Many patients are grateful and relieved by acknowledgment of the profound loss intrinsic to abandoning the lifestyle associated with substance use. Twelve-step programs tend to place a premium on cultivating gratitude, and patients may encounter little tolerance in meetings for natural feelings of anxiety, disillusionment, or loss associated with changing people, places, and things. Similarly, some patients may simply be unaware of the loss involved and of the need to replace the positive emotion, social networks, and sense of purpose and structure that the substance-abusing lifestyle included. Often overlooked in substance abuse treatment is the structuring function served by the rituals associated with active substance abuse. This is particularly crucial given the emphasis on promoting structure and a sense of purpose in the treatment both of substance and mood disorders.

It is our impression that interpersonal deficits are pervasive with mood-disordered substance abuse patients, and these can represent a serious impediment to recovery. Unfortunately, "this IPT area has been least used, least studied, and least conceptually developed" (Markowitz and Weissman, 1995, p. 382). Therefore, we recommend that for these patients the IPT approach should be supplemented with cognitive and behavioral techniques. We have also found it helpful to supplement formal treatment interventions with bibliotherapy. Larsen's (1985) work on stage II recovery can serve as a helpful guide for those plagued with maladaptive, longstanding interpersonal problems. Larsen identifies six destructive interpersonal styles common to substance abusers (caretakers, people pleasers, martyrs, workaholics, perfectionists, and tap dancers) and outlines simple strategies for implementing a formal program of self-change.

Bipolar Disorder

Bipolar disorder, known colloquially as manic-depression, is marked by dramatic alternations between periods of depression and of mania. Ten to 15 percent of those diagnosed with major depression will eventually develop bipolar symptoms. Depressive phases in bipolar patients are similar to those in depressed patients, although bipolar patients are more likely to exhibit lethargy, overeating and oversleeping, and psychotic symptoms (Maxmen and Ward, 1995). Manic phases are characterized by excessive activity, racing thoughts, grandiosity and/or irritability, decreased need for sleep, and excessive involvement in pleasurable activities (American Psychiatric Association, 1994). Manic phases typically develop gradually, and patients may initially present simply as unusually energetic, optimistic, loquacious, or buoyant. Increasingly, they are likely to exhibit more irritability, excessive activity, and poor judgment. In severe cases the manic patient may recklessly indulge in alcohol or drugs, indiscriminate sexual activity, or excessive spending, sometimes with disastrous results. For all these reasons, bipolar disorder can generally be considered a more severe mood disorder than depression.

Substance use disorders are found in about 60 percent of bipolar patients, more than twice the rate observed in unipolar depression (Regier et al., 1990). Outcomes are typically poor (Feinman and Dunner, 1996), which is particularly unfortunate given the potentially catastrophic consequences of substance abuse in this population. There is a regrettable absence of integrated treatment approaches for these patients. It is likely that principles of dual recovery therapy would also be applicable to bipolar patients, although we have yet to test this empirically.

One recently developed group model seems promising (Weiss et al., 2000). The treatment consists of 12–20 weekly therapy groups, each of which focuses on a topic relevant to both disorders. Topics can include denial, ambivalence, and acceptance; self-help groups; and the identification and fighting of triggers. The group is based on a relapse prevention model, which was adapted to integrate the treatment of bipolar and substance abuse disorders by focusing on similarities between the recovery and relapse processes for each. For instance, just as many substance abusers are tempted to abandon attempts at abstinence after a "slip," those with bipolar disorder may feel like stopping their medications after experiencing a mood disorder episode despite complying with their medications. The group reviews strategies for coping with a temporary setback, emphasizing the role of thoughts and behaviors that can either improve or worsen such a situation in either disorder.

As with our DRT approach, each session begins with a check-in, during which patients report on their previous week's (1) drug and alcohol use, (2) mood, (3) medication adherence, (4) encounters with high-risk situations, and (5) use of coping skills. Then follows a review of the previous week's group, a didactic presentation, and a group discussion of the current week's topic. Treatment is guided by a therapist manual and patient handouts. For a more detailed account of this promising approach, see Weiss, Najavits, and Greenfield (1999).

Medication management is central to the treatment of this disorder. This is particularly true of the manic phase, which is virtually nonresponsive to psychosocial interventions. A variety of mood stabilizers have demonstrated remarkable efficacy with bipolar patients. Unfortunately, medication compliance is of greater concern with bipolar than with depressed patients, perhaps because of the chaotic lifestyles and substance use disorders more prevalent in this group. Many patients find the hypomanic or manic phases immensely pleasurable and will episodically discontinue medications to achieve the intense peaks associated with hypomania or mania. Clinicians should be particularly wary of boredom as a trigger for substance use or medication noncompliance.

Clinical management of the depressive phase is similar to the treatment of unipolar depression. However, the following adjustments in technique should be considered. First, treatment should include an educational component emphasizing the role of genetic and biological factors in the illness and the critical role of medications in its treatment. Patients also should be made aware of the potential for substances of abuse, especially stimulants, to trigger a manic episode. Second, medication compliance should be strongly emphasized and inquired about at every session. The cyclical nature of the disorder, frequently punctuated by bouts of deliberate medication noncompliance, can test clinicians' patience, and it is crucial to convey an understanding of the allure of the manic episode. Many bipolar patients describe initial hypomanic or manic symptoms as exhilarating. They possess tremendous confidence and energy and may become more productive, active, and socially popular than at any other time. Consequently, they may ward off therapeutic interventions through the use of defense mechanisms such as intellectualization and denial. Third, given that many patients are ambivalent about giving up mania, with some it is useful to treat their affinity for mania as analogous to a substance abuse disorder. Motivational interviewing and relapse prevention strategies can be useful in this regard. Fourth, family members should be enlisted, when possible, to be vigilant for initial symptoms of mania or depression.

Conclusion

Dual recovery therapy suggests an approach to blending and modifying traditional mental health treatments for depression and traditional addiction treatments. The level of motivation to change and the stage of recovery for both disorders influence the timing and specific emphasis of dual recovery treatment. With regard to blending psychosocial treatments, there is little empirical evidence to guide the clinician in selecting among the above treatment options, and a strategic eclectic approach might provide the greatest flexibility. Patients with highly internalized, negative, and self-critical thoughts and attributions may respond best to a cognitive approach. Those with a symptom picture marked by social withdrawal and disengagement from activities or who have pervasive and enduring deficits in social skills should be ideally suited for a behaviorally informed treatment. Finally, those with a readily identified problem area involving grief or a focused role dispute or transition seem ideal for IPT.

In addition, we have found two rules to be useful. First, the emphasis on behavioral interventions should be proportional to the level of impairment. Those with cognitive deficits, poor verbal skills, minimal insight, or vegetative symptoms are probably poorly suited for techniques requiring the capacity for self-expression, reflection, and abstraction and may respond best to simple, focused behavioral tasks. Second, patients may present at different motivational levels for different treatments and are likely to be most readily engaged in the approach that they find the most intuitively appealing or plausible. It is incumbent on the clinician to recommend an intervention, but it is foolhardy to insist on one to which the patient is highly resistant.

REFERENCES

Alcoholics Anonymous World Services. 1984. *The AA Member: Medications and Other Drugs.* New York: Alcoholics Anonymous World Services.

American Psychiatric Association. 1993. Practice guidelines for major depressive disorder in adults. *American Journal of Psychiatry* 150 (suppl 4):1–26.

———. 1994. *Diagnostic and Statistical Manual of Mental Disorders*, 4th ed. Washington, D.C.: American Psychiatric Association.

Anthony, W. A. 1993. Recovery from mental illness: The guiding vision of the mental health service system in the 1990s. *Psychosocial Rehabilitation Journal* 16:11–23.

Beck, A. T., F. D. Wright, C. F. Newman, and B. S. Liese. 1993. *Cognitive Therapy of Substance Abuse*. New York: Guilford Press.

Bemporad, J. R. 1995. Long-term analytic treatment of depression. In *Handbook of Depression*, 2d ed., edited by P. M. Lewinsohn and I. H. Gotlib, 391–403. New York: Guilford Press.

Burns, D. B. 1999. *Feeling Good: The New Mood Therapy*. New York: William Morrow.

Coyne, J. C. 1976. Toward an interactional description of depression. *Psychiatry* 39:28–40.

Cummings, C., J. Gordon, and G. A. Marlatt. 1980. Relapse: Strategies of prevention and prediction. In *The Addictive Behaviors*, edited by W. R. Miller, 291–321. Oxford, England: Pergamon Press.

D'Zurilla, T. J. 1988. Problem-solving therapies. In *Handbook of Cognitive-Behavioral Therapies*, edited by K. S. Dobson, 85–135. New York: Guilford Press.

Elkin, I., M. T. Shea, J. T. Watkins, S. D. Imber, S. M. Sotsky, J. F. Collins, D. R. Glass, P. A. Pilkonis, W. R. Leber, J. P. Docherty, S. J. Fiester, and M. B. Parloff. 1989. National Institute of Mental Health Treatment of Depression Collaborative Research Program: General effectiveness of treatments. *Archives of General Psychiatry* 46:971–82.

Feinman, J. A., and D. L. Dunner. 1996. The effect of alcohol and substance abuse on the course of bipolar affective disorder. *Journal of Affective Disorders* 37:43–49.

Gomberg, E. S. L. 1999. Women. In *Addictions: A Comprehensive Guidebook*, edited by B. S. McCrady and E. E. Epstein, 527–41. New York: Oxford University Press.

Helzer, J. E., A. Burnham, and L. T. McEvoy. 1991. Alcohol abuse and dependence. In *Psychiatric Disorders in America: The Epidemiologic Catchment Area Study*, edited by L. Robins and D. A. Regier, 81–115. New York: Free Press.

Higgins, S. T., D. D. Delaney, A. J. Budney, W. K. Bickel, J. R. Hughes, F. Foerg, and J. W. Fenwick. 1991. A behavioral approach to achieving initial cocaine abstinence. *American Journal of Psychiatry* 148:1218–24.

Klerman, G. L., M. M. Weissman, B. J. Rounsaville, and E. Chevron. 1984. *Interpersonal Psychotherapy of Depression*. New York: Basic Books.

Larsen, E. 1985. *Stage II Recovery: Life beyond Addiction*. New York: Harper Collins.

Markowitz, J. C., and M. M. Weissman. 1995. Interpersonal psychotherapy. In *Handbook of Depression*, 2d ed., edited by P. M. Lewinsohn and I. H. Gotlib, 376–90. New York: Guilford Press.

Marlatt, G. A., and J. R. Gordon. 1985. *Relapse Prevention: Maintenance Strategies in the Treatment of Addictive Behaviors*. New York: Guilford Press.

Maxmen, J. S., and N. G. Ward. 1995. *Essential Psychopathology and Its Treatment*. New York: W. W. Norton.

McConnaughy, E. A., J. O. Prochaska, and W. F. Velicer. 1983. Stages of change in psychotherapy: Measurement and sample profiles. *Psychotherapy: Theory, Research, and Practice* 20:368–75.

Miller, W. R., and S. Rollnick. 2002. *Motivational Interviewing: Preparing People for Change*. New York: Guilford Press.

Miller, W. R., and J. S. Tonigan. 1996. Assessing drinkers' motivation for change: The Stages of Change Readiness and Treatment Eagerness Scale (SOCRATES). *Psychology of Addictive Behaviors* 10:81–89.

Miller, W. R., A. Zweben, C. C. DiClemente, and R. G. Rychtarik. 1995. *Motivational Enhancement Therapy Manual*, NIH Publication No. 94-3723. Rockville, Md.: U.S. Department of Health and Human Services.

Nace, E. P. 1997. Alcoholics Anonymous. In *Substance Abuse: A Comprehensive Textbook*, 3d ed., edited by J. H. Lowinson, P. Ruiz, R. B. Millman, and J. G. Langrod, 383–90. Baltimore: Williams & Wilkins.

Narcotics Anonymous. 1984. *Narcotics Anonymous*. Van Nuys, Calif.: World Service Office.

Nezu, A. M. 1987. A problem-solving formulation of depression: A literature review and proposal of a pluralistic model. *Clinical Psychology Review* 7:121–44.

Prochaska, J. O., C. C. DiClemente, and J. C. Norcross. 1992. In search of how people change: Applications to addictive behaviors. *American Psychologist* 47:1102–14.

Regier, D. A., M. E. Farmer, D. S. Rae, B. Z. Locke, S. J. Keith, L. L. Judd, and F. K. Goodwin. 1990. Comorbidity of mental disorders with alcohol and other drug abuse: Results from the Epidemiologic Catchment Area (ECA) Study. *Journal of the American Medical Association* 264:2511–18.

Robles, E., M. L. Stitzer, E. C. Strain, G. E. Bigelow, and K. Silverman. 2002. Voucher-based reinforcement of opiate abstinence during methadone detoxification. *Drug and Alcohol Dependence* 65:179–89.

Rollnick, S., N. Heather, R. Gold, and W. Hall. 1992. Development of a short "Readiness to Change" Questionnaire for use in brief opportunistic interventions. *British Journal of Addictions* 87:743–54.

Sacco, W. P., and A. T. Beck. 1995. Cognitive theory and therapy. In *Handbook of Depression*, 2d ed., edited by E. E. Beckham and W. R. Leber, 329–51. New York: Guilford Press.

Stewart, S. H. 1996. Alcohol abuse in individuals exposed to trauma: A critical review. *Psychological Bulletin* 120:83–112.

Sweeney, P. D., K. Anderson, and S. Bailey. 1986. Attributional style in depression: A meta-analytic review. *Journal of Personality and Social Psychology* 50:974–91.

Weiss, R. D., L. M. Najavits, and S. F. Greenfield. 1999. A relapse prevention group for patients with bipolar and substance use disorders. *Journal of Substance Abuse Treatment* 16:47–54.

Weiss, R. D., M. L. Griffin, S. F. Greenfield, L. M. Najavits, D. B. A. Wyner, J. A. Soto, and J. A. Hennen. 2000. Group therapy for patients with bipolar disorder and substance abuse dependence: Results of a pilot study. *Journal of Clinical Psychiatry* 61:361–67.

Wilsnack, S. C., and R. W. Wilsnack. 1993. Epidemiological research on women's drinking: Recent progress and directions for the 1990's. In *Women and Substance*

Abuse, edited by E. S. L. Gomberg and T. D. Nirenberg, 62–99. Norwood, N.J.: Ablex.

Ziedonis, D. M. 1992. Comorbid psychopathology and cocaine addiction. In *Clinician's Guide to Cocaine Addiction: Theory, Research and Treatment*, edited by T. R. Kosten and H. D. Kleber, 335–58. New York: Guilford Press.

Ziedonis, D. M., and W. Fisher. 1996. Motivation based assessment and treatment of substance abuse in patients with schizophrenia. *New Directions in Psychiatry* 16:1–8.

Ziedonis, D. M., and R. Stern. 2001. Dual recovery therapy for schizophrenia and substance abuse. *Psychiatric Annals* 31:255–64.

SUGGESTED READINGS

Bean, M. H., and N. E. Zimberg. 1981. *Dynamic Approaches to the Understanding and Treatment of Alcoholism*. New York: Free Press.

Becker, R. E., R. G. Heimberg, and A. S. Bellack. 1987. *Social Skills Training for Depression*. Elmsford, N.Y.: Pergamon Press.

Beckham, E. E., and W. R. Leber. 1995. *Handbook of Depression*, 2d ed. New York: Guilford Press.

Gomberg, E. S. L., and T. D. Nirenberg (eds.). 1993. *Women and Substance Abuse*. Norwood, N.J.: Ablex.

Kranzler, H. R., and B. J. Rounsaville. 1998. *Dual Diagnosis and Treatment: Substance Abuse and Comorbid Medical and Psychiatric Disorders*. New York: Marcel Dekker.

Lewinsohn, P. M., and I. H. Gotlib. 1995. Behavioral theory and treatment of depression. In *Handbook of Depression*, 2d ed., edited by P. M. Lewinsohn and I. H. Gotlib, 352–75. New York: Guilford Press.

Riba, M. B., and R. Balon. 1999. *Psychopharmacology and Psychotherapy: A Collaborative Approach*. Washington, D.C.: American Psychiatric Press.

Rosenthal, R. N., and L. Westreich. 1999. Treatment of persons with dual diagnoses of substance use disorder and other psychological problems. In *Addictions: A Comprehensive Guidebook*, edited by B. S. McCrady and E. E. Epstein, 439–76. New York: Oxford University Press.

Solomon, J., S. Zimberg, and E. Shollar. 1993. *Dual Diagnosis: Evaluation, Treatment, Training, and Program Development*. New York: Plenum Press.

Zimberg, S. 1993. Introduction and general concepts of dual diagnosis. In *Dual Diagnosis: Evaluation, Treatment, Training, and Program Development*, edited by J. Solomon, S. Zimberg, and E. Shollar, 3–21. New York: Plenum Press.

6

Pharmacotherapy for Co-occurring Mood and Substance Use Disorders

Roger D. Weiss, M.D.

The topic of pharmacological treatment of individuals with depression and substance use disorder has long generated a great deal of controversy. As with psychotherapy, the use of medications to treat negative mood states in substance-abusing patients has sometimes created a rift between substance abuse clinicians and mental health practitioners, particularly psychiatrists. Added to that controversy was the strange phenomenon that, despite some research data supporting the potential efficacy of antidepressant treatment in depressed alcoholic patients, the prevailing clinical wisdom until only very recently was that antidepressant treatment of alcoholic patients with coexisting depression was ineffective at best. More recent studies have challenged that view, however, and have presented accumulating evidence for the role of pharmacotherapy in the treatment of patients with substance use disorders and coexisting mood disorders.

In this chapter, we review the recent research evidence for the efficacy of antidepressants among chemically dependent patients with coexisting depression, discuss the sparse information available about pharmacotherapy of substance-dependent patients with coexisting bipolar disorder, and discuss the critical issue of medication compliance among substance-dependent patients.

General Considerations

Considering the high rate of comorbidity between substance use disorders and psychiatric disorders in general, and mood disorders in particular, it is striking how few well-designed studies of pharmacotherapy have been conducted with this population. In the studies that have taken place, however, the medications tested have almost exclusively been those agents used in the treatment of psychiatric illness. Thus, for example, pharmacotherapy studies involving depressed alcoholic patients have primarily investigated the efficacy of antidepressants with this population. By the same token, pharmacotherapy studies of patients with coexisting bipolar disorder and substance use disorder have studied mood stabilizers. Although different researchers have investigated a variety of medications, there is no evidence that any particular psychiatric medication is uniquely effective with substance abusers. Thus, there is no specific antidepressant that should be used just because a patient has coexisting alcohol or cocaine dependence. Factors influencing the choice of a specific agent in this population are discussed later in this chapter.

The Reluctance to Prescribe Psychotropic Medications to Substance Abusers

For several reasons, the prospect of prescribing psychotropic medications to current or recently active substance abusers generally strikes fear in the hearts of physicians. First, there is the possibility of a toxic interaction between the prescribed medication and the nonprescribed drug(s) of abuse that the patient will take in addition. This phenomenon was illustrated by a question I was once asked by a patient with bipolar disorder and polysubstance dependence: "Doctor, yesterday I drank about a dozen beers, smoked a couple of joints, and smoked a lot of cocaine. Was it safe to take my lithium afterward?"

Second, physicians may believe that the treatment of choice is abstinence, not an antidote to what they perceive as substance-induced symptoms. This belief is based on the opinion that, if a patient is depressed and is taking large amounts of a drug that can adversely affect mood (e.g., alcohol or cocaine), then the treatment of choice is to stop the substance abuse, not to take a drug that is supposed to reverse the unwanted effect of the abused agents. The corollary to this view is the belief that an antidepressant cannot work effectively in the face of heavy substance use.

Third, substance abusers make physicians nervous. Physicians often feel that they are being manipulated by these patients into prescribing medication, even if they do not clearly understand the motivation behind the perceived manipulation. They believe they are enabling these patients rather than treating them effectively, and they worry about poor outcomes.

Recent Research

Recently, several published studies have changed the "wait and see" paradigm for the treatment of individuals with alcohol dependence and depression. Specifically, three studies have shown that antidepressant treatment of depressed alcoholic patients who have recently been drinking has, on average, led to a reduction in depressive symptoms and some (though less robust) improvement in drinking, without serious adverse consequences. Two studies published in 1996 showed the potential helpful role of tricyclic antidepressants in the treatment of depressed alcoholic patients. McGrath and collaborators (1996) at Columbia University conducted a 12-week, double-blind, placebo-controlled study of imipramine, combined with weekly relapse prevention therapy, with 69 actively drinking alcoholic patients who had a coexisting primary depressive disorder. These investigators found statistically significant, albeit modest, improvement in depressive symptoms; no serious adverse events, including among those who continued to drink heavily while receiving imipramine; and decreased alcohol consumption among those patients who experienced an improvement in their depression.

Mason and colleagues (1996) at the University of Miami studied desipramine in a population that most people would hypothesize to be least likely to respond to antidepressant pharmacotherapy: depressed alcoholic patients in whom the alcohol dependence was primary and the depression secondary. In this study of 71 patients, depressive symptoms among the patient group receiving desipramine decreased significantly. Interestingly, depressed patients receiving desipramine also abstained from alcohol for a longer period. Thus, treating a major depressive disorder even in patients with primary alcoholism may be helpful in reducing the risk of relapse to drinking.

Finally, Cornelius and collaborators (1997) at the Western Psychiatric Institute and Clinic in Pittsburgh randomly assigned 51 patients with coexisting major depressive disorder and alcohol dependence to receive either fluoxetine or placebo for 12 weeks. These researchers found a significantly greater reduction in depressive symptoms among the fluoxetine-treated patients. Moreover, total alcohol consumption was lower in the group that received fluoxetine.

A naturalistic outcome study of depression and alcoholism conducted by our research group at McLean Hospital and Harvard Medical School, led by Dr. Shelly Greenfield (1998), showed the potential negative sequelae of *not* treating patients for major depressive disorder. This study prospectively followed for a year 101 patients hospitalized for alcohol dependence; patients were evaluated each month for their drinking, other substance use, mood, and treatment utilization. Within 4 months, all study subjects who had met DSM-III-R criteria for major depression within the 6 months before hospitalization (regardless of their drinking status at the time when they met those criteria) returned to drinking if they were not discharged with a prescription for an antidepressant. Moreover, nearly two-thirds of this dually diagnosed population who did not receive antidepressants had returned to drinking within a month after discharge.

Our study was conducted before the publication of the three studies described above, during which time the general guidelines for the evaluation and treatment of depression in alcoholic patients involved observing patients for as long as possible while they were alcohol-free to avoid unnecessary prescription of medications to treat potentially alcohol-induced depressive symptoms. However, the publication of three successful reports of double-blind, placebo-controlled studies of antidepressants, combined with our naturalistic study showing the extremely poor outcomes of alcoholic patients with coexisting major depressive disorder in the absence of antidepressant treatment, supports the current trend toward earlier treatment with antidepressants in this population.

The Treatment of Patients with Drug Dependence and Depression

Opioids

The treatment of comorbid depression and opioid dependence has been the topic of several research studies, most of which have reported some, though not spectacular, efficacy resulting from this approach. In the 1970s and 1980s, several studies with this population used tricyclic antidepressants, most commonly doxepin, a relatively sedating agent. For the most part, patients in these studies experienced an improvement in their depressive symptoms, but the effect on drug use was less impressive, ranging in different studies from mildly successful to ineffective. As in the alcohol studies described above, however, drug use did not worsen with antidepressant treatment.

Virtually all studies of the pharmacotherapy of depression and opioid dependence have been performed with patients receiving methadone maintenance treatment. Because the daily administration of methadone may mask some depressive symptoms and alter the metabolism of certain antidepressant drugs, the dearth of research with depressed, opioid-dependent patients not taking methadone is unfortunate.

Another methodological limitation of some of the research conducted with opioid-dependent patients is that the diagnoses of depression in these studies were made by a variety of criteria, frequently relying on depression rating scales rather than strict syndromal diagnostic criteria. A study by Nunes and colleagues (1998) at Columbia University used strict syndromal diagnostic criteria as they tested imipramine versus placebo in 137 methadone-maintained patients who had coexisting primary major depressive disorder. Among those patients who received an adequate trial of at least 6 weeks of medication, those receiving imipramine experienced a significantly greater reduction in depressive symptoms than did those receiving placebo. Patients who experienced mood improvement generally had an associated reduction in drug use, although the overall effect of treatment on drug use was less dramatic than the effect on mood. Thus, for this population, antidepressants can be said to treat depression effectively but are not terribly efficacious in the treatment of drug use.

Cocaine

Although many pharmacological agents have been studied for the treatment of cocaine abuse and dependence, no published research has focused strictly on cocaine abusers with depression. Some medication treatment studies of cocaine-dependent patients in general have shown reduction of cocaine use in the subset of patients with coexisting depression (Nunes et al., 1995), but these data must be considered preliminary.

The Pharmacotherapy of Bipolar Disorder and Substance Abuse

Although the topic of pharmacotherapy of patients with depression and substance abuse has generated a great deal of controversy, the subject of pharmacotherapy for individuals with bipolar disorder and substance dependence suffers from the opposite problem, namely, too little attention. Only four studies have been performed with this population, with a total of 49 subjects having been studied. Moreover, only one of these studies was a double-blind, placebo-controlled trial. An open-label study (Gawin and Kleber, 1984) of 5 patients given lithium was modestly successful, while another open study (Nunes et al., 1990) of 10 patients given lithium was less successful. An open-label study (Brady et al., 1995) of 9 patients given valproate was relatively promising. However, each of these studies utilized an open-label design, meaning that the patients in these studies all knew what medication they were receiving. This can lead to a biased result, as the expectation of a beneficial outcome may help to produce such a result. This is the reason for double-blind, placebo-controlled pharmacotherapy studies, in which neither the patient nor the clinician knows what the patient is receiving; this minimizes the form of bias related to a positive expectancy. Indeed, the reluctance to perform a study involving a placebo for patients with bipolar disorder is one reason that so little pharmacological research has been done with this patient population. Only one such study has been performed; Dr. Barbara Geller and her collaborators (1998) randomly assigned lithium or placebo to 25 adolescents with bipolar disorder and substance dependence that had begun after the bipolar disorder. Those patients who received lithium had better overall functioning and a greater percentage of negative (i.e., drug-free) urine screens than did those receiving placebo.

Choosing a Medication

How, then, should one decide which antidepressant or mood stabilizer to use for a depressed or bipolar patient with a comorbid substance use disorder? There are several factors to bear in mind when making this choice; most of these considerations are not substantially different from the type of decision-making process that a clinician needs to undertake when treating a patient with a mood disorder who does not have a substance abuse problem. These include the side effect profile of the medication, the patient's history or family history with similar medications, the potential drug-drug interactions with other medications and/or drugs of abuse that the patient is taking, and compliance issues, specifically whether there is a different likelihood of compliance with one agent versus another.

Side Effect Profile

One consideration in choosing a medication for a particular patient is its characteristic side effect profile, both undesirable and desirable. This powerful factor helps to determine specific medication choice for many patients. For substance abusers, a question that frequently arises is whether one should prescribe medications that are similar to or different from the patient's drug of choice. For example, should a depressed cocaine abuser be given a stimulating antidepressant because it is reminiscent of a drug that the patient likes, or should the clinician prescribe a drug that does not resemble the patient's drug of choice? There are virtually no research data to inform us on this subject (i.e., no studies that have compared sedating versus stimulating antidepressants in depressed cocaine abusers or opioid addicts). However, clinicians often have strong and conflicting opinions about this issue. It could easily be argued, for example, that compliance would be better if an individual were given a medication that he or she "liked." Thus, if an individual chose to self-administer stimulating drugs, one might intuitively hypothesize that such an individual would be more likely to take as prescribed a stimulating antidepressant than a sedating agent. Moreover, since withdrawal syndromes are generally characterized by symptoms that are the opposite of those of drug intoxication (e.g., fatigue and increased appetite during cocaine withdrawal, insomnia and anxiety during benzodiazepine withdrawal), the use of a drug with side effects similar to the effects of the original drug may help to ameliorate early withdrawal symptoms. It is for this reason that sedating agents such as trazodone are often useful during early abstinence from opioids.

Two reasons arguing *against* the use of a medication with side effects similar to those of an individual's drug of choice are (1) the likelihood of overuse of the agent and (2) the possible stimulation of craving for the original drug of choice. Overuse of prescribed medication is one of the potential risks inherent in treating substance abusers pharmacologically. In addition to the well-known risks of overuse of medications such as benzodiazepines or stimulants, these patients may take greater than prescribed doses of medications not ordinarily associated with abuse. In a study with patients who had bipolar disorder and substance dependence (Weiss et al., 1998), we found that some of these patients took higher than prescribed doses of tricyclic antidepressants, usually claiming that they were impatient waiting for the drug to work. Thus, a patient who was prescribed imipramine, 100 mg a day, might take 200 mg, saying, "I don't want to wait for the drug to work; I'm too depressed." Interestingly, we did not find this pattern among patients who received the newer generation antidepressants such as selective serotonin reuptake inhibitors (SSRIs). Perhaps this is related to the fact that the target therapeutic doses are reached more quickly with SSRIs than with tricyclic antidepressants, which is an advantage of the former compounds.

Another potential risk of using medications with side effects that are similar to those of the patient's drugs of choice is that these medications may at times trigger conditioned craving responses. Weiss (1988) reported three such cases of cocaine-dependent patients who experienced the "tricyclic jitteriness syndrome" soon after being prescribed desipramine. These patients all stated that this sensation of jitteriness reminded them of their experiences with cocaine and, thus, through a classically conditioned response, served as a trigger to increase their desire for the drug. Each of these three patients relapsed soon after being prescribed desipramine despite early reports of that medication's potential efficacy in the treatment of cocaine-dependent patients.

The Patient's History or Family History with Similar Medications

Past history can help to predict future antidepressant response. A previous good response to a medication or a class of medication is a favorable prognostic sign for that medication or a similar agent in the future. Conversely, a poor response to a specific type of antidepressant would lead a clinician to eschew the use of that particular medication again, although it is not necessarily true that other medications within that drug class would have to be avoided. For example, there are individuals who respond well to fluoxetine and not to sertraline, and vice versa. It is also important to distinguish between poor response and intolerance of side effects when gathering a history regarding antidepressant use. Patients may have to stop using a medication because of untoward side effects, sometimes despite having achieved an excellent antidepressant response. In other instances, patients may stop using the antidepressant before they have had the opportunity to undergo an adequate trial to see whether it could improve their mood. This distinction between poor response and premature discontinuation because of side effects is important in planning future pharmacotherapy. Dosing strategies, for instance, could be quite different, with a more aggressive approach for individuals who have previously failed to respond to antidepressants and a very slow and gradual dose escalation for people who have experienced intolerable side effects during previous medication trials.

Family history may also help to guide the prescribing clinician in deciding upon a specific pharmacological agent. For example, if a patient's biological relative has responded well to a particular antidepressant, it would be advisable to try that medication early in the course of his or her treatment if there is no good reason (e.g., hypersensitivity to similar drugs) to avoid that medication in this patient.

Drug-Drug Interactions

The potential for drug-drug interactions is another phenomenon that should be considered when prescribing an antidepressant or mood stabilizer to a substance-dependent patient. Several such interactions have been described in the literature. It is known, for instance, that alcoholic patients who have recently stopped drinking require a substantially higher dose of the tricyclic antidepressants imipramine and desipramine to reach an adequate therapeutic blood level. This is probably less prominent with the newer antidepressants such as SSRIs. Clinicians treating patients who are receiving methadone maintenance treatment need to be aware of two potentially important drug-drug interactions. The first involves the use of certain anticonvulsant drugs, such as carbamazepine or phenytoin; these agents may induce liver enzymes that accelerate the metabolism of methadone, thus precipitating opiate withdrawal symptoms. This interaction does not occur, however, among patients receiving valproate (Saxon, Whittaker, and Hawker, 1989). Thus, valproate is preferred over carbamazepine if an anticonvulsant is being considered as a mood stabilizer for a patient receiving methadone maintenance treatment. Unfortunately, methadone-maintained patients may be accused of drug seeking when they complain of withdrawal symptoms after receiving carbamazepine. Therefore, it is important to be aware of these potential drug-drug interactions with this population.

Patients receiving methadone maintenance treatment who receive fluvoxamine for the treatment of obsessive-compulsive disorder or depression may, conversely, experience an increased blood level of methadone (Bertschy et al., 1994). This drug-drug interaction is less likely to generate patient complaints, but such patients may appear intoxicated, raising staff suspicion about surreptitious drug use. When a patient receiving methadone maintenance treatment discontinues fluvoxamine therapy, on the other hand, he or she will experience withdrawal symptoms and be quite uncomfortable.

Compliance Issues

Regardless of the disorder and the medication prescribed to treat it, one inviolable tenet holds true: no medication works unless the patient takes it. Unfortunately, in many cases, any resemblance between the medication that is prescribed and the medication that a patient takes is purely coincidental. Patients with coexisting substance use and mood disorders are particularly unlikely to take medications as prescribed. Research by Dr. Paul Keck and his colleagues (1996) at the University of Cincinnati has shown that, among patients with bipolar disorder, a coexisting substance use disorder is the single biggest risk factor for medication noncompliance. Because studies have shown that failure to take medication as prescribed generally leads to poor outcomes in bipolar patients, focusing on compliance issues with this population is critical. In a naturalistic 6-month study that we conducted with a relatively small sample of patients with coexisting bipolar and substance use disorders, less than half of the patients took their medication as prescribed in any of the 6 months.

Interestingly, this dually diagnosed patient population may be more likely to take some medications properly than others. For example, our research group (Weiss et al., 1998) asked a sample of 48 bipolar substance abusers to list all of the psychotropic medications they had taken in their lifetimes and then asked them how often they had taken each of these agents as prescribed. We found that patients were significantly more likely to have always taken valproate than lithium as prescribed: approximately half of those who had been prescribed valproate reported that they had always taken that medication as prescribed, while only about a quarter of those who had been prescribed lithium reported full compliance with that medication throughout their lifetimes.

Enhancing Medication Compliance

Why don't patients take their medications as prescribed? There are several reasons, and prescribing clinicians can adopt corresponding strategies to try to deal with these issues.

First, some medication regimens are overly complicated. Patients are more likely to comply with a once-a-day regimen than a twice-a-day regimen. When a medication has to be taken more often than twice daily, the likelihood of full compliance with the regimen falls off further. Thus, when possible, it is optimal to prescribe medications that can be taken once a day, or twice a day at most.

A second reason for noncompliance is nonacceptance of illness. Many patients with substance use disorders and mood disorders (particularly bipolar disorder) deny or minimize the seriousness of their disorders. Addiction has frequently been called "a disease of denial," and many patients in the early stages of mood disorder find it difficult to accept their diagnosis. This is particularly true for relatively young people who have experienced primarily manic episodes (as opposed to depression); they may find aspects of their illness pleasurable and are thus reluctant to take medication to ward it off. In our study of reasons for medication noncompliance among bipolar substance abusers, for example, nearly a quarter of patients who did not take lithium as prescribed stated that their primary reason for noncompliance was the belief that they did not need to take medication (Weiss et al., 1998).

There is no simple approach to help patients overcome the lack of acceptance of their illness. In many instances, denial is overcome more by the gradual intrusion of harsh reality (e.g., losses, arrests, hospitalizations) than by a specific clinician's persuasive powers. However, asking patients how they feel about taking medication, particularly in the early stages, may help to foster discussions that will ultimately increase their level of acceptance. Frequently, acceptance grows with time. Therefore, clinicians should encourage patients to think about taking medication for manageable chunks of time: "Why don't you take this for the next 3 months, see how things are going, and then we'll talk about where we go from there?" For patients who may need to be taking medication for a very long time, perhaps for life, this approach allows them gradually to become accustomed to the idea of taking medication. The prospect of a long-term medication regimen may lead some patients to say "forget this" right at the beginning.

Even the most motivated individual sometimes has difficulty remembering to take medication regularly, however. At the first visit in which a patient is given a prescription, the clinician should ask if the patient has ever taken any other pills on a daily basis (e.g., vitamins, birth control pills, or antihypertensive medication). If the answer is yes, the clinician should inquire about the degree to which the patient was successful at sticking to the prescribed regimen in the past. If this past episode worked out well, the clinician should ask about what was helpful then. If the patient was unable to follow a previous regimen, it is important to understand the factors that interfered with that attempt. To take medication successfully, the patient should ideally incorporate the process into his or her life routine. For many patients, taking a pill with orange juice in the morning, placing the bottle of pills on the night table, or posting a note on a bathroom mirror can serve as a reminder. An alarm watch can be helpful for people who have a less-structured routine or who have to take medication doses in the middle of the day. Unfortunately, patients with substance use and mood disorders frequently lead unstructured lives and do not have a routine into which a medication regimen can easily fit. However, the prescribing clinician should still work with the patient to figure out a strategy to increase the likelihood of medication compliance. To the extent that the patient and the doctor are working on this issue together, taking medication is likely to be seen as a team effort rather than something that is being forced on the patient.

Side effects can also limit medication compliance. In our study of bipolar substance abusers (Weiss et al., 1998), the most common reason for not taking lithium as prescribed was the presence of physical side effects. Thus, the prescribing clinician should inquire about side effects at each visit. Moreover, in taking an initial medication history, it is important to find out whether certain specific side effects led a patient to stop taking a medication in the past. This piece of data can inform the clinician's choice of medication in the future. For example, if a patient stopped two antidepressants in the past because of intolerable anticholinergic side effects, then the clinician should obviously try to choose a new medication that has few such side effects.

There are certain symptoms that patients are less likely to discuss with their doctor, and these may lead to discontinuation of the drug. Foremost among these are sexual side effects (e.g., decreased libido, inability to achieve orgasm), which are unfortunately quite common among individuals taking antidepressants. It is thus crucial that the prescribing clinician warn patients about the possibility of these side effects and systematically ask about them at each visit. Patients are then likely to volunteer information about their sexual functioning, and problem-solving strategies (e.g., dose adjustment, switching medications) can be developed to deal with these symptoms.

Another reason for medication noncompliance is the perception, correct or otherwise, that the medication is ineffective. Patients with mood disorders, substance use disorders, and especially the combination of the two are at great risk to discontinue medications abruptly because they are notoriously impatient. Impatience can lead to two forms of noncompliance: premature discontinuation of medication or the use of higher than prescribed doses in an attempt to make the medication work sooner. In our study of medication compliance among bipolar substance abusers, we found that it was relatively common for patients to use excessive dosages because they were impatient with waiting for the drug to work. This was particularly prevalent in patients taking tricyclic antidepressants; 4 of the 10 patients who did not take these drugs as prescribed took higher than prescribed doses because of their impatience with the process of reaching a therapeutic dose and a beneficial effect.

Finally, when prescribing medications to patients with substance use and mood disorders, one should anticipate noncompliance as well as try to prevent it. If a clinician expects some degree of noncompliance, then the use of a medication with a longer half-life might have advantages over shorter-acting drugs. For example, a drug such as fluoxetine, which has a long half-life, may retain some of its effectiveness even if a patient takes it less often than prescribed and may thus be a good choice for some depressed substance abusers.

The Use of Medications to Treat Substance Abuse Itself in Patients with Coexisting Mood Disorders

In addition to drugs that act on mood, patients with coexisting substance use and mood disorders can be treated with medications that are designed to treat the substance abuse itself. Several different categories of drugs are commonly used to treat substance use disorders, in addition to those medications that are used to treat withdrawal syndromes. These include maintenance drugs, such as methadone; drugs that block or attenuate the reinforcing properties of specific substances of abuse (e.g., naltrexone for opioid or alcohol abuse); and drugs that induce aversive consequences from substance use (e.g., disulfiram for alcohol abuse). Very little has been written about the use of these medications for patients with coexisting mood disorders. Salloum and colleagues (1998) reported some positive results with naltrexone in a group of depressed alcoholic persons, but little else has been written about the use of medications to treat substance use in affectively ill patients. As mentioned above, the potential for drug interaction between substance-related and mood-related medications needs to be considered when prescribing both types of drugs for a dually disordered patient. Specifically, adjustments in methadone dose may need to be made when prescribing specific agents that can affect the rate of its metabolism (e.g., carbamazepine or fluvoxamine). Alternatively, the prescribing clinician should consider using a different medication for the same purpose if clinically indicated and appropriate (e.g., valproate rather than carbamazepine for the treatment of bipolar disorder).

One controversial question that frequently arises in treating this population is whether one should prescribe disulfiram to a patient who is seriously depressed, specifically whether one should give disulfiram to a suicidal patient. There are reasonable arguments to support either answer to this dilemma. Although prescribing disulfiram can be viewed as giving a patient a potentially lethal weapon to use in combination with alcohol to attempt suicide, our experience at McLean Hospital is that drinking with disulfiram is a highly unusual, inefficient method of attempting to kill oneself. Moreover, since so many suicide attempts (both successful and unsuccessful) are made after ingesting alcohol, the capacity of disulfiram to deter drinking may consequently prevent suicide attempts. Of course, there is no hard and fast rule about whether one should prescribe disulfiram to a suicidal patient. Disulfiram is a very powerful drug, which should be prescribed only in the context of a good doctor-patient relationship. The patient must thoroughly understand the drug and be both willing and able to avoid alcohol in its beverage and its disguised forms (e.g., foods and over-the-counter liquid medicines). As part of my evaluation of an individual's appropriateness for disulfiram, I simply ask any patient for whom I am considering prescribing the drug, "Can you imagine yourself drinking while you're taking this medication?" If a patient unhesitatingly says, "No way! I'm not interested in poisoning myself," I feel more confident, although I realize that even patients who emphatically give this response may nevertheless drink while taking disulfiram. If, on the other hand, a patient answers, "Doctor, I'm alcoholic, and when I want to drink, nothing is going to stop me from drinking," I would eschew the use of disulfiram.

For patients with serious psychiatric illness, the willingness to forgo drinking is not enough; the clinician must decide whether a patient is capable of avoiding alcohol in its disguised forms. Taking disulfiram requires a level of vigilance that some patients with serious mood disorders do not possess, particularly when symptomatic. Patients who are using this medication must read labels carefully to make sure that they are not ingesting alcohol unknowingly and must have the ability and willingness to ask waiters in restaurants if items they are considering have alcohol in them. While this can be embarrassing for people with or without psychiatric illness, patients with mood disorders may not remember to follow through on all of these behaviors and may thus be at risk to experience unintentional alcohol-disulfiram reactions. The severity of such a reaction is largely related to the amount of alcohol ingested and the dose of disulfiram being taken, and the accidental ingestion of a small amount of alcohol that was not cooked off in a bowl of soup generally does not precipitate the same type of medical crisis that can occur when someone intentionally imbibes beverage alcohol. However, it is important to evaluate a patient's level of organization and ability to follow the very strict rules incumbent on someone taking disulfiram before prescribing this medication.

An Algorithm for the Pharmacological Treatment of the Depressed Alcoholic Patient

Although patients with mood and substance use disorders are a heterogeneous group, the most common presentation of these two disorders involves the combination of depression and alcohol abuse or dependence. In many such cases, the patient is not interested in having both disorders treated. Rather, such a patient commonly enters treatment with a request for an antidepressant. When the treating clinician takes a drinking history and points out that alcohol may be exacerbating the patient's depression, a frequent response is, "When I get less depressed, I'll be able to handle my drinking better." How should one proceed in such a case? Should the clinician urge the patient to stop drinking before prescribing medication, to see what happens to the depressive symptoms in the absence of alcohol? Is it reasonable to insist on abstinence as a precondition for medical treatment? Or should the clinician treat the depression in the face of continued drinking?

This is an extraordinarily common dilemma, with no clear answer. Ideally, the patient will agree to stop drinking for long enough (at least 2 weeks, preferably a month) for the clinician to evaluate the effect of the patient's drinking on his or her mood. In some cases, merely stopping drinking will have such a powerful effect on the patient's mood that medication will not be necessary. Moreover, when abstinence does not produce substantial mood elevation, the prescribing clinician has a much more informed assessment of the patient's baseline mood state and, thus, a better sense of the effects of pharmacotherapy.

In many cases, however, the patient will be unwilling or unable to stop drinking. In such cases, the first obligation of the treating clinician is to evaluate whether the patient is acutely dangerous because of the alcohol use, the depression, or both. It is important to determine whether the patient requires immediate medical detoxification or hospitalization because of suicidal risk or dangerous alcohol-related behaviors. If this is not the case and there is no other medical or psychiatric contraindication, then the clinician should carefully evaluate the patient for the presence of major depressive disorder, as opposed to depressive symptoms alone. If the patient meets criteria for the former, then treatment with an antidepressant such as a serotonin-selective reuptake inhibitor (e.g., fluoxetine, sertraline, paroxetine, citalopram) is a reasonable choice. The patient should be told, however, that abstaining from alcohol is highly advisable during an antidepressant trial, since there is some evidence from a Harvard Medical School (Worthington et al., 1996) study suggesting that even social drinkers have an attenuated antidepressant response when compared with those who abstain from alcohol. If the patient stops drinking during this time, so much the better. If not, then the clinician has concrete evidence of the significance of the alcohol problem: the patient is willing to risk a suboptimal antidepressant response in order to continue drinking. By thus focusing the initial treatment plan on an area of agreement with the patient (i.e., the wish to improve the patient's mood), the clinician can build an alliance and gain some credibility when later discussing an area of initial disagreement (i.e., the need to stop drinking).

The Reluctance to Take Psychotropic Medication

While some patients with substance use and mood disorders enter treatment specifically looking for antidepressants, some individuals with substance use disorders are reluctant to take psychotropic medication. Some such patients assume that taking medication implies that they are "crazy." Many substance abusers see themselves as quite distinct from individuals with psychiatric illness and are quite frightened by the idea of psychiatric symptoms. Some substance abusers are confused about whether the medications that they are being prescribed are, in fact, addictive. Thus, some patients see the use of antidepressants as merely substituting a pharmaceutical medication for a substance of abuse. The phrase "chewing your booze" is used by some individuals with alcoholism and, indeed, by some treaters in the substance abuse field to describe the phenomenon of substitution. Some patients will hear this phrase at Alcoholics Anonymous (AA) meetings and will believe that they are relapsing by taking medications. It is important to point out that AA does not, in fact, discourage the appropriate use of psychotropic medications to treat coexisting psychiatric disorders. In fact, an official AA publication encourages AA members to follow their doctor's advice regarding proper medication use. Having this booklet on hand and giving it to patients can help to overcome this source of resistance to taking medication.

Conclusion

Nowhere is the gradual healing of the historical rift between the substance abuse and mental health treatment communities more evident than in the area of psychopharmacological treatment of patients with coexisting substance use and mood disorders. Research conducted over the past several years has shown that the judicious prescription of psychotropic medication to appropriately diagnosed patients in this dually diagnosed subgroup can improve outcome of the mood disorder and, to a lesser extent, the substance use disorder as well. Of course, positive outcomes depend on not only the prescription of the proper medication but also a solid doctor-patient relationship, attention to compliance issues, and a commitment to work on both the addiction and the mood disorder. Such an approach can improve the prognosis of this commonly seen patient population.

ACKNOWLEDGMENTS
Preparation of this chapter was supported by grants DA09400 and DA00326 from the National Institute on Drug Abuse; grant AA09881 from the National Institute on Alcohol Abuse and Alcoholism; and a grant from the Dr. Ralph and Marian C. Falk Medical Research Trust.

REFERENCES
Bertschy, G., P. Baumann, C. B. Eap, et al. 1994. Probable metabolic interaction between methadone and fluvoxamine in addict patients. *Therapeutic Drug Monitoring* 16:42–45.
Brady, K. T., S. C. Sonne, R. Anton, et al. 1995. Valproate in the treatment of acute bipolar affective episodes complicated by substance abuse: A pilot study. *Journal of Clinical Psychiatry* 56:118–21.
Cornelius, J. R., I. M. Salloum, J. G. Ehler, et al. 1997. Fluoxetine in depressed alcoholics. *Archives of General Psychiatry* 54:700–705.

Gawin, F. H., and H. D. Kleber. 1984. Cocaine abuse treatment: Open pilot trial with desipramine and lithium carbonate. *Archives of General Psychiatry* 41:903–9.

Geller, B., T. B. Cooper, K. Sun, et al. 1998. Double-blind and placebo-controlled study of lithium for adolescent bipolar disorders with secondary substance dependency. *Journal of the American Academy of Child and Adolescent Psychiatry* 37:171–78.

Greenfield, S. F., R. D. Weiss, L. R. Muenz, et al. 1998. The effect of depression on return to drinking. *Archives of General Psychiatry* 55:259–65.

Keck, P. E., Jr., S. L. McElroy, S. M. Strakowski, et al. 1996. Factors associated with pharmacologic noncompliance in patients with mania. *Journal of Clinical Psychiatry* 57:292–97.

Mason, B. J., J. H. Kocsis, E. C. Ritvo, et al. 1996. A double-blind, placebo-controlled trial of desipramine for primary alcohol dependence stratified on the presence or absence of major depression. *Journal of the American Medical Association* 275:761–67.

McGrath, P. J., E. V. Nunes, J. W. Stewart, et al. 1996. Imipramine treatment of alcoholics with primary depression. *Archives of General Psychiatry* 53:232–40.

Nunes, E. V., P. J. McGrath, S. Wager, et al. 1990. Lithium treatment for cocaine abusers with bipolar spectrum disorders. *American Journal of Psychiatry* 147:655–57.

Nunes, E. V., P. J. McGrath, F. M. Quitkin, et al. 1995. Imipramine treatment of cocaine abuse: Possible boundaries of efficacy. *Drug and Alcohol Dependence* 39:185–95.

Nunes, E. V., F. M. Quitkin, S. J. Donovan, et al. 1998. Imipramine treatment of opiate-dependent patients with depressive disorders. *Archives of General Psychiatry* 55:153–60.

Salloum, I. M., J. R. Cornelius, M. E. Thase, et al. 1998. Naltrexone utility in depressed alcoholics. *Psychopharmacology Bulletin* 34:111–15.

Saxon, A. J., S. Whittaker, and C. S. Hawker. 1989. Valproic acid, unlike other anticonvulsants, has no effect on methadone metabolism. Two cases. *Journal of Clinical Psychiatry* 50:228–29.

Weiss, R. D. 1988. Relapse to cocaine abuse after initiating desipramine treatment. *Journal of the American Medical Association* 260:2545–46.

Weiss, R. D., S. F. Greenfield, L. M. Najavits, et al. 1998. Medication compliance among patients with bipolar disorder and substance use disorder. *Journal of Clinical Psychiatry* 59:172–74.

Worthington, J., M. Fava, C. Agustin, et al. 1996. Consumption of alcohol, nicotine, and caffeine among depressed outpatients: Relationship with response to treatment. *Psychosomatics* 37:518–22.

7

Evaluating and Managing Patients Who Are Not Responding to Treatment

Jill M. Williams, M.D., and Caroline Eick, M.A.

In this chapter, we discuss some of the factors involved in the response to treatment and present a conceptual framework for dealing with a lack of treatment response (often termed *treatment nonresponse*). It can be important to define treatment response, since clinical outcomes can be very different from those used in research settings. The term *treatment nonresponse* is somewhat of a misnomer and should be interpreted broadly to include any failure of a therapeutic response. As many as 15 percent of depressed patients will fail to respond to treatment, although this percentage is much larger when one considers that as many as 70 percent achieve only a symptom response to treatment and not a true remission. There are several diagnostic and treatment issues to consider, ranging from general considerations like the therapeutic setting and diagnosis to specific treatment modalities, including psychotherapy and medications.

Clients who fail to respond to typical treatments can provide the clinician with opportunities to re-evaluate and reconsider the case. Countertransference issues may be relevant, indicating that the goals of the patient and those of the clinician are not concordant. Successfully working with a treatment-resistant client may require taking time to reconsider the case, using a fresh perspective, and even consider the input of a consultant.

One of the first issues to consider is the possibility of an inaccurate diagnosis. Related is the issue of comorbidity, which can be complex, as there can be one or more coexisting psychiatric disorders and coexisting substance use disorders, as well as medical problems and conditions that may be related to the substance use or present with overlapping symptoms. In addition, failure to respond to treatment can be a result of treatment issues. Treatments may simply be of too little intensity or duration to be effective. In the treatment of depression, for example, patients who are initially termed *nonresponders* often do well on higher medication doses or longer durations of treatment.

In the treatment of addictions, much has been written about treatment matching based on the particular needs or problem areas of the individual patient. Too often patients receive a generic or programmatic treatment not tailored to their needs, and this may contribute to a lack of treatment response. Matching treatments based on the patient's motivational level can prevent the offering of overly intensive therapies to patients not ready to use them. Additionally, the treatment setting may not be best suited to the patient. Levels of care developed by the American Society on Addiction Medicine (ASAM) can help guide the clinician in using criteria to best justify the need for inpatient versus outpatient and other levels of care. Common reasons that contribute to treatment nonresponse include

- inaccurate diagnosis
- insufficient treatment
- comorbidity: axis I, axis II, axis III
- clinician-client mismatch or failure to understand current motivational level

Process "addictions" are an important and often unrecognized aspect of treatment that may also contribute to a client's difficulty in treatment. These nonchemical compulsive behaviors are frequently seen in clinical practice as complicating the course of treatment, yet relatively little is known about their occurrence. These compulsive behaviors and their relationship to substance use disorders can have an effect on treatment outcomes.

Inaccurate Diagnosis

An inaccurate diagnosis can be the result of several different factors. Unfortunately, many patients present to the clinician with a diagnosis that is never confirmed or verified. Clinicians should reconsider for diagnostic clarity patients who fail to respond to treatment. Careful interviewing and chart review can help delineate the timing and severity of symptoms and the relationships of symptoms to periods of substance use and sobriety and can help clarify previous patterns of illness and response. Prior episodes of treatment response and true remission of illnesses such as depression can be predictors of future treatment response. Structured interviews and standardized instruments can be used as a more rigorous measure of diagnosis and can assist in more complex cases. Ancillary and verifying information can be elicited from interviews with family and friends of the patient.

An incorrect diagnosis of unipolar depression rather than bipolar disorder may account for some lack of treatment response. Patients diagnosed by clinicians as having unipolar depression were found to have a bipolar type II depression when interviewed using a Structured Clinical Interview assessment (SCID) (Benazzi, 1997). Clinicians should consider bipolar disorder when patients present with a mixed state of agitation, hypomanic symptoms, and depression, as it has important implications for treatment. Antidepressants may aggravate the condition and worsen the hypomania or cause frank mania, and patients may do better with discontinuation of antidepressants and treatment with a mood stabilizer.

Clinicians should use diagnostic references with specific sets of criteria like DSM-IV, not vague and nonspecific symptoms, to guide the process of diagnosis. For example, attention should be paid to a patient's report of feeling "panicky," which is associated with several diagnostic entities. It is important to distinguish whether symptoms occur during substance use or withdrawal, with sufficient frequency and associated symptoms to warrant the diagnosis of panic disorder, or in the context of a major depressive episode. The treatment issues would be quite different for each diagnosis, making the need for clarity vital. Similarly, the presence of nonspecific depressive symptoms such as low mood and energy may be the cause or the result of the addictive behavior, warranting different treatments. Systematic assessments like structured interviews used in research settings are not routinely used in clinical practice but might lower the probability of diagnoses being missed or misclassified.

Insufficient Treatment

The clinician must assess whether the client has received adequate and appropriate treatment for the diagnosis. Additional studies might be performed to help clarify the diagnosis or rule out other contributing factors. Important issues to consider include the following:

- Was the treatment appropriate?
- Was the client on an adequate dose for a sufficient period?
- Was the client likely to have complied with treatment?
- After an adequate trial, were appropriate attempts made to try alternative treatments?

In the treatment of depression, failure to respond to a medication treatment can lead the clinician to vary the dose or duration of the treatment. Greenhouse et al. (1987) found that the remission rate with imipramine was 25 percent at the end of 4 weeks of treatment for depression but increased to 50 percent when treatment continued for 12 weeks and to 80 percent at 6 months.

Switching antidepressants is a popular technique when there is treatment-resistant depression, yet there are few scientific data to guide clinicians on how best to do this. Switching medications, also termed *crossover monotherapy*, offers some advantages over augmentation, which adds medications. Using a single agent lowers the risks of drug-drug interactions and side effects, offers medications with potentially different mechanisms of action, and is usually less expensive (Thase and Rush, 1997). Switching within a class of medications was previously avoided, yet now may be beneficial with selective serotonin reuptake inhibitors (SSRIs), since they have somewhat different properties with regard to dopaminergic and noradrenergic activity. Switching outside of the class is also commonly done, and newer atypical antidepressants, such as venlafaxine, mirtazapine, and bupropion, can be useful alternatives, offering possible different mechanisms of action. Tricyclic antidepressants and monoamine oxidase inhibitors (MAOIs) are alternatives but have more side effects and may be used as third-line options. MAOIs are effective for treatment-resistant depression, but their side effects and the inconvenience of a special diet limit their clinical usefulness and may be undesirable to patients. A disadvantage in switching antidepressants is the need for a washout period between agents and the possibility of a discontinuation syndrome, which causes uncomfortable flulike symptoms.

Additional strategies include adding secondary augmenting medications to increase the benefit of the initial response. This allows continued use and longer trial of the original agent. Augmentation may be preferred when there is a partial or initial response to the original agent. Lithium is the best-studied augmenting agent. Meta-analysis of lithium augmentation reveals almost twice the likelihood of response of adding placebo to the antidepressant (Bauer, 1999). Commonly used augmenting agents that need further controlled study to determine efficacy include thyroid medications, buspirone, stimulants, mood stabilizers, and anticonvulsants such as gabapentin, lamotrigine, divalproex, and topiramate, as well as dopamine agonists and dopamine antagonists. It can be difficult to decide whether to switch to another antidepressant or add an augmenting agent, and data are lacking to support their usefulness; clearly, this is an area that needs more study. Treating with two antidepressants simultaneously, such as an SSRI and bupropion, is promising in small case reports but needs further study.

Other modalities — psychotherapy, group treatments, and electroconvulsive therapy (ECT) — may be substituted or added to the regimen. Newer treatments are being investigated, including repetitive transcranial magnetic stimulation and direct vagal nerve stimulation. Although promising, these treatments are only in preliminary studies and probably will not be available for several years.

As with affective disorders, treatments for addictions can be varied when there is a poor response. Psychosocial treatments are most common, and the frequency, timing, and type of interventions can be made more intense when appropriate. Self-help groups like Alcoholics Anonymous (AA) include this rationale in their program and speak of the need for "90 meetings in 90 days" for those in early recovery or coming back from a relapse, signifying the need for the support and assistance of more frequent meetings. The treatment setting can be changed to be more structured or supervised, if appropriate to the needs of the client (e.g., requiring inpatient detoxification). Programs providing a continuum of care through outpatient, intensive outpatient, and residential or inpatient treatment create the smoothest transitions for clients needing to pass through these levels at different stages in their recovery.

Many pharmacological treatments for addictive disorders are now available. Although all are effective, they have different mechanisms of action, which range from substitution of drug effects to reducing craving, decreasing the reinforcing properties of the substance, or creating an aversive effect when the drug is taken. The use of these agents is becoming more widespread and accepted in addiction treatment as our knowledge of the biological underpinnings of addictions increases. Clinicians should consider pharmacotherapies in the treatment-resistant case, especially if patients are highly motivated or want to receive all available treatments. Some physicians are reluctant to prescribe certain medications for fear of fostering the addiction component. Medications should always be used as part of a comprehensive substance abuse program, and the use of sedating and addicting medications, such as benzodiazepines, should be avoided.

Another reason for insufficient treatment is the potential for nonadherence to a treatment regimen. Medication noncompliance is quite common in a variety of medical and psychiatric disorders, particularly mood disorders and substance use disorders. Among patients with bipolar disorder, having a coexisting substance use disorder puts patients at very high risk for medication noncompliance and, subsequently, a poor outcome. Medication noncompliance can occur for a variety of reasons. Some patients with substance use disorders are afraid to mix drugs of abuse with prescribed medications and sometimes unfortunately choose the former rather than the latter. Alternatively, these patients are often quite disorganized and cannot remember to take medications; this argues for a simpler rather than a more complex medication regimen in this population. Denial of illness is another common reason for medication noncompliance, particularly among patients with bipolar disorder and substance abuse.

Medication noncompliance does not always mean that patients fail to take their medications or take too little medication. In many cases, persons with substance use disorder who are prescribed medications for their mood disorders take more than prescribed, either because they are impatient for the drug to work or because they find some side effect from the medication to be reinforcing (Weiss et al., 1998). Patients with substance use disorders often take excessive doses of a variety of different medications, including over-the-counter headache remedies and cold preparations. Therefore, it is critical that clinicians monitor medication compliance carefully and address this issue regularly. Further strategies for addressing medication compliance in this population are described in chapter 6.

Comorbidity

Axis I Comorbidity

The overlap of substance use disorders and other psychiatric disorders is well known. Comorbidity is more often the rule than the exception in treatment. The significance of this overlap is that it often complicates making accurate diagnoses and results in inadequate treatment or in treatment nonresponse. These issues can become more complex if one considers the coexisting psychiatric disorders, substance abuse disorders, and medical problems. Axis I diagnoses that may be unrecognized and contribute to comorbidity include anxiety disorders (such as panic disorder, generalized anxiety disorder, and phobias) and disorders with behavioral manifestations (such as attention deficit/ hyperactivity disorder).

Of patients with an alcohol use disorder, 19.4 percent also have an anxiety disorder. Of patients with drug use disorders, 28.3 percent also have an anxiety disorder (Regier et al., 1990). The syndromes most commonly associated with alcoholism include panic disorder, social phobia, and generalized anxiety disorder (Kranzler, 1996; Kushner, Sher, and Beitman, 1990). The relationship between anxiety and alcohol is complex and perhaps reciprocal, in that anxiety has been shown to be both a cause and a consequence of heavy drinking. The high prevalence of anxiety symptoms does not always mean that patients will demonstrate a chronic anxiety disorder, however. Anxiety is prominent during drug and alcohol withdrawal, and the anxiety level in alcoholic persons will decline as they gain increased abstinence from alcohol (Brown, Irwin, and Schukit, 1991). Even after protracted withdrawal syndromes, there is evidence that most anxiety syndromes decrease dramatically or disappear, although studies are inconclusive and not definitive at this point (Schuckit and Hesselbrock, 1994).

The treatment of anxiety disorders in individuals with a substance use disorder can be complicated, and pharmacological therapy is often warranted. Abnormalities in serotonin (5-HT) are suspected to be related to alcohol consumption and anxiety, with findings of low 5-hydroxyindoleacetic acid (5-HIAA), the major metabolite of serotonin in the cerebrospinal fluid of more severe alcoholics who have an onset of excessive consumption before 25 years of age (Fils-Aime et al., 1996). While no one agent has been demonstrated to be more efficacious than another, a SSRI is often considered first-line treatment. Advantages include safety in overdose, simple dosing, few side effects, and no dependence liability. Although SSRIs are also used to treat depressive disorders, doses needed for anxiety disorders are generally higher, which might explain a lack of an initial response. Buspirone, a direct serotonin agonist, is associated with greater retention in treatment, reduced anxiety, and fewer drinking days in anxious alcoholic persons (Kranzler et al., 1994). In addition to pharmacological therapy, the client can benefit from specific behavioral therapies that target relaxation, the overcoming of anxiety urges, and coping skills.

Clients with substance use disorders have high rates of attention deficit/hyperactivity disorder (ADHD). Twenty-four percent of patients in substance use treatment settings meet DSM-IV criteria for ADHD, with higher rates in men and more likely lifetime patterns of cocaine, stimulant, hallucinogen, and cannabis use (Schubiner et al., 2000).

Axis II Comorbidity

Personality disorders, classified on axis II in the DSM-IV, represent chronic maladaptive interpersonal styles of behavior, which can have a significant effect on treatment in many settings. It is estimated that at least 60 percent of patients with substance use disorders also have personality disorders. Strongest associations occur between substance use disorders and cluster B, or "dramatic," personality types, which include antisocial, borderline, narcissistic, and histrionic personality. For clients with cocaine, hallucinogen, opioid, sedative, or stimulant use disorders, the odds of having a cluster B personality disorder increase more than 12 times (Skodol, Oldham, and Gallagher, 1999). In addition, patients with early-onset substance abuse (before age 18) have significantly higher rates of antisocial, borderline, and passive-aggressive personality than do patients with a later onset (Franken and Hendriks, 2000).

Unfortunately, it can be difficult to make correct assessments of personality disorders with coexisting substance use, since similar impulsive, violent, or self-destructive behaviors are observed transiently in substance use disorders. Without prior history, it can be difficult to differentiate substance-induced personality traits from more pervasive axis II conditions cross-sectionally.

Much has been written about the effects of axis II comorbidity on outcomes of substance abuse treatment. The diagnosis of antisocial personality disorder (APD) among substance abusers is associated with earlier onset of substance use (Buydens-Branchley, Branchley, and Noumair, 1989), more severe substance dependence (Regier et al., 1990), more criminal activity (Cottler et al., 1995), higher rates of depression (Kosten and Rounsaville, 1986; Rounsaville et al.,

1987), more treatment noncompliance (Alterman et al., 1998), and poorer treatment outcomes (Rounsaville et al., 1986; Woody et al., 1985). Many of these studies have been with opiate-dependent clients in methadone maintenance treatment centers. Interestingly, APD and non-APD patients with cocaine dependence do not differ in treatment retention, substance use outcomes, or social function outcomes (McKay et al., 2000). Clients with a related condition, adult antisocial behavior (AAB), often lack the childhood criteria for conduct disorder, although clinically they may be indistinguishable from those with APD in terms of the severity of substance use (Cecero et al., 1999). APD clients with depression show greater response to treatment, suggesting that negative affects can increase motivation to change (Rounsaville et al., 1983). Clients with APD and other axis II disorders are more prone to emotional distress and instability.

Borderline personality disorder (BPD) is associated with substance use disorders as well as multiple other axis I diagnoses (Zimmerman and Mattia, 1999). Comorbidity of borderline personality within substance abuse settings ranges from 5 to 32 percent (Weiss et al., 1993). Patients with BPD have significantly more psychiatric problems, use of health care resources, behavioral dyscontrol, suicidal thoughts, and legal problems than patients without a personality disorder (Linehan et al., 1999; Trull et al., 2000). Treatment with borderline patients is often compromised by noncompliance and self-destructive behaviors. Recent studies have shown that dialectical behavior therapy for borderline patients results in not only global functional gains, less suicidal behavior, and improved social adjustment but also significantly reduced drug abuse (Linehan et al., 1999).

Other manualized treatments attempt to integrate treatment for substance abuse and personality disorders. Since personality traits are often enduring and making changes is a lengthy process, these treatments do not focus on personality change. Instead, there is emphasis on developing personality awareness, which allows patients to have a greater understanding of how their personality traits either facilitate or hinder substance abuse recovery (Weiss and Daley, 1994).

Medical Comorbidity

Medical conditions and some medications cause syndromes that mimic depression and complicate the treatment course or contribute to a lack of response. A variety of disorders can lead to behavioral abnormalities, including nearly all broad categories of illness (trauma, tumor, infection, cardiovascular disease, hereditary conditions, and metabolic, demyelinating, degenerative, and immune disorders). A discussion of all of these is beyond the scope of this chapter; only those commonly seen with substance use disorders are included.

Central nervous system (CNS) disorders like delirium, dementia, and other so-called organic disorders occur independently or as the result of substance use and can complicate both diagnosis and treatment. These conditions interfere with treatment by affecting the person's ability to understand and process information. Individuals with a CNS disorder may exhibit lower motivation, greater frustration, poorer coping, and increased psychological stress that complicate recovery and lead to a relapse. CNS disorders related to trauma or anoxia can cause impulse dysregulation, which may impair the person's judgment regarding substance use. Human immunodeficiency virus (HIV) is prevalent among substance users, and high-risk groups include those who share infected needles and practice unsafe sex; HIV infection can present with a variety of mood, cognitive, or psychotic symptoms.

Endocrinopathies

Many endocrinopathies present with psychiatric symptoms, particularly affective symptoms, leading clinicians to consider the relationships between these disorders. Two of the most common disorders related to affective disorders are Cushing disease and hypothyroidism. It is important to use blood tests to screen for these disorders and to retest when antidepressants don't seem to work. The neuroendocrine network is highly complex and involves the release of several hormones and a feedback loop system for regulation.

The hypothalamic-pituitary-adrenal axis regulates the release of cortisol from the adrenal cortex. This system has been a focus of intense research because of its widespread effects on other parts of the brain, including the neocortex, limbic system, locus ceruleus, and hippocampus, and it has been implicated in the understanding of depression. Glucocorticoid excess is hypothesized to contribute to treatment-refractory depression, and treatments that suppress adrenal steroid production and reduce cortisol have been promising in a few studies (Amsterdam et al., 1987). Depressed patients have been found to have enlarged adrenal glands on imaging studies, and this enlargement has also been correlated with completed suicides (Nemeroff, Krishnan, and Reed, 1992).

Head Trauma

Drugs and alcohol play a significant role in head trauma. One study found that approximately 43 percent of subjects presenting to an emergency room for head injury had one or more substances in their urine (Boyle, Vella, and Moloney, 1991). Another study revealed that 46 percent of patients admitted for head injury had drugs or alcohol in their system (Parkinson, Stephensen, and Phillips, 1985). The effects of head trauma on the treatment of a substance use disorder can be quite dramatic. Individuals with injury to the frontal and prefrontal cortex may display impulse dysregulation and mood lability. This impulsivity will complicate treatment in several ways. The affected individual is more likely to act on urges to use drugs and alcohol and not employ techniques learned in treatment. Further, behavioral dyscontrol is likely to result in reduced tolerance for frustration; this may trigger a relapse or hinder sobriety.

Behavioral dyscontrol can be treated with behavioral techniques and medication management. Medications that can be used include valproate (Depakote), gabapentin (Neurontin), and other newer antiepileptic drugs (AEDs). Clinicians should take special precautions when using these medications. The liver metabolizes valproate, and hence an assessment of liver function should be done before starting medication. Gabapentin is a relatively safe and well-tolerated medication that is excreted almost entirely unchanged via the kidney. For patients with kidney impairment, the dose may need to be lessened. It is also a good idea to obtain 24-hour urine creatinine clearance in individuals with suspected kidney disease to help determine dosing.

In addition to impulse dysregulation, head trauma survivors will sometimes display rage reactions and aggressive behavior. Serotonin has been shown to exert an inhibitory control over impulsive aggression (Volavka, 1999). In addition, research has demonstrated abnormalities in tryptophan hydroxylase activity in impulsive-aggressive male clients with personality disorders (New et al., 1998). Although the exact role of serotonin in head trauma survivors is not known, a trial of a SSRI is often warranted.

Direct Effects of Substance Use on the Brain

Because alcohol is a neurotoxin, chronic alcohol use has a direct effect on neuronal tissue. A major effect of chronic alcohol use is shrinkage of brain material (atrophy), which has been demonstrated on computed tomographic (CT) scans of the brains of alcoholic patients. Pathological evidence suggests that chronic use of alcohol results in a decrease in the weight of the brain in both cortical and subcortical structures. After long-term use, individuals may develop an alcoholic dementia that may be due to either the direct effects of the alcohol, nutritional deficiencies, or a combination of both. The clinician must be sure to assess the cognitive status of the client and factor into the equation whether the individual is resistant to treatment because of the cognitive effects of the alcohol.

Nutritional Deficiencies

Substance-abusing patients risk deficiencies of essential nutrients. Effective therapeutic techniques may fail if there is an undetected medical problem. Chronic alcohol abuse is most commonly associated with nutritional deficiencies; however, they may be associated with other drugs of abuse as well. Peripheral neuropathies and memory disorders are linked to vitamin B_{12} deficiency, which may be a result of poor intake or malabsorption. Acute thiamine deficiency can cause a severe and dramatic presentation, termed Wernicke encephalopathy, or a more chronic disorder, Korsakoff psychosis, which is a syndrome of memory loss and confabulation.

Korsakoff syndrome represents pathology in the diencephalic and frontal lobe regions of the brain due to a deficiency in thiamine. Atrophy of the mammillary bodies affects short-term memory and recall. Frontal lobe deficits will produce delayed recall, deficits on the Wisconsin Card Sorting Test, and decreased temporal order memory, which involves recall of items in sequence. The syndrome consists of significant anterograde and retrograde amnesia and is permanent in up to 70 percent of patients. Recent memory is more affected, and it is estimated that about 9 percent of alcoholic persons have Korsakoff psychosis (Eckardt and Martin, 1986).

Wernicke encephalopathy is an acute form of thiamine deficiency associated with a triad of mental confusion, ophthalmoplegia, and ataxia. This requires urgent treatment with parenteral thiamine and may be reversible. However, studies have demonstrated that up to 90 percent of alcoholic persons with Wernicke encephalopathy will develop Korsakoff psychosis (Charness, 1993; Victor, Adams, and Collins, 1989). Only 20 percent of patients with Korsakoff psychosis will make a complete recovery, while 55 percent have deficits severe enough to require some type of residential or supervised care.

Essential nutrients like calcium, potassium, magnesium, and zinc are often depleted in substance users because of poor nutrition. These deficiencies cause electrical conduction disturbances in neuronal, cardiac, and muscular systems. Of particular concern is the depletion of calcium and magnesium. Routine laboratory tests check for calcium but often do not address magnesium. However, if magnesium is low, supplementing calcium will often not be of use, as magnesium is required to maintain normal calcium levels.

Infections

The incidence of HIV infection among intravenous (IV) drug users is quite high. Of acquired immune deficiency syndrome (AIDS) cases in 1997, IV drug abusers accounted for 24 percent of the men and 47 percent of the women, according to the Centers for Disease Control and Prevention. HIV infection and other infections associated with drug abuse are widespread. Knowledge of the illness may enhance compliance with substance abuse treatment to prevent the worsening of the disease. On the other hand, an individual may feel hopeless, even if he or she is not ill from HIV, making the individual unable to deal with the substance use disorder.

The infections that may occur in substance abusers can affect general health and response to treatment. These infections can occur in the absence of IV drug abuse, and many are transmitted sexually. Substance abusers engage in risky behaviors, putting them at increased risk of transmission, including using sex as a means of obtaining substances. The presence of one or more sexually transmitted diseases is associated with increased rates of HIV.

Viral hepatitis is associated with substance use, and chronic forms are disabling, with high comorbidities of depressive disorders and chronic fatigue. Treatments for hepatitis, such as interferon, can cause similar syndromes of fatigue and depressed mood and can contribute to lack of a treatment response.

Client-Clinician Mismatch and Mismatch of Motivational Level

In every aspect of life, two individuals are not guaranteed to like or work well with each other. This is true in the therapeutic context as well, and it is important for the clinician to be mindful of this. In cases of treatment nonresponse, the clinician should consider whether a therapeutic relationship has been established. These difficulties may be particularly hard for the clinician to recognize and may require frank discussions with the client or review of the case with a supervisor.

Consultation or gaining a second opinion from someone uninvolved with the case may be helpful. If there is a problem in the therapeutic relationship that cannot be resolved, it is probably necessary to have a different clinician treat the client to prevent continuing on a path of unproductiveness.

Another problem that arises in treatment is when the clinician does not correctly assess the client's level of motivation for change. What the clinician perceives as treatment nonresponse may be a misinterpretation of the client's motivation for change. This can lead to differing expectations and the clinician's working at a motivational level that the client has not yet reached. Patients with lower motivation to change, who do not feel that their substance use is a problem or who feel unable to make changes in the next 6 months, still warrant treatment but perhaps cannot make use of intensive treatment modalities created for patients who are actively working to abstain from substances. Prochaska and DiClemente's (1983) five stages of change are a useful guide in understanding levels of readiness to change.

Motivational enhancement therapy (MET) improves a client's ability and readiness for change. The usefulness of MET is most evident when the clinician has assessed the client correctly. Employing contemplation strategies for clients in the precontemplation stage is likely to be met with nonresponse. Likewise, to approach the client from a precontemplation standpoint when the client is in the preparation stage may be interpreted by the client as the clinician's not listening.

For the less-motivated patient, the short-term goals include increasing motivation and harm reduction related to the substance use. This might include decreasing associated risks such as sharing needles or helping a client to reduce current usage. As motivation to change increases, the goals of treatment include shifting from harm reduction to abstinence. MET techniques for the less-motivated patient include being empathic, eliciting self-motivational statements, gathering information, handling nonresponse, collaborating with a significant other, and summarizing information presented by the client.

Patients with coexisting substance use disorders and mood disorders may be unmotivated in large part because of their depression. One of cardinal symptoms of major depressive disorder is hopelessness, and individuals who are hopeless about their futures generally do not demonstrate a great deal of motivation to work at tasks (e.g., substance abuse treatment) that they see as having no chance of positively affecting their lives. Thus, although these patients may seem primarily unmotivated, their lack of motivation cannot be disentangled from their depression. An integrated treatment approach can be particularly helpful. Pointing out ways in which depression is making substance abuse treatment more difficult can help the patient put this into perspective and be less likely to give up. Pointing out similarities in mood-disordered thinking and addictive thinking is the foundation of the treatment that Weiss and colleagues (1998, 2000) developed for patients with bipolar disorder and substance dependence; this approach has had promising results.

Gambling and Other Habitual Problematic Behaviors

In some cases, patients have other problematic behaviors that are inappropriate or excessive and cause distress or impairment in functioning. Some of the behaviors, such as gambling, have a richer research base (Blume, 1995). Most of the other behaviors, such as overeating, sexual compulsions, codependence, overworking, and overspending, are described in the recovery clinical literature and have a smaller research base.

Clinically these problematic behaviors are characterized by a repetitive pattern, a loss of control, escalation despite attempts to reduce behavior, and a tolerance of or need for greater risk to produce the desired sensation. These problematic behaviors also show patterns of an inordinate amount of time spent in thinking about and preparing for the behavior as well as recovering from the experience; persistent desire and unsuccessful efforts to control the behavior; chronic and progressive course marked by preoccupation, loss of control, and cravings; denial of behavior and consequences; and continued engagement in behavior even when it causes serious family, financial, occupational, health, and social problems.

The coexistence of pathological gambling and substance abuse in treatment populations seems well established, with considerably higher rates of gambling in substance abusers than in the general population (Ciarrocchi, 1993). It is estimated that 39–52 percent of pathological gamblers have coexisting alcohol or drug problems (Linden, Pope, and Jonas, 1986; Ramirez et al., 1984). Hypersexuality or problematic sexuality is estimated to have a prevalence of 3–6 percent in the U.S. population, although there is lack of consensus regarding an accurate name for this phenomenon. Some authors have raised concerns about its existence (Carnes, 1991; Gold and Heffner, 1998). Levine and Troiden (1988) contested that conceptualizing sexual behavior as disease threatens the civil liberties of sexually variant peoples. In contrast, others have asserted that problematic sexuality is not just an excess of activity but a maladaptive pattern associated with distress, depression, guilt, and an inability to control sexual behavior (Coleman, 1992).

Comorbidity between eating disorders and substance abuse occurs more often than expected by chance, with familial patterns for both. Alcohol and drugs can affect eating and food preferences, with marijuana leading to increased eating and nicotine decreasing intake through its central effects on satiety centers in the brain (Gold, Johnson, and Stennie, 1997).

The greatest obstacle to identifying the presence of other problematic behaviors during active addiction is that many associated behaviors resemble those linked to substance abuse. It has long been the belief in the field that the first year of recovery is dedicated to achieving physical sobriety and that byproducts of the disease and deeper issues should be addressed only later. In fact, many of the dangerous and self-destructive behaviors displayed during active substance abuse do not vanish at the beginning of sobriety. Even after addiction has been treated, existing problematic behaviors (Esterly and Neely, 1997) and personality disorders (Thomas, 1999) do not disappear.

Differentiating the "high anxiety" addicted person from the "sensation seeking" addicted person helps predict the kind of problematic behavior in which the addict is most likely to engage. A "high anxiety" addicted person is more likely to be "workaholic" (i.e., focus on work to the exclusion of other activities and relationships) or to have an eating disorder. A "sensation seeking" addicted person is more likely to be a gambler and sex/relationship addict or to engage in high-risk behaviors. More recently, other problematic behaviors have been emerging — devotion to computer and exercise to the exclusion of other activities and relationships. See table 7.1 for examples of problematic behaviors and their common manifestations.

Addressing Problematic Behaviors during Treatment

We need to educate the client about the manifestations of addiction and problematic behaviors. One treatment model exemplifying this approach is the Desjardins Unified Model of Addiction Treatment, which is an integrated, manualized addictions treatment (Eick, 1998). This therapy approach blends ego-identity and spirituality concepts with aspects of cognitive-behavioral therapy, motivational enhancement therapy, 12-step meetings, psychoeducation, and peer support. The technique relies heavily on shifting of the self-percep-

Table 7.1. Categories and Examples of Behavior Disorders and Problematic Behaviors

Problem Categories	Examples of Problematic Behaviors
Eating disorders	A repetitive pattern of eating more food than one wishes to eat; continued eating after the appetite has been satisfied to the point of physical discomfort; eating even when one is not hungry; eating to alter mood.
Pathological gambling	Preoccupation with gambling, gambling action, and gambling strategies; gambling activity used to alter mood; preoccupation with anticipated future wins.
Sexual-relationship problems	A pattern of sexual behaviors or relationships used to alter mood; a need for increased amount or intensity of the sexual behavior to achieve the desired effect; markedly diminished effect with continued involvement in the sexual behavior at the same level of intensity; preoccupation with pornography; repeated, increasing brief romantic involvement.
Work problems	An inordinate amount of time spent at work at the expense of family time; decreased socializing and recreation; alienation from spouse or children; friendless; social isolation.

tion identity from the "addict-self" to the "true-self," which is more forgiving, compassionate, and spiritual. Problem behaviors are defined and linked to the substance use so their interactions and role in recovery can be understood. Consider the following case.

Case 1. John is a 31-year-old, single man with a history of bipolar disorder. He entered treatment after an arrest for driving under the influence of alcohol. John initially began drinking while in college and soon found that he was able to drink significantly more than his friends in a heavy-drinking fraternity. He had two visits to the emergency room for alcohol poisoning while in college and was arrested for driving while under the influence at the age of 24.

In his mid-20s, John began to experience episodes of "moodiness," with periods of depression "like a cloud descending on me" lasting up to several weeks. During these times, he slept much of the time, ate very little, felt extremely anxious, and went to work only sporadically. He worked at a series of entry-level jobs and lost them for sporadic attendance. He rarely drank, however, during these periods because "I didn't have the energy to drink when I was that depressed." Although he was not actively suicidal, he often thought that he would be better off dead.

At the age of 26, John began to see a psychiatrist, who initiated treatment with a serotinergic antidepressant. His mood improved initially, but after several months he experienced a hypomanic episode, with grandiosity, flight of ideas, increased energy, very little need to sleep, and, in his mind, a new "creative spirit." The psychiatrist recommended that he take lithium, but the patient was only intermittently compliant "because it made me feel dead." He liked the extra energy that he experienced while his mood was elevated. When he was hypomanic, he frequented the racetrack. At the track, he typically drank heavily, occasionally used cocaine, and gambled heavily. He piled up debts and began borrowing and eventually stealing money from his parents to finance his gambling activities. When his mood dropped, however, and he became very depressed, he would not go to the racetrack and his drinking would fall off greatly.

This pattern continued for several years. His psychiatrist frequently urged him to go to AA meetings and Gamblers Anonymous meetings, but John refused to do so. When his girlfriend left him because he had stolen money from her purse while hypomanic, he was convinced to enter Gamblers Anonymous and AA as well. However, he was unable to abstain from both gambling and drinking for more than several weeks at a time. During the past 2 years, his relapse to drinking has been preceded by gambling. Even when he had been compliant with his medications, attending the racetrack would so excite him that his sleep patterns would be disrupted. Moreover, his medication compliance was erratic after his gambling. Thus, in John's case, the mixture of pathological gambling, alcohol dependence, and bipolar disorder led to frequent relapses among the other disorders.

Conclusion

Failure of response to treatment for addiction should alert the clinician to the usual causes for treatment nonresponse:

- inaccurate diagnosis
- inadequate treatment of correct diagnosis
- failure to recognize an underlying medical condition
- clinician-client mismatch or mismatch of motivation to change stage
- failure to detect a secondary drug use or compulsive behavior

Making these distinctions during active substance use or in the early weeks of abstinence poses a challenge. As the weeks and months go by, familiarity with the usual course of recovery alerts the clinician that the patient is manifesting nonresponse to treatment.

REFERENCES

Alterman, A. I., M. J. Rutherford, J. S. Cacciola, et al. 1998. Prediction of 7 months methadone maintenance treatment response by four measures of antisociality. *Drug and Alcohol Dependence* 49:217–23.

Amsterdam, J. D., D. L. Marinelli, P. Arger, et al. 1987. Assessment of adrenal gland volume by computerized tomography in depressed patients and health volunteers: A pilot study. *Psychiatry Research* 21:189–97.

Benazzi, F. 1997. Presence of bipolar II disorder in outpatient depression: A 20-3 case study in private practice. *Journal of Affective Disorders* 43:163–66.

Blume, S. B. 1995. Pathological gambling. *BMJ* 31:522–23.

Boyle, M. J., L. Vella, and E. Moloney. 1991. Role of drugs and alcohol in patients with head injury. *Journal of the Royal Society of Medicine* 84(10):608–10.

Brown, S. A., M. Irwin, and M. A. Schuckit. 1991. Changes in anxiety among abstinent male alcoholics. *Journal of Studies on Alcohol* 52:55–61.

Buydens-Branchley, L., M. H. Branchley, and D. Noumair. 1989. Age of alcoholism onset: Relationship to psychopathology. *Archives of General Psychiatry* 46:225–30.

Carnes, P. 1991. *Don't Call It Love: Recovery from Sexual Addiction.* New York: Bantam Books.

Cecero, J. J., S. A. Ball, H. Tennen, et al. 1999. Concurrent and predictive validity of antisocial personality disorder subtyping among substance abusers. *Journal of Nervous and Mental Disease* 187:478–86.

Charness, M. E. 1993. Brain lesions in alcoholics. *Alcoholism, Clinical Experimental Research* 17:2–11.

Ciarrocchi, J. W. 1993. Rates of pathological gambling in publicly funded outpatient substance abuse treatment. *Journal of Gambling Studies* 9:289–93.

Coleman, E. 1992. Is your patient suffering from compulsive sexual behavior? *Psychiatric Annals* 22(6):320–25.

Cottler, L. B., R. K. Price, W. M. Compton, et al. 1995. Subtypes of adult antisocial behavior among drug abusers. *Journal of Nervous and Mental Disease* 183:154–61.

Eckardt, M. J., and P. R. Martin. 1986. Clinical assessment of cognition in alcoholism. *Alcoholism, Clinical Experimental Research* 10:123–27.

Eick, C. 1998. *The Desjardins Unified Model of Addictions Therapy Manual.* Millspring, N.C.: Pavilion International.

Esterly, R. W., and W. T. Neely. 1997. *Chemical Dependency and Compulsive Behaviors.* Mahwah, N.J.: Lawrence Erlbaum Associates.

Fils-Aime, M. L., M. J. Eckardt, D. T. George, et al. 1996. Early-onset alcoholics have lower cerebrospinal fluid 5-hydroxyindoleacetic acid levels than late-onset alcoholics. *Archives of General Psychiatry* 53:211–16.

Franken, I. H., and V. M. Hendriks. 2000. Early-onset of illicit substance use is associated with greater axis II comorbidity, not with axis I comorbidity. *Drug and Alcohol Dependence* 59:305–8.

Gold, M. S., C. R. Johnson, and K. Stennie. 1997. Eating disorders. In *Substance Abuse: A Comprehensive Textbook*, 3d ed., edited by J. H. Lowinson, P. Ruiz, R. B. Millman, and J. G. Langrod, 319–20. Baltimore: Williams & Wilkins.

Gold, S. N., and C. L. Heffner. 1998. Sexual addiction: Many conceptions, minimal data. *Clinical Psychology Review* 18(3):367–81.

Greenhouse, J. B., D. J. Kupfer, E. Frank, et al. 1987. Analysis of time to stabilization in the treatment of depression: Biological and clinical correlates. *Journal of Affective Disorders* 13:259–66.

Kosten, T. R., and B. J. Rounsaville. 1986. Psychopathology in opioid addicts. *Psychiatric Clinics of North America* 9:515–32.

Kranzler, H. R. 1996. Evaluation and treatment of anxiety symptoms and disorders in alcoholics. *Journal of Clinical Psychiatry* 57(suppl 7):15–21; discussion 22–24.

Kranzler, H. R., J. A. Burleson, F. K. Del Boca, et al. 1994. Buspirone treatment of anxious alcoholics. *Archives of General Psychiatry* 51:720–31.

Kushner, M. G., K. R. Sher, and B. D. Beitman. 1990. The relation between alcohol problems and the anxiety disorders. *American Journal of Psychiatry* 147(6):685–95.

Levine, M. P., and R. R. Troiden. 1998. The myth of sexual compulsivity. *Journal of Sex Research* 25:347–63.

Linden, R. D., H. D. Pope, and J. M. Jonas. 1986. Pathological gambling and major affective disorder: Preliminary findings. *Journal of Clinical Psychiatry* 134:558–59.

Linehan, M. M., H. Schmidt, L. A. Dimeff, et al. 1999. Dialectical behavior therapy for patients with borderline personality disorder and drug-dependence. *American Journal on Addictions* 4:279–92.

McKay, J. R., A. I. Alterman, J. S. Cacciola, et al. 2000. Prognostic significance of antisocial personality disorder in cocaine-dependent patients entering continuing care. *Journal of Nervous and Mental Disease* 188(5):287–96.

Nemeroff, C. B., K. R. Krishnan, and D. Reed. 1992. Adrenal gland enlargement in major depression: A computerized tomographic study. *Archives of General Psychiatry* 49:384–87.

New, A. S., J. Gelernter, Y. Yovell, et al. 1998. Tryptophan hydroxylase genotype is associated with impulsive-aggressive measures: A preliminary study. *American Journal of Medical Genetics* 81:13–17.

Parkinson, D., S. Stephensen, and S. Phillips. 1985. Head injuries: A prospective, computerized study. *Canadian Journal of Surgery* 28(1):79–83.

Prochaska, J. O., and C. C. DiClemente. 1983. Stages and processes of self-change of smoking: Toward an integrative model of change. *Journal of Consulting and Clinical Psychology* 51(3):390–95.

Ramirez, L. F., R. A. McCormick, A. M. Russo, et al. 1984. Patterns of substance abuse in pathological gamblers undergoing treatment. *Addictive Behaviors* 8:425–28.

Regier, D. A., M. E. Farmer, D. S. Rae, et al. 1990. Comorbidity of mental disorders with alcohol and other drug abuse: Results from the Epidemiologic Catchment Area (ECA) study. *Journal of the American Medical Association* 264:2511–18.

Rounsaville, B. J., S. L. Eyre, M. M. Weissman, et al. 1983. The antisocial opiate addict. In *Psychosocial Constructs: Alcoholism and Substance Abuse*, edited by B. Stimmel. New York: Haworth Press.

Rounsaville, B. J., T. R. Kosten, M. M. Weissman, et al. 1986. Prognostic significance of psychopathology in treated opiate addicts. *Archives of General Psychiatry* 43:739–45.

Rounsaville B. J., Z. S. Dolinsky, T. F. Babor, et al. 1987. Psychopathology as a predictor of treatment outcome in alcoholics. *Archives of General Psychiatry* 44:505–13.

Schubiner, H., A. Tzelepis, S. Milberger, et al. 2000. Prevalence of attention-deficit/hyperactivity disorder and conduct disorder among substance abusers. *Journal of Clinical Psychiatry* 61:244–51.

Schuckit, M. A., and V. Hesselbrock. 1994. Alcohol dependence and anxiety disorders: What is the relationship? *American Journal of Psychiatry* 151(12):1723–34.

Skodol, A. E., J. M. Oldham, and P. E. Gallagher. 1999. Axis II comorbidity of substance use disorders among patients referred for treatment of personality disorders. *American Journal of Psychiatry* 156(5):733–38.

Thase, M. E., and A. J. Rush. 1997. When at first you don't succeed: Sequential strategies for antidepressant nonresponders. *Journal of Clinical Psychiatry* 58(suppl 13):23–29.

Thomas, V. 1999. Substance dependence and personality disorders. *Journal of Studies on Alcohol* 60(2):271–77.

Trull, T. J., K. J. Sher, C. Minks-Brown, et al. 2000. Borderline personality disorder and substance use disorders: A review and integration. *Clinical Psychology Review* 20(2):235–53.

Victor, M., R. D. Adams, and G. H. Collins. 1989. *The Wernicke-Korasakoff Syndrome and Related Neurologic Disorder Due to Alcoholism and Malnutrition*, 2d ed. Philadelphia: F. A. Davis Co.

Volavka, J. 1999. The neurobiology of violence: An update. *Journal of Neuropsychiatry and Clinical Neuroscience* 11:3307–14.

Weiss, R. D., and D. C. Daley. 1994. *Understanding Personality Problems and Addiction*. Center City, Minn.: Hazelden.

Weiss, R. D., S. M. Mirin, M. L. Griffin, et al. 1993. Personality disorders in cocaine dependence. *Comprehensive Psychiatry* 34:145–49.

Weiss, R. D., S. F. Greenfield, L. M. Najavits, et al. 1998. Medication compliance among patients with bipolar disorder and substance use disorder. *Journal of Clinical Psychiatry* 59:172–74.

Weiss, R. D., M. E. Kolodziej, L. M. Najavits, et al. 2000. Utilization of psychosocial treatments by patients diagnosed with bipolar disorder and substance dependence. *American Journal on Addictions* 9:314–20.

Woody, G. E., A. T. McLellan, L. Luborsky, et al. 1985. Sociopathy and psychotherapy outcome. *Archives of General Psychiatry* 42:1081–86.

Zimmerman, M., and J. I. Mattia. 1999. Axis I diagnostic comorbidity and borderline personality disorder. *Comprehensive Psychiatry* 40(4):245–52.

8

Addressing Tobacco Dependence in Integrated Treatment

John Slade, M.D., and
Betty Vreeland, M.S.N., R.N., N.P.-C., C.S.

Addressing tobacco use and dependence will reduce illness and death. Smoking may play a more insidious role than drinking in the use and development of dependence on illicit substances and in depression (Hanna and Grant, 1999). Compared to the general population, people with addictive and other psychiatric disorders have extremely high rates of tobacco use. The rate of smoking among substance abusers is two to three times that of the general population (National Institute on Alcohol Abuse and Alcoholism [NIAAA], 1998).

Striking interrelationships exist between tobacco use and depression. Cigarette smoking is associated with major depressive disorder. Depressive symptoms and a history of depression are associated with a substantially increased difficulty in quitting (Glassman et al., 1988, 1990; Hall, Muñoz, and Reus, 1994). Nicotine withdrawal provokes depressive symptoms in some individuals, and depressive symptoms have been shown to trigger cravings to smoke. Health risks increase in persons with depression and substance use disorders who smoke (Linkins and Comstock, 1990; NIAAA, 1998). Tobacco-related diseases are the leading cause of death in patients previously treated for alcoholism or other nontobacco dependence disorders (Hurt et al., 1996). Dr. Bob and Bill W., the cofounders of Alcoholics Anonymous, died from tobacco-related illnesses.

As the culture becomes less accepting of smoking, this problem becomes more tractable for clinicians interested in addictions and mental disorders. Patients with comorbid psychiatric and other addictive disorders frequently need skilled intervention. Professionals and systems often lack the specific expertise needed to treat psychiatric patients with comorbid nicotine addiction.

Epidemiology

Nicotine is one of the most widely abused substances. Given the health problems caused by tobacco products and the public's general awareness of those problems, its use is surprisingly prevalent. Recent data estimate that 25 percent of the U.S. adult population smoke cigarettes (about 48 million people), 25 percent used to smoke but have quit, and 50 percent have never smoked regularly (National Health Interview Survey, 1995). Smoking is becoming less prevalent. In 1965, 42.4 percent of adults in the United States smoked, 13.6 percent were former smokers, and 44.0 percent had never smoked.

As the casual smokers are eliminated from the smoker pool or discouraged from ever starting smoking, smoking is becoming increasingly concentrated among people with comorbid psychiatric and addictive disorders. Depending on the diagnosis, the prevalence of smoking in this population ranges from 50 percent to 95 percent (Buchanan, Huffman, and Barber, 1994; Glassman, 1993; Goff, Henderson, and Amico, 1992; Hughes et al., 1986; Kaplan and Saddock, 1994; NIAAA, 1998; Ziedonis et al., 1994).

Extensive research confirms the common observation that "smokers drink and drinkers smoke" (NIAAA, 1998). The rate of smoking among substance abusers is 2–3 times that of the general population, with as many as 80–95 percent of alcoholics smoking (Hurt et al., 1996; NIAAA, 1998). Approximately 70 percent of alcoholic persons are heavy smokers (smoke more than one pack of cigarettes per day), compared with 10 percent of the general population. Adolescents who smoke are 3 times as likely to use alcohol, and smokers are 10 times more likely than nonsmokers to develop alcoholism (NIAAA, 1998).

There is an increased likelihood of smoking among patients with mood disorder. There is an extremely high prevalence (70%) of smoking among patients with mania (Hughes et al., 1986). Studies by Glassman and colleagues (1988,

1993, 1999) found that both major depression and depressive symptoms are associated with a high rate of cigarette smoking, and the more cigarettes that a person smokes, the more likely they are to have a history of depression. Sixty percent of smokers in one of his clinical studies, all of whom wanted to quit smoking, had a history of depression. He also found that individuals with a lifetime history of depression are more likely to have "ever smoked" (76%) than are those without such a history (52%) and that a history of depression doubled the chances of failing to quit smoking.

The Rationale for Addressing Tobacco Dependence

Treatment Works

A large and growing body of literature demonstrates the benefits of helping people address their tobacco use (Agency for Health Care Policy and Research [AHCPR], 1996a, 1996b; American Psychiatric Association [APA], 1996; Fiore et al., 2000; Orleans and Slade, 1993). Scientifically established clinical methods, often supported by adjunctive medication, help people stop using tobacco. Although treatment is more complicated for individuals with a prior history of depression and clinicians need to monitor these individuals for the re-emergence of depressive symptoms, specialized treatment is effective (Hall et al. 1994, 1996, 1998).

How well treatment works depends on a lot of things. It depends on the set and setting of the client; the skill, interest, and experience of the clinician; whether there is a coexisting psychiatric condition; and whether special strategies are used to deal with smokers with coexisting mood disorder. In general, the more intensive and extensive the treatment, the better the outcome. Overall, using an adjunctive medication (nicotine replacement therapy [NRT] or bupropion) doubles the chances of success from any one attempt to quit.

Tobacco Dependence Is a Chronic, Relapsing Disease

Tobacco dependence begins in childhood or early adolescence and generally persists for decades. Along the way, people try to stop, with more or less success, repeatedly. Relapse is common. Once a sustained abstinence is achieved, it can be undermined by slips and relapse. In the general population, one-third of smokers try to stop each year, but less than 10 percent of those succeed. With repeated tries, about half of ever-smokers have quit. Those who continue to smoke despite repeated tries are regarded as more heavily addicted (Fagerstrom et al., 1997) and often have comorbid conditions such as depression or another substance disorder. Some persons who have had multiple drug problems describe nicotine as the most difficult drug to stop (Kozlowski et al., 1989). However, many of these people have not had an opportunity to receive appropriate treatment for their tobacco dependence.

Stopping Tobacco Use Averts Unnecessary Illness and Early Death

There is a high correlation between increased health risks and the abuse of alcohol or other drugs or the use of tobacco in depressed persons. For example, the risks for developing mouth and throat cancer are 7 times greater for those who use tobacco, 6 times greater for those who use alcohol, and 38 times greater for those who use both tobacco and alcohol (NIAAA, 1998). Hurt and colleagues (1996) found that the death rate among persons previously treated for alcoholism or for other nonnicotine drug dependencies was twice that of the general population. Moreover, the major finding in this study was that tobacco-related diseases were the leading cause of death among patients previously treated for alcoholism or other nonnicotine drug dependence. Additionally, there is evidence that depressed persons are at increased risk of dying of smoking-related and non-smoking-related cancers versus nondepressed smokers (Linkins and Comstock, 1990).

When a person stops smoking, the carbon monoxide is gone within a day. The nicotine is gone that fast, too, unless the person is using NRT. Even then, the nicotine the person takes in with NRT does not come in surges like it does with smoking, making it less reinforcing and probably less likely to cause circulatory problems (Benowitz, Zevin, and Jacob, 1998). These changes can improve exercise tolerance and, for people with angina, reduce pain right away.

Patients Often Want to Deal with It

Simultaneous treatment of smoking and other addictions, once considered undesirable, has been shown to be mutually reinforcing (Howard and Hughes, 1995; Hurt et al., 1993). Smoking is a predictor of greater problem severity and poorer treatment response (Roll et al., 1996; Stuyt, 1997). Similarly, both acute cocaine administration (Roll, Higgins, and Tidey, 1997) and methadone administration (Schmitz, Grabowski, and Rhoades, 1994) have been shown to increase cigarette consumption, and at least one clinical study has shown re-duced cigarette use after successful treatment for cocaine dependence (Wise-man and McMillan, 1998).

Alcohol and drug users are interested in smoking cessation treatment (Clem-ney et al., 1997; Kozlowski et al., 1989). This is especially so when the clinical setting invites discussion of tobacco as a problem it is willing to address. When clients are asked about tobacco cessation, many want to attempt it (Buchanan, Huffman, and Barbour, 1994; Orleans and Slade, 1993).

Although many individuals with mental illness are not ready to quit smok-ing, some want to address their addiction to tobacco. Buchanan and colleagues (1994), in a study in a state hospital, found that 90 percent of patients smoked. Nurses believed that 88 percent of these patients were not interested in quit-ting smoking, whereas nearly two-thirds of the patients said they would use help from a nurse if it were available. Patients identified assistance with with-drawal (46%), coping skills (42%), exercise and activities (34%), and emotional support (34%) as the interventions that would be most helpful to them in quit-ting smoking.

Addressing Tobacco Problems in Clients Is a Necessary Part of Controlling Environmental Tobacco Smoke

Tobacco smoke harms exposed nonsmokers as well as smokers (California En-vironmental Protection Agency, 1997; U.S. Environmental Protection Agency, 1992; Woodward and Laugesen, 2001). Because it is such a common exposure, the level of harm places environmental tobacco smoke among the top causes of illness and death from pollution. It is a cause of lung cancer, heart disease, exacerbations of asthma, nasal sinus cancer, and a range of respiratory prob-lems in young and old alike.

In a clinical setting, limiting or eliminating places where smoking is per-mitted serves an additional purpose beyond pollution control. For clients who are trying to stop smoking, seeing others smoke or knowing that others are smoking can undermine efforts to stop. The sight or smell of another person smoking is the leading trigger for relapse. If the rule is that there is no smok-ing, both for pollution control and for the sake of those who are trying to learn how not to smoke, then everyone who uses tobacco in a clinical setting where addictions and mental illness are treated should have treatment for tobacco de-pendence readily available.

Smoke-Free Psychiatric Settings

Many psychiatric inpatient units have a policy of being smoke-free. The APA
(1996) recommends a smoke-free psychiatric unit because it is very difficult to
motivate inpatients to stop smoking unless the unit is smoke-free.

Patients need to be educated about the public health rationale for a smoke-
free unit. They should also be educated about the goals of therapy, which include treatment of their tobacco dependence, including withdrawal symptoms. In part because of the absence of smoking cues, nicotine withdrawal
during hospitalization is often not as severe as anticipated. The APA practice
guideline (1996) recommends that patients be assessed for nicotine withdrawal
and be monitored for changes in psychiatric symptoms, nicotine withdrawal
symptoms, and side effects of medications because levels of several psychiatric
medications can be altered. The use of psychosocial treatments and pharmacological therapies should be considered.

Some Patients Have an Urgent Need to Address
Their Tobacco Dependence

Complications from tobacco often seem a distant, merely theoretical matter,
but they are an immediate problem for many clients. Persons with asthma, diabetes, sickle cell disease, or human immunodeficiency virus (HIV) infection
will have immediate improvements in health if they stop smoking. Similarly,
persons who are or who might become pregnant and persons who already have
complications of tobacco use such as chronic obstructive pulmonary disease
(COPD) or heart disease should not be delayed by institutional inertia in coming to terms with their tobacco problem. A newly diagnosed tobacco-induced
medical problem can be an ideal motivator for a patient to quit smoking.

Insurance Coverage for Treating Tobacco Dependence Is Usually Limited

While it is common for a person to have health insurance coverage for treatment of depression, cocaine dependence, or alcohol dependence, it is uncommon for a person to have insurance coverage for the treatment of tobacco
dependence. At a practical level, this means that treatment will not be provided
unless it happens during treatment for another condition. Fifteen years ago,

cocaine dependence was often not a covered condition. At that time, it was not unusual for a treatment program to search for another diagnosis to use for insurance purposes while addressing the cocaine problem at the same time. In these times, the same approach is appropriate for tobacco dependence.

There are encouraging signs of change among insurance carriers. Minnesota Blue Cross/Blue Shield has begun paying for treatment of tobacco dependence by physicians on the same basis as it pays for any other medical treatment (Blue Cross/Blue Shield of Minnesota, 2000). A consortium of carriers in California have added a moderate benefit for treatment of tobacco dependence to their coverage (Harris et al., 2001).

Tobacco Use Is Often a Trigger for Other Drug Use

Smoking is often linked with other drug use. There are probably both behavioral and pharmacological reasons for this association, and tobacco dependence is usually the first addiction a person develops. People who do not smoke have a greater likelihood of remaining abstinent after treatment for alcohol or heroin problems than do people who smoke (Stuyt, 1997). Both acute cocaine administration (Roll, Higgins, and Tidey, 1997) and methadone administration (Chait and Griffiths, 1984; Schmitz, Grabowski, and Rhoades, 1994) have been shown to increase cigarette consumption, and at least one clinical study has shown reduced cigarette use after successful treatment for cocaine dependence (Wiseman and McMillan, 1998). Cues to smoke cigarettes lead to cravings for other drugs in those with multiple drug problems (National Institute on Drug Abuse, 2000). This finding strongly suggests that continued tobacco use poses a major risk of relapse to other drug use and strongly argues for dealing with tobacco in the course of other treatment for addictions.

Pathophysiology and Pharmacology

Nicotine dependence, like other drug addictions, is a progressive, chronic, relapsing disorder. Three distinct nicotine-related disorders have been recognized by the American Psychiatric Association (APA, 1994): (1) Nicotine Dependence; (2) Nicotine Withdrawal; and (3) Nicotine-Related Disorder, Not Otherwise Specified.

The International Classification of Diseases (ICD-10) also has a category for Tobacco Dependence. The pathophysiology of these disorders is now understood to involve the effects of nicotine at specific receptors, on cerebral metabolism, and on hormonal systems (Henningfield, 1994). The reward system that underlies nicotine addiction may play an important role in the psychopathology of addictive and other psychiatric disorders (Blum et al., 1995; Pomerleau, 1992). Dopaminergic reward pathways have frequently been implicated in the etiology of addictive behaviors. Nicotine, similar to several other drugs of abuse, activates the mesolimbic dopamine system, and this effect has been shown to play an important role in mediating the reinforcing effect of various drugs of abuse (Nisell, Nomikos, and Svensson, 1995). Thus, nicotine-like chemicals directly influence motivational systems.

Although many harmful health consequences are due to cigarettes, nicotine is frequently perceived to improve mood, especially among those with a predisposition toward negative affect. Smokers consistently report that smoking serves to reduce stress and anxiety. However, these reports come largely from persons addicted to nicotine and subject to withdrawal and withdrawal relief from drug ingestion. These beneficial effects may simply be the result of reduced withdrawal symptoms. Substantial evidence indicates that smoking actually increases overall levels of stress and negative affect (Parrott, 1999). For many people, particularly those with comorbid psychiatric conditions, the perceived benefits of smoking outweigh the perceived risks (Pomerleau, 1997) and certainly make it more difficult to quit.

Research has revealed that up to 60 percent of the variance associated with cigarette smoking is attributable to genetic factors (cf. Bergen and Caporoso, 1999). Studies suggest a genetic association between smoking and depression that predisposes an individual to both smoking and depression (Kendler et al., 1993). Data also have confirmed an association between dopamine D2 receptor gene variants and alcoholism, drug dependency, smoking, obesity, pathological gambling, and other related compulsive behaviors (Blum et al., 1995).

Managing Tobacco Dependence

Several ways to help psychiatric patients stop smoking have been described (Hall et al., 1994, 1996, 1998; Ziedonis and George, 1997). This section focuses on effective general treatment approaches and on methods that have helped people with mood disorders or other addictions quit smoking.

General Treatment Approaches

Clinical Practice Guidelines for Smoking Cessation. Both the Agency for Health Care Policy and Research and the American Psychiatric Association have developed clinical practice guidelines for smoking cessation. The AHCPR offers two sets of guidelines, both of which are based on the best available science (AHCPR, 1996a, 1996b), one for primary care clinicians and one for specialists in the treatment of tobacco dependence. These guidelines are available in their entirety through the Internet (www.ahcpr.gov/clinic/) or by phoning 800-358-9295.

Helping Smokers Quit: A Guide for Primary Care Clinicians (AHCPR, 1996a) primarily targets primary care providers. It recommends that *all* clinicians integrate the following guidelines into their clinical practice to be effective in helping smokers quit:

- Ask about smoking at every visit.
- Advise tobacco users to quit.
- Assist the patient with a quit plan.

Steps for the clinician to follow include:

- Offer smoking cessation treatment at every office visit.
- Ask about and record the tobacco-use status of every patient.
- Offer intensive smoking cessation programs.
- Consider three particularly effective treatment strategies: (1) nicotine replacement therapy, (2) clinician-provided social support, and (3) skills-training/problem-solving techniques.
- Schedule follow-up contact, either in person or by telephone.
- Prevent relapse: offer ex-smokers reinforcement.

The APA Practice Guideline for the Treatment of Patients with Nicotine Dependence (APA, 1996) details specific guidelines that target smokers for whom primary care treatment has failed, psychiatric patients, and patients in smoke-free facilities. It builds on the AHCPR guideline by focusing on specific populations and by providing detail on more intensive treatments.

The recommended strategies for all psychiatric patients who smoke are

- Assess smoking behavior, motivation to quit, motivators and barriers to quitting.
- Establish a therapeutic alliance.
- Advise patient to stop.
- Assist in cessation.
- Arrange follow-up.

The APA guideline recommends that psychiatrists should assess the smoking status of all their patients regularly and, if the patient is a smoker, should discuss interest in quitting and give personalized advice to help motivate the patient to stop smoking. The guideline recognizes that many psychiatric patients are not ready to stop smoking and that the goal of advice will often be to motivate patients to contemplate cessation (APA, 1996).

Medications. The Food and Drug Administration has approved four forms of nicotine replacement (patch, gum, oral inhaler, and nasal spray) and one antidepressant (bupropion) for the management of tobacco dependence. Each of these drugs can double the chances of success with quitting, but success is often hindered when people do not use these medicines effectively, for long enough, or with effective behavioral support. Research reveals that combining patch with gum or patch with bupropion may increase the quit rate compared with any single treatment (Hughes et al., 1999). This combination approach should be considered and may be particularly effective in patients with a history of depression or treatment resistance.

Nicotine replacement therapy is designed to suppress withdrawal symptoms. For gum, inhaler, and nasal spray, the medicine can also be mildly reinforcing, so these medicines can be used in situations that would otherwise lead to smoking a cigarette. NRT products deliver nicotine more slowly than tobacco products do, and they deliver only nicotine, not any of the thousands of other materials found in tobacco smoke.

Both patch and gum are available over the counter. Although package instructions ask consumers not to use tobacco products once either product is started, many patients find that they are not completely abstinent at first. This should not cause panic or discouragement. It simply means that quitting is often difficult. If the person has substantially reduced tobacco use and is using NRT consistently, then the therapeutic plan should attend to problem solving around the remaining cigarettes, paying close attention to the circumstances in which smoking still occurs, with an immediate goal of achieving a cigarette-free day.

The dose of NRT should be individualized. The idea is for patients to feel comfortable and, once comfortable, to reduce the dose at a pace that is, well, comfortable. Achieving this often means raising or lowering the dose from the starting level and continuing the medication for a highly variable length of time, from a few weeks to many months. Sometimes, it is helpful to supplement nicotine patch with nicotine gum. The patch serves as baseline medicine, and the gum both permits finer titration and facilitates response to external and internal cues.

Patients should be instructed in the use of the gum:

• Use enough. Each dose lasts about 30 minutes and provides less nicotine than an average cigarette.

• Use it more like chewing tobacco, holding it in the cheek most of the time, instead of like chewing gum. If it is chewed like chewing gum, less nicotine is absorbed through the mouth and more is swallowed. The swallowed nicotine can produce an upset stomach and, because of hepatic metabolism, less reaches the brain.

• Do not use gum within about 30 minutes of having something to drink. Most beverages (water, coffee, soda) are acidic and will shut down the oral absorption of nicotine from the gum.

The other approved medicine for the treatment of tobacco dependence is bupropion, marketed for this indication as Zyban. Bupropion consistently doubles quit rates compared to placebo and seems to work equally effectively in smokers with and without a history of depression (Hughes et al., 1999). Smokers with a history of seizures, anorexia, heavy alcohol use, or head trauma should not use bupropion. The other trade name given to bupropion is Wellbutrin. It is frequently prescribed for depression. Bupropion would be a likely antidepressant to consider in depressed persons who want to quit smoking. If the patient is already on bupropion and is still smoking, an assessment as to whether the patient is on an effective dose should be made. Although the labeling suggests a limited duration of therapy, this simply follows the design of the clinical trials used to show efficacy. In practice, some patients benefit from using this drug for shorter or for longer periods. Some find that depressive symptoms lift and so continue the medicine for that reason.

Nortriptyline has also been reported to help people stop smoking (Hall, Reus, and Muñoz, 1998). In this study, nortriptyline produced higher abstinence rates than placebo in persons with and without a prior history of depression. It also alleviated negative affect that occurred after quitting smoking. To date, there are no compelling data indicating that the selective serotonin reuptake inhibitors (SSRIs) are beneficial in helping people stop smoking.

Motivational Issues

A key factor, perhaps the most important, is the attitude of the clinical staff and its willingness to deal with tobacco dependence and the ramifications of addressing it (Resnick, 1993; Rustin, 1998). Although behavioral health professionals are in the ideal position to integrate treatment of tobacco dependence, this is not routinely done. For instance, although many treatment programs have been developed to address the mentally ill chemical abuser (MICA), and a high percentage of MICA patients smoke, treatment for tobacco dependence is rarely included in programming. In fact, in a recent staff survey by one of the authors, MICA staff had not even considered listing nicotine dependence as a diagnosis on their patients. To a great extent, if the staff thinks dealing with tobacco dependence can and should be done, then it can be done.

We have found that, to effect change among patients, it is essential to direct efforts at changing agency and staff attitudes first. As agency and staff attitudes changed, a corresponding change was seen among the patients. Patients move from the precontemplation to the contemplative stage of being ready to quit smoking. Patients who have successfully quit smoking often report that mental health professionals were key in their efforts at quitting.

Factors affecting internal motivation also should be addressed. Since many depressed patients are not ready to quit, the goal of treatment will often be to motivate patients to contemplate quitting. Mental health professionals should be prepared to assist them in moving through the stages of change (Prochaska, DiClemente, and Norcross, 1992). Psychotherapeutic strategies such as motivational interviewing (Miller and Rollnick, 2002) can be modified to address tobacco in various addiction and psychiatric settings. The goal of these motivational strategies is to match the intervention with the particular stage of change of the patient. A fundamental assumption underlying motivational interviewing is that interventions appropriate for one level of motivation may be entirely inappropriate for another. For instance, the intervention for a patient in the precontemplation stage of quitting smoking would not be to advise the patient to attempt to cut down on the number of cigarettes smoked. Such an approach would probably be met with noncompliance and resistance. A more appropriate intervention would be to ask the patient to consider the advantages and disadvantages of quitting smoking, to offer education about the health risks associated with smoking, and to discuss openly the patient's ambivalence around quitting. Motivational interviewing is as much a matter of fundamental attitudes and assumptions as it is of techniques. Respect, patience, empathy, and a willingness to listen are combined with an active approach that emphasizes Socratic questioning and guided reflection. Clients are assumed to be ambivalent rather than purely resistant. For more information about this powerful approach to working with addictive behaviors, see Miller and Rollnick (1991) or Ziedonis and Krejci (2000; chap. 5 in this volume).

Clinical Issues Concerning Patients with a History of Depression

Numerous research reports suggest that depression is one of the major obstacles to quitting smoking. In fact, smokers with a history of major depressive disorder fail at their attempts to quit smoking more than twice as often as those without such a history (Glassman, 1993). The reasons that persons with a propensity for depression have difficulty quitting are not clearly understood. In part, it is hypothesized that the stimulating, mood-elevating properties of nicotine may be used by depressed smokers as a mood management technique (Kinnunen et al., 1996). Although depression is not a common symptom of nicotine withdrawal, it does occur frequently among smokers with a prior history of major depression and occurs more often among those who relapse. Additionally, all of the withdrawal symptoms from nicotine, especially difficulty concentrating, are worse in persons with a history of depression (Glassman, 1999).

The link between new-onset major depression after tobacco dependence treatment in persons with a prior history of depression deserves special consideration. In one study, the 3-month incidence of new major depression after treatment for tobacco dependence was 2 percent, 17 percent, and 30 percent among subjects with histories of no major depression, single major depression, and recurrent major depression, respectively (Covey, Glassman, and Stetner, 1997). Glassman (1999) found that 2–4 percent of persons without a history of depression become depressed after quitting, whereas 20–25 percent of people with a prior history of major depression become depressed during the acute treatment phase. He further found that there continues to be a serious rate of re-exacerbation of major depressive disorder when these patients are weaned off medication that treats their nicotine dependence. The period of vulnerability of developing a new depressive episode ranges from a few weeks to several months after abstinence is achieved (Covey, Glassman, and Stetner, 1998).

Glassman (1999) points out that a difficulty in interpreting these data is that people with a history of depression are likely to experience another episode of major depression even without a potential precipitant such as stopping smoking. It is unclear how many of these subjects would have experienced a re-exacerbation of depression if they had not quit smoking. However, it does seem that for some of these people smoking may self-medicate symptoms of depression. In fact, in one study, nicotine patches produced short-term improvement of depression in nonsmoking patients with major depression (Salín-Pascual et al., 1996).

Although treatment is more complicated for individuals with a prior history of depression, specialized treatment works. For example, Ziedonis and George (1997) describe a smoking cessation model using NRT, motivational enhancement therapy, and relapse prevention therapy. Although developed for patients with schizophrenia, this model also is applicable to people with depression. For patients who state that depression intensified with smoking cessation or that cessation caused depression, the APA treatment guideline recommends that the clinician consider starting or restarting psychotherapy or pharmacology. This recommendation is based on research findings that cognitive behavioral therapy for depression and antidepressants improved smoking cessation rates in those with a past history of depression or symptoms of depression.

The Timing of Treatment for Tobacco Dependence in Patients with Comorbid Mood Disorders

Concerns are often expressed about when tobacco dependence should be addressed in the course of treating persons with other addictions and with psychiatric comorbidity. Clinical data suggest that smoking by mood-disordered patients may represent an attempt to self-medicate symptoms of their illnesses. High levels of nicotine dependence, psychiatric comorbidity, low levels of motivation to quit, and poor support systems predict a greater likelihood of relapse with attempts to quit smoking.

The clinician should emphasize several principles when helping psychiatric patients stop smoking:

- Attempt abstinence during a noncrisis period.
- Go slow, and be patient.
- The psychiatric condition (including symptoms and medication side effects) should be watched carefully by someone with psychiatric expertise.

It is harder for people with psychiatric problems to quit smoking, but many are successful. We have worked with patients with depression who were able to quit smoking without adverse psychiatric consequences. We have also witnessed patients with mood disorders who have attempted to stop smoking and who have had increased symptoms or been unable to tolerate nicotine withdrawal symptoms and have returned to smoking. Some of these patients have later been successful in their attempts at quitting.

Specialized Treatments for Depression and Smoking

Pharmacological Treatment. As with the nondepressed smoker, effective pharmacotherapy management is an important tool in aiding smokers with a history of depression. In one study, the benefits of nicotine gum were particularly apparent among depressed smokers. Only 12.5 percent of depressed smokers on placebo gum quit smoking as compared to 29.5 percent of depressed smokers on nicotine gum. However, clinicians should be aware that nicotine replacement treatments often relieve many but not all of the mood symptoms related to nicotine withdrawal and that depressed mood, restlessness, and hostility frequently remain (Hall, Muñoz, and Reus, 1993). We also found that treatment with NRT needs to be extended beyond the standard time frame in some psychiatric patients. Nortriptyline has been reported to help people stop smoking (Hall, Reus, and Muñoz, 1998). Nortriptyline produced higher abstinence rates than placebo in persons with and without a prior history of depression. It also alleviated negative affect that occurred after quitting smoking.

For a minimum of 6 months after the achievement of abstinence from tobacco, clinicians should monitor all patients with a past history of depression, particularly those with recurrent depressive episodes, for a re-emergence of depressive symptoms. These patients should receive a combined treatment approach using pharmacotherapy, motivational enhancement therapy, cognitive behavioral therapy, and relapse prevention therapy. If a client with a past history of depression who was no longer on an antidepressant medication wanted to quit smoking, the clinician should consider restarting antidepressant medication. Bupropion or nortriptyline would be good choices of medication. If the patient is already on an SSRI (fluoxetine, paroxetine, sertraline, citalopram, or fluvoxamine), there is no contraindication to adding bupropion (Wellbutrin, Zyban) to aid in quitting—although monitoring for serotonin toxicity should be implemented. Increasing the bupropion dose a little more slowly is warranted for such a patient. Perhaps the clinician may then consider tapering the SSRI if the patient remains stable after several months. If the patient is receiving venlafaxine (Effexor), the clinician would want to ensure monitoring of the patient's blood pressure. Zyban (bupropion) should not be added if the patient is already taking Wellbutrin (also bupropion) for depression. If the patient taking bupropion continues to smoke, its dose should be re-evaluated and the addition of nicotine replacement therapy should be considered, along with a thoughtful review of the behavioral and environmental factors that may be affecting the patient.

Smoking-Antidepressant Interactions. Tobacco smoke alters the way people respond to various medications. Tobacco smoke is an inducer of the cytochrome P450 enzyme system. It contains substances that can cause the cytochrome P450 enzymes in the liver to make drugs less effective and therefore reduce the serum levels of some medications. Consequently, some medication levels should be expected to rise on smoking cessation, and levels and side effects should be monitored carefully. Smoking cessation causes the blood levels of some antidepressants to rise (clomipramine, desipramine, doxcpin, imipramine, and nortriptyline). For the antidepressants amitriptyline and bupropion, smoking cessation does not cause their blood levels to rise. Thus far, there are no reported interactions between smoking, smoking cessation, and the SSRI medications (fluoxamine, fluoxetine, paroxetine, sertraline, or citalopram) or the newer, novel antidepressants, such as venlafaxine (Effexor), nefazodone (Serzone), or mirtazapine (Remeron).

Cognitive-Behavioral Interventions. Hall and colleagues (1994, 1996, 1998) developed an impressive model for treating smokers who have a history of depression. They demonstrated the effectiveness of a cognitive-behavioral intervention designed specifically for individuals with a history of depression (Hall, Muñoz, and Reus, 1994; Hall, Reus, and Muñoz, 1998). The main focus of the initial sessions is on smoking cessation, with a gradual shift in focus in later sessions to mood management techniques designed to prevent relapse to smoking. The protocol was designed to inform the participants of the relationship between negative mood and relapse and of the importance of teaching mood management techniques to reduce the probability that they would become demoralized enough to begin smoking. Initial sessions focus on developing plans for coping with a variety of negative mood states, including irritability, sadness, and anxiety. Strategies include self-distraction, deep breathing, imagining a relaxing scene, and reminding oneself that withdrawal and negative mood states are unpleasant but tolerable and will eventually end. The connection between negative thoughts and negative emotions is explained, and clients are encouraged to develop more realistic but positive responses to their negative internal monologue, particularly with regard to passive or fatalistic beliefs about achieving abstinence from tobacco. Clients learn to recognize negative cognitive styles, including tendencies toward all-or-nothing thinking, jumping to conclusions, magnifying failures and minimizing successes, and basing conclusions purely on emotional reactions. Treatment also addresses excessively negative and all-encompassing self-evaluations and the tendency to overattribute failures to permanent personality traits. The interested reader is referred to the detailed treatment manual by Muñoz, Organista, and Hall (1991).

Particularly important in working with the depressed smoker are smoking-related thoughts and beliefs. As noted earlier, many smokers attribute to smoking an almost magical power to alleviate negative affect and enhance concentration and motivation. These smokers are likely to view with extreme trepidation the prospect of giving up what they perceive to be their only tool for maintaining their happiness and equilibrium. The skilled clinician will gently but persistently begin to encourage clients to identify and question such overvalued ideas about the beneficial effects of smoking and to focus instead on the known dangers and on alternative sources of gratification and relaxation.

Also important are cognitive factors in managing nicotine withdrawal. As noted earlier, patients with a history of depression tend to suffer more extreme withdrawal symptoms, particularly in the domains of mood and concentration. It is likely that both physiological and psychological processes play a role in the patient's withdrawal experience. Those who tolerate frustration or discomfort poorly, who interpret withdrawal symptoms as medically dangerous, or who convince themselves that these negative symptoms are intolerable are probably at higher risk of resumed smoking. Cognitive techniques, many drawn from mainstream addictions treatment, can help clients to reinterpret withdrawal symptoms as finite and tolerable. One such technique, drawn from a relapse prevention procedure known as "urge surfing" (Marlatt and Gordon, 1985), encourages clients to attend closely but objectively to the physical sensations that accompany withdrawal and craving, while distancing themselves emotionally from the perceived urgency to smoke.

Behavioral Interventions. Many of the behavioral interventions recommended for tobacco dependence are based upon the principles of behavioral therapy and on the theory that learning processes operate in the development, maintenance, and cessation of smoking. The major goals of behavioral therapy for treating tobacco dependence are to change the antecedents to smoking, to reinforce nonsmoking, and to teach the patient new skills to avoid smoking. Behavioral therapy generally doubles success rates (APA, 1996) and is usually multimodal. Specific techniques include skills training and relapse prevention; stimulus control; aversive therapy, including aversive rapid smoking (Houtsmuller and Stitzer, 1999); cue exposure; social support; relaxation; nicotine fading; and physiological feedback. Different behavioral interventions have demonstrated effectiveness in predicting positive outcomes associated with smoking cessation.

Substance abuse clinicians can incorporate behavioral principles from addiction treatment into the treatment of tobacco dependence. Smoking is both a physiological dependence and a powerfully conditioned habit. The average smoker inhales more than one million times over the course of a lifetime. Cigarettes also tend to be strongly associated with particular mood states, activities, and times of day. Research and clinical experience suggest that strategies designed to interrupt the automatic connection between smoking and smoking-related cues and triggers is likely to be helpful. Calling a friend, taking a bath, watching television, writing in a journal, and taking a walk are all substitute activities that can serve to delay the first cigarette and thus to reduce the probability of succumbing to cravings. Self-reinforcement can also be a powerful tool. One such strategy involves encouraging clients to reward themselves with a special purchase bought with money saved by not smoking. Alternatively, clients can reward themselves with a valued activity after each day of abstinence from cigarettes.

Self-reward strategies can be particularly effective with depressed clients experiencing pervasive difficulties with motivation. An important behavioral technique in the treatment of depression involves having clients record for 1 week their pleasurable activities. The therapist then works with the client to create a behavioral plan intended to increase the frequency of pleasurable activities. Adapting this technique to include pleasurable activities as a reward for successful abstinence can act simultaneously to increase client activity and self-reinforcement for not smoking.

Learned helplessness theory suggests that depression is an understandable consequence of a failure or inability to exercise healthy control over one's environment. Confronted with stressors, those vulnerable to depression may react with anxiety and fear, appraising the situation as fraught with danger or potential failure. In response, they react with avoidance and withdrawal. Such clients will require patience and active support to maintain their resolve to quit smoking. The clinician should explain that relapses are the rule rather than the exception and that each failure is an opportunity to learn new strategies for maintaining abstinence.

Both cognitive and behavioral therapies demand that the practitioner be comfortable with an active, engaged, directive, and educational role. Treatment is typically highly focused and time limited, with a strong emphasis on the role of the patient in developing and maintaining the depressive disorder. Therapists typically present in clear, prosaic language the assumptions of the approach, mechanisms believed to underlie change, and the expected roles of the therapist and patient. A forthright and collaborative tone is cultivated, with the treatment provider sometimes portrayed as a consultant rather than a doctor.

Conclusion

The cigarette kills 435,000 Americans each year, more than alcohol, cocaine, crack, heroin, homicide, suicide, car crashes, fires, and AIDS combined (U.S. Department of Health and Human Services, 1990). Treatment of tobacco addiction should be as high a priority as the treatment of other addictions. Smoking has been deeply embedded in the culture, and tobacco has been important to powerful commercial interests. Consequently, it has been difficult for

health care professionals to grasp the enormity of the problem and organize effective actions to control the resulting epidemic of illness and death. Recently,
this has begun to change, and health care professionals are learning how to address tobacco addiction.

Patients with comorbid mood and other addictive disorders can successfully
address their addiction to tobacco. Many patients who suffer from addictive
and mood disorders eagerly address tobacco dependence as part of their treatment regime. Mental health and addiction professionals, once committed to
the need to treat tobacco dependence, can integrate guidelines for managing
tobacco dependence into their everyday practices. Professionals should urge
patients to attempt quitting during noncrisis periods and be patient, while
monitoring the psychiatric condition (including mental status and medications) carefully. (This does *not* mean that smoking should be permitted for hospitalized patients in crisis. The rules of the unit should prevail. A person merely
suspends smoking while hospitalized on a nonsmoking unit, just as the patient
suspends alcohol or heroin use during an inpatient stay, whether or not there
is a plan to stop after discharge.)

Patients with a history of depression should be monitored carefully for the
re-emergence of a depressive episode. Recent advances, including cognitive
behavioral therapy and pharmacotherapy, have been useful in this population.
Many standard psychotherapeutic strategies, such as motivational interviewing and harm reduction, can be modified to address tobacco as part of a holis-
tic treatment plan in various addiction and psychiatric settings.

REFERENCES

Agency for Health Care Policy and Research. 1996a. Clinical Practice Guideline #18:
    Helping Smokers Quit, AHCPR Publication No. 96-0693. Washington, D.C.: U.S.
    Government Printing Office.
————. 1996b. *Smoking Cessation: Information for Specialists*, AHCPR Publication
    No. 96-0694. Washington, D.C.: U.S. Government Printing Office.
American Psychiatric Association. 1994. *Diagnostic and Statistical Manual of Mental
    Disorders*, 4th ed. Washington, D.C.: American Psychiatric Association.
————. 1996. Practice guideline for the treatment of patients with nicotine depen-
    dence. *American Journal of Psychiatry* 153(10,suppl):1–31.
Benowitz, N. L., S. Zevin, and P. Jacob. 1998. Suppression of nicotine intake during
    ad libitum cigarette smoking by high dose transdermal nicotine. *Journal of Pharma-
    cology and Experimental Therapeutics* 287:958–62.
Bergen, A. W., and N. Caporoso. 1999. Cigarette smoking. *Journal of the National Can-
    cer Institute* 91(16):1365–75.

Blue Cross/Blue Shield of Minnesota. 2000. Blue Cross awarded top national indus-
try honor for helping smokers quit. Blue Cross/Blue Shield of Minnesota News Center, October. Bluecross.com/news/htdocs/releases/smokingaward.html. Accessed Au-
gust 11, 2002.

Blum, K., P. J. Sheridan, R. C. Wood, E. R. Braverman, T. J. Chen, and D. E. Com-
ings. 1995. Dopamine D2 receptor gene variants: Association and linkage studies in
impulsive-addictive-compulsive behavior. *Pharmacogenetics* 5(3):121–41.

Buchanan, C., C. Huffman, and V. Barbour. 1994. Smoking health risk: Counseling
of psychiatric patients. *Journal of Psychosocial Nursing and Mental Health Services*
32(1):27–31.

California Environmental Protection Agency. 1997. Health Effects of Exposure to Environmental Smoke, 6–28.

Chait, L. D., and R. R. Griffiths. 1984. Effects of methadone on human cigarette smoking and subjective ratings. *Journal of Pharmacology and Experimental Therapeutics*
29:636–40.

Clemney, P., R. Brooner, M. A. Chutuape, et al. 1997. Smoking habits and attitudes in
a methadone maintenance treatment population. *Drug and Alcohol Dependence*
44(2–3):123–32.

Covey, L. S., A. H. Glassman, and F. Stetner. 1997. Major depression following smoking cessation. *American Journal of Psychiatry* 154(2):263–65.

———. 1998. Cigarette smoking and major depression. *Journal of Addictive Diseases*
17(1):35–46.

Fagerstrom, K. O., R. Tejding, A. Westin, et al. 1997. Aiding reduction of smoking with
nicotine replacement medications: Hope for the recalcitrant smoker? *Tobacco Control* 6:311–16.

Fiore, M. C., W. C. Bailey, S. J. Cohen, et al. 2000. *Treating Tobacco Use and Dependence: Clinical Practice Guideline.* Rockville, Md.: U.S. Department of Health and
Human Services.

Glassman, A. 1993. Cigarette smoking: Implications for psychiatric illness. *American
Journal of Psychiatry* 150(4):546–52.

Glassman, A. H. 1999. *Smoking, Smoking Cessation, and Major Depression.* Cassette
recording, vol. 28, no. 7. Glendale, Calif.: Audio-Digest Foundation.

Glassman, A. H., F. Stetner, B. T. Walsh, P. S. Raizman, J. L. Fleiss, T. B. Cooper, and
L. S. Covery. 1988. Heavy smokers, smoking cessation, and clonidine: Results of a double-blind, randomized trial. *Journal of the American Medical Association* 259:2863–66.

Glassman, A. H., J. E. Helzer, L. S. Covey, L. B. Cottler, F. Stetner, J. E. Tipp, and J.
Johnson. 1990. Smoking, smoking cessation, and major depression. *Journal of the
American Medical Association* 264:1546–49.

Goff, D., D. Henderson, and E. Amico. 1992. Cigarette smoking in schizophrenia: Relationship to psychopathology and medication side effects. *American Journal of Psychiatry* 149(9):1189–94.

Hall, S. M., R. F. Muñoz, and V. I. Reus. 1993. Nicotine, negative affect, and depression. *Journal of Consulting and Clinical Psychology* 61(5):761–67.

————. 1994. Cognitive-behavioral intervention increases abstinence rates for depressive-history smokers. *Journal of Consulting and Clinical Psychology* 62(1):141–46.

Hall, S. M., K. L. Sees, R. F. Muñoz, V. I. Reus, C. Duncan, G. L. Humgleet, and D. T. Hartz. 1996. Mood management and nicotine gum in smoking treatment: A therapeutic contact and placebo controlled study. *Journal of Consulting and Clinical Psychology* 64(1):1003–9.

Hall, S. M., V. I. Reus, and R. F. Muñoz. 1998. Nortriptyline and CBT in the treatment of cigarette smoking. *Archives of General Psychiatry* 55:683–90.

Hanna, E. Z., and B. F. Grant. 1999. Parallels to early onset alcohol use in the relationship of early onset smoking with drug use and DSM-IV drug and depressive disorders: Findings from the national longitudinal epidemiologic survey. *Alcoholism, Clinical Experimental Research* 23(3):513–22.

Harris, J. R., H. H. Schauffler, A. Milstein, et al. 2001. Expanding health insurance coverage for smoking cessation treatments: Experience of the Pacific Business Group on Health. *American Journal of Health Promotion* 15:350–56.

Henningfield, J. E. 1994. Pharmacology of nicotine. Adapted from educational material prepared by L. M. Schwandt and J. E. Henningfield as an In-Service Training Program for the American Association for Clinical Chemistry, Inc. (AACC TDM/Tox, vol. 14, no. 10, pp. 249–62, October 1993).

Houtsmuller, E. J., and M. L. Stitzer. 1999. Manipulation of cigarette craving through rapid smoking: Efficacy and effects on smoking behavior. *Psychopharmacology* 142:149–57.

Howard, T. S., and J. R. Hughes. 1995. Smoking cessation and the nicotine patch. *Journal of the American Medical Association* 274:214.

Hughes, J., D. Hatsukami, J. Mitchell, and L. Denlgree. 1986. Prevalence of smoking among psychiatric outpatients. *American Journal of Psychiatry* 143(8):993–97.

Hughes, J. R., M. G. Goldstein, R. D. Hurt, and S. Shiffman. 1999. Recent advances in the pharmacotherapy of smoking. *Journal of the American Medical Association* 281(1):72–76.

Hurt, R. D., K. M. Ebermna, J. Slade, and L. Karan. 1993. Treating nicotine addiction in patients with other addictive disorders. In *Nicotine Addiction: Principles and Management*, edited by C. T. Orleans and J. Slade. New York: Oxford University Press.

Hurt, R. D., K. P. Offord, I. T. Croghan, L. Gmez-Dahl, T. E. Kottke, R. M. Morse, and L. J. Melton. 1996. Mortality following inpatient addictions treatment. *Journal of the American Medical Association* 275(14):1097–1103.

Kaplan, H., and B. Saddock (eds.). 1994. *Synopsis of Psychiatry*. Baltimore: Williams & Wilkins.

Kendler, K. S., M. C. Neale, C. J. MacLean, A. C. Heath, L. J. Eaves, and R. C. Kessler. 1993. Smoking and major depression: A causal analysis. *Archives of General Psychiatry* 50(1):36–43.

Kinnunen, T., D. Doherty, F. S. Militello, and A. J. Garvey. 1996. Depression and smoking cessation: Characteristics of depressed smokers and effects of nicotine replacement. *Journal of Consulting and Clinical Psychology* 64(4):791–98.

Kozlowski, L. T., W. Skinner, C. Kent, and M. A. Pope. 1989. Cigarette smoking among alcohol abusers: A continuing and neglected problem. *Canadian Journal of Public Health* 77:205–7.

Linkins, R. W., and G. W. Comstock. 1990. Depressed mood and development of cancer. *American Journal of Epidemiology* 132(5):962–72.

Marlatt, G. A., and J. R. Gordon. 1985. *Relapse Prevention: Maintenance Strategies in the Treatment of Addictive Behaviors.* New York: Guilford Press.

Miller, W. R., and D. Rollnick (eds.). 2002. *Motivational Interviewing: Preparing People to Change Addictive Behavior,* 2d ed., 3–390. New York: Guilford Press.

Muñoz, R. F., K. Organista, and S. M. Hall. 1991. *Mood Management Training to Prevent Smoking Relapse: A Cognitive-Behavioral Treatment Manual.* Unpublished manuscript. San Francisco: University of California at San Francisco.

National Health Interview Survey: Percentage of Adults Who Are Current, Former, or Never Smokers (1965–95). In Tobacco Information and Prevention Source (on-line). Available at www.cdc.gov/tobacco/adstat1.htl.

National Institute on Alcohol Abuse and Alcoholism. 1998. Alcohol and tobacco. *Alcohol Alert* 39.

National Institute on Drug Abuse. 2000. Nicotine craving and heavy smoking may contribute to increased use of cocaine and heroin. *NIDA Notes* 15(5):October.

Nisell, M., G. G. Nomikos, and T. H. Svensson. 1995. Nicotine dependence, midbrain dopamine systems and psychiatric disorders. *Pharmacology and Toxicology* 76:57–62.

Orleans, C. T., and J. Slade (eds.). 1993. *Nicotine Addiction: Principles and Management,* 1–455. New York: Oxford University Press.

Parrott, A. C. 1999. Does cigarette smoking cause stress? *American Psychologist* 54(10): 817–20.

Pomerleau, C. S. 1997. Co-factors for smoking and evolutionary psychobiology. *Addiction* 92(4):397–408.

Pomerleau, O. F. 1992. Nicotine and the central nervous system: Biobehavioral effects of cigarette smoking. *American Journal of Medicine* 93(suppl 1A):2S–7S.

Prochaska, J., C. DiClemente, and J. Norcross. 1992. In search of how people change: Applications to addictive behaviors. *American Psychologist* 47(9):1102–14.

Resnick, M. P. 1993. Treating nicotine addiction in patients with psychiatric comorbidity. In *Nicotine Addiction: Principles and Management,* edited by C. T. Orleans and J. Slade, 327–36. New York: Oxford University Press.

Roll, J. M., S. T. Higgins, A. J. Budney, W. K. Bickel, and G. J. Badger. 1996. A comparison of cocaine-dependent cigarette smokers and non-smokers on demographic, drug use and other characteristics. *Drug and Alcohol Dependence* 40:195–201.

Roll, J. M., S. T. Higgins, and J. Tidey. 1997. Cocaine use can increase cigarette smoking: Evidence from laboratory and naturalistic settings. *Experimental and Clinical Psychopharmacology* 5:263–68.

Rustin, T. A. 1998. Incorporating nicotine dependence into addiction treatment. *Journal of Addictive Diseases* 17:83–108.

Salín-Pascual, J. J., M. Rosas, A. Jimenez-Genchi, B. L. Rivera-Meza, and V. Delgado-

Parra. 1996. Antidepressant effect of transdermal nicotine patches in nonsmoking patients with major depression. *Journal of Clinical Psychiatry* 57(9):387–89.

Schmitz, J. M., J. Grabowski, and H. Rhoades. 1994. The effects of high and low doses of methadone on cigarette smoking. *Drug and Alcohol Dependence* 34:237–42.

Stuyt, E. B. 1997. Recovery rates after treatment for alcohol/drug dependence: Tobacco users vs. non-tobacco users. *American Journal on Addictions* 6:159–67.

U.S. Department of Health and Human Services. 1990. *The Health Benefits of Smoking Cessation,* DHHS Publication No. (CDC) 90-8416. Washington, D.C.: U.S. Government Printing Office.

U.S. Environmental Protection Agency. 1992. Respiratory Health Effects of Passive Smoking: Lung Cancer and Other Disorders, 8–14. EPA/600/6–90/006F.

Wiseman, E. J., and D. E. McMillan. 1998. Relationship of cocaine use to cigarette smoking in cocaine-dependent outpatients. *American Journal of Drug and Alcohol Abuse* 24:617–25.

Woodward, A., and M. Laugesen. 2001. How many deaths are caused by secondhand smoke? *Tobacco Control* 10:383–88.

Ziedonis, D., T. Kosten, W. Glazer, and R. Frances. 1994. Nicotine dependence and schizophrenia. *Hospital and Community Psychiatry* 45(3):204–6.

Ziedonis, D. M., and T. P. George. 1997. Schizophrenia and nicotine use: Report of a pilot smoking cessation program and review of neurobiological and clinical issues. *Schizophrenia Bulletin* 23(2):247–54.

Resources

Suggested Readings

The articles, books, and manuals listed here can supplement materials presented in this book. The National Clearinghouse of Alcohol and Drug Information in Washington, D.C., provides focused manuals on hundreds of topics related to substance use disorders. The Hazelden Foundation in Central City, Minnesota, publishes enlightening manuals and books for people recovering from substance use disorder as well as for their families.

The American Psychiatric Association has sponsored a practice guideline for the treatment of depression and another guideline for the treatment of substance abuse. The American Psychiatric Press, Inc. (1400 K Street N.W., Washington, D.C.), distributes these guidelines. Although they are meant for psychiatrists, other physicians and mental health workers may benefit from them as well. Some extrapolation is needed to bridge from these guidelines to the care of both disorders in the same patient.

Institutes and programs within the National Institutes of Health have prepared hundreds of publications addressing specific areas related to depression and substance abuse. These are generally available through the National Clearinghouse noted above. However, the institutes fund treatment studies to which citizens might want access. The relevant institutes and programs include the following:

- National Institute of Mental Health (NIMH)
- National Institute of Alcohol Abuse and Alcoholism (NIAAA)
- National Institute of Drug Abuse (NIDA)
- Substance Abuse and Mental Health Services Agency (SAMHSA)

The Surgeon General's Report on Mental Health (1999) is a landmark document that should guide government and societal efforts over the next few decades.

International organizations have increasingly turned their attention to depression and substance abuse over the last few decades, since these disorders comprise major sources of disability, death, and societal costs throughout the world. Publications may be obtained through the United Nations, in New York City. United Nations–sponsored organizations include the following:

- Mental Health Division of the World Health Organization
- United Nations agencies for narcotic drug control and drug abuse prevention

Reference lists on published articles are available through medical libraries. These are designed to access specific topics. Librarians can assist interested people in learning to search the national MEDLINE references.

One journal commonly publishes articles on comorbid depression and substance abuse. This is the *American Journal of Addiction*, published by the American Academy of Addiction Psychiatrists, whose members are particularly concerned with comorbid substance abuse and other psychiatric disorders. In addition, many journals in the mental health arena accept manuscripts on comorbid depression and substance disorder from time to time. These latter include:

- *American Journal of Psychiatry* (from the American Psychiatric Association)
- *Archives of General Psychiatry*
- *Journal of Clinical Psychiatry*
- *Journal of Consulting and Clinical Psychology*
- *Journal of Nervous and Mental Disorders*
- *Psychiatric Services* (from the American Psychiatric Association)

Likewise, several journals emphasizing substance abuse also publish occasional articles on comorbid substance disorder and depression. These include the following:

- *American Journal of Drug and Alcohol Abuse*
- *Journal of Addictive Diseases*
- *Journal of Studies on Alcohol*

Advocacy, Self-help, and Support Groups

Advocacy groups welcome the involvement of mental health professionals, current and former patients, relatives and friends of patients, and concerned citizens. They provide a format within which patients, family members, and professionals can promulgate care, resources, and enlightened public attitudes regarding mental disorders and substance use disorders. The largest national chapters have state and local offices around the United States. They include:

- National Alliance for the Mentally Ill (NAMI)
- National Mental Health Association (NMHA)

Resource-referral groups serve as a source of information, referral, and support. These groups especially focus on depression and anxiety disorders.

- Depression and Related Affective Disorders Association

Self-help organizations for substance use disorder are present in virtually all cities and towns and increasingly in rural areas as well. They include the following:

- Alcoholics Anonymous
- Cocaine Anonymous
- Narcotics Anonymous
- SMART Recovery

Self-help organizations for family members of people with substance use disorder serve to support the family members and guide them toward appropriate interventions as well as the importance of attending to their health and well-being. They include:

- Alanon — for adult partners and family members
- Alateen   for teenaged offspring of parents with substance use disorder
- various parent support groups for those whose adolescent children are abusing substances, often while engaging in disturbed or disturbing behavior

Self-help organizations for mental disorders tend to be present in cities and larger towns. They often use concepts and methods borrowed from Alcoholics Anonymous and other self-actualization movements.

- National Depressive and Manic Depressive Association — This group composed of people with mood disorders offers support and education.
- Recovery — This group largely composed of people who have been hospitalized for severe mental illness offers a structured group process aimed at identifying symptoms and developing personal strategies for managing symptoms.
- Emotions Anonymous — Similar to Recovery, this group is oriented to those who, while not necessarily hospitalized, have been impaired or limited as a result of their symptoms.

Web Sites
Increasingly, web sites supplement texts and manuals in providing recent findings. The quality and reliability of these resources depend almost entirely on the individual or group that sponsors the web site. We have found the following web sites to be authoritative resources:

- American Academy of Addiction Psychiatry: www.aaap.org
- American Association of Educators and Researchers in Substance Abuse: www .med.nyu.edu.substanceabuse

- American Journal of Psychiatry: ajp.psychiatryonline.org
- American Psychiatric Association: www.psych.org
- Group for the Advancement of Psychiatry: www.groupadpsych.org
- National Institute of Alcohol Abuse and Alcoholism (NIAAA): www.niaaa.nih.gov
- National Institute of Drug Abuse (NIDA): www.nida.nih.gov
- National Institute of Mental Health (NIMH): www.nimh.nih.gov
- National Library of Medicine: www.nlm.nih.gov
- World Health Organization: www.who.int/whr, www.who.ch

Other web sites have articles or bulletins on comorbid mood and substance disorder, although with varying frequency:

- Internet Mental Health: www.mentalhealth.com/p.html
- Mayo Clinic: www.mayohealth.org
- Medical World Search: www.mwsearch.com
- Mental Health Infolink: www.onlinepsych.com/index.html
- Mental Health Net and Mental Health Psychiatry: www.cmhc.com

A nonprofit corporation has a web site to provide information on dubious health information:

- www.quackwatch.com

Educational Videos

Daley, D. 1994. *Living Sober: An Interactive Video Recovery Program*. Skokie, Ill.: Gerald T. Rogers Productions. Segment topics: Resisting Social Pressure to Use Chemicals, Coping with Cravings and Thoughts of Using, Managing Anger in Recovery, Managing Feelings of Boredom and Emptiness, Coping with Family and Interpersonal Conflict, Building a Recovery Network and Sponsorship, Coping with Relapse Warning Signs, Recovering from Crack/Cocaine Addiction.

———. 1995. *The Promise of Recovery*. Skokie, Ill.: Gerald T. Rogers Productions. Part I: Psychiatric Illness, An Overview, Understanding Psychiatric Illness and the Process of Recovery, How to Use Therapy or Counseling, The Role of Medication in Recovery, Developing a Relapse Plan, Psychiatric Illness and the Family. Part II: Specific Psychiatric Disorders, Depression, Borderline Personality Disorder, Bipolar Illness, Anxiety/Panic Disorder, Schizophrenia, Eating Disorders (Bulimia).

———. 1997. *Living Sober II: An Interactive Video Recovery Program*. Skokie, Ill.: Gerald T. Rogers Productions. Segment topics: Motivation and Recovery, Relationship Issues. Part I: Amends, Assertiveness, and Honesty, Relationship Issues. Part II: Passion, Rejection, and Criticism, Relationship Issues. Part III: HIV, Quick Sex, and Early Recovery Romances, Other Addictions, Balanced Living.

————. 1998. *Living Sober III: An Interactive Video Recovery Program*. Skokie, Ill.: Gerald T. Rogers Productions. Segment topics: Compliance with Aftercare and Outpatient Counseling, Low Motivation to Change or Seek Treatment, Relationship to Therapist and Treatment Group, Compliance with Medications and Self-help Programs, Compliance with Lifestyle Changes.

Index

Page numbers in *italics* refer to figures and tables.